FISHING FROM THE ROCK OF THE BAY

The Making of an Angler

Learning to be an angler around the world,
then settling in Cornwall and fishing for bass

James 'Leakyboots' Batty

Merlin Unwin Books

First published in Great Britain by Merlin Unwin Books 2021

Merlin Unwin Books Ltd
Palmers House
7 Corve Street
Ludlow
Shropshire SY8 1DB   UK

www.merlinunwin.co.uk

ISBN 978-1-913159-34-4

Typeset in 11.5 point Minion Pro by Merlin Unwin Books
Printed by CPI Antony Rowe, Chippenham, England

Dedication

I spent many years moving around the world to find better jobs and interesting fishing. This book is for the millions of people who have to leave their homes because of war, oppression, and poverty.

In retirement I work with a small charity that tries to help one group of such people, Yezidis in northern Iraq whose communities were targeted by the ISIS genocide of 2014.

https://sites.google.com/site/oneandallaid/
or https://www.facebook.com/groups/1619802224759642/

Part One
ALL OVER THE WORLD

Part Two
THE UK
MOSTLY BASS

PART ONE

ALL OVER THE WORLD

Fishing Talk

'High voltage man'
Captain Beefheart & His Magic Band, *Electricity*

I hardly remember life without a rod in my hand. I dimly recall a steamer voyage through Egypt just before the Aswan High Dam was finished. We saw the temple at Luxor where I made my mother buy me an earthenware scarab beetle. But the highlights of the trip were bunk beds with furry ladders and my father asking for a pear from a Greek steward by sketching it with his propelling pencil. That apart, my childhood memories revolve around fishing.

When I met my wife Shelley she flipped through our old family albums. I'm the second of three sons, it was no surprise that the photographic record of my early life was sparse. For the first child parents religiously document the first bowel movement, smile, tooth, tantrum, upright step, haircut, and day at kindergarten; before moving on to primary and secondary school sports teams, driving lessons, boyfriends and girlfriends, graduation ceremonies, jobs, and criminal convictions as relevant. With later arrivals you get birth, marriage, and that's about it. But what amazed my bride was that nearly all the snapshots were of a boy holding a fish, or just as often of the fish on its own. No birthday parties or posed studio portraits, no family groups, none of those holiday scenes of a small blurry human figure in front of a famous building or landscape. She seemed to think this showed some sort of neglect, perhaps extravagant abuse of thirty-five millimetre film. I disagree. Why would a doting father or mother want a memento of a scowling child who's blanked or – even worse – not been fishing at all? What's more every picture was written up with species, size, and location; clear evidence of responsible parenting. If you were picky you might ask why Mother failed to mention bait, water temperature, and time of day, but she made a good start.

My angling career began at the age of four or five when my older brother was shipped off to boarding school, leaving me without a live-in playmate and tormentor. Home was in Khartoum where my father was a manager in the Sudan's utility company. He was obsessive about tennis, squash, and cricket, none of which are thrilling for a small boy to sit and watch. My mother loved gardening, that's not much of a spectator sport either. Also she was taking care of my younger brother and he was under a year old. In my sixties I see him as a contemporary but when I was an inquisitive young lad and he was a horizontal blob we didn't have much in common. I must have been bored.

I've no idea how I hit on fishing as a way to amuse myself. I don't believe the nursery school library had a picture book copy of *The Compleat Angler*. Mr. Crabtree inspired a lot of young dabblers, but he showed up in the *Daily Mirror*. My parents read the airmail edition of *The Times*, usually two weeks out of date so – as with today's papers – only the obituaries and the crossword puzzle were worth a damn. Maybe I saw people catching things from the Nile as we walked the dog along its banks. Maybe I overheard grown-ups telling the sort of tall tales that have sustained me for the last sixty years. All I know is that I was mad keen to wet a line.

Parental planning's a mystery to a youngster but after what felt like an age I found out that a junior engineer, Mr. Hansome, had agreed to take me along on his afternoon sessions. My father wasn't the sort of man to arm-twist a subordinate into a favour so I reckon Mr. Hansome was just a typical angler, eager to corrupt the youth, to turn potentially productive citizens into obsessive nutters who'll waste thousands of hours by the water's edge and hundreds of pay cheques on tackle they never use. I have scant memory of Mr. Hansome's appearance. He was tall to the eye of a five year old, so at least four foot six, and he was never to be seen without a battered felt hat. What I remember clearly are his hands, rough and weather-beaten, dark with tobacco stains, and wonderfully nimble. As he threaded a worm, tied up a new hook, or nipped on lead-shot it was impossible to keep up with the movements of his fingers, fluttering like the tentacles of an octopus on a caffeine binge. I was a keen student so one day he dug out some heavy monofilament and sent me home with guidance on the half-blood knot. Good guidance as well, Mr. Hansome never could have written software manuals or instructions for flat pack furniture, his diagrams made perfect sense; and on our next outing he inspected my homework, grunted cheerfully, and declared me a qualified junior angler.

My tackle came from his store cupboard, an Aladdin's cave – if Aladdin had never thrown anything away and had managed his inventory by stuffing everything on top of everything else. From this adult toy box Mr Hansome found an old greenheart rod that had snapped off about five feet from the butt. It had been rescued from the scrapheap with the addition of a tip ring at the point of fracture. The action, as a modern catalogue might say, was stiff – it would have splintered before it bent. The rod was teamed up with a small brass centre pin reel with a permanent ratchet. Mr. Hansome himself used a cutting edge fibreglass rod with a fixed spool reel. I was in awe of the way he cast with this lot, his terminal tackle flying like a longhop hoicked over the cow corner boundary, splashing down so far away that we squinted to keep track of his float. My gear flopped like a nervous defensive prod as I pulled a few yards of line from my reel then flicked out into the margin.

We fished for bulti (*Tilapia nilotica*) – apart from tigerfish (*Hydrocynus vittatus*) we used the local names for all the species we ran into – using a float, a couple of split shot, and a size four or six hook baited with worm. Bulti are good to eat, in those days they were as common as fruit flies in a genetics laboratory, and we'd often come home with a decent meal. And although I longed to try a fixed spool reel and hurl my worm half way to Egypt I caught plenty in the reedy gullies a few feet from my Clarks' sandals.

Bulti

One day bites were slow. Mr. Hansome took off his float and fished a leger in the deepest channels, eking out a catfish or two. He'd given me a few chats about the benefits of sticking at it, so I carried on drifting my worms around the tufty reeds beside the bank. Finally my float budged. It lay on its side for a moment then slid underwater at a heart-stopping rate.

I tightened and the rod was almost yanked from my grasp as line began to vanish from the reel. To his credit Mr. Hansome didn't grab the gear out of my hands, he just offered a stream of breathless advice. 'Let it go, let it go. Now wind as fast as you can, keep the rod up. It's turning, let it go again.' After what felt like a whole cricket match I drew my fish into the shallows. 'A barada, an electric fish (*Malapterus electricus*), and a really big one too, at least five pounds. Don't try to lift it, I'll get the landing net.' There followed a torrent of words I didn't recognise, many of them short and voiced in a yelp. The net's frame and handle were aluminium. 'And I've spent twenty years as an electrical engineer,' said Mr. Hansome, rubbing his hands on his shorts, 'I should know better than to shock myself. But I tell you what, young man, we'll call her a six pounder. We'll unhook her with the insulated pliers and we'll slip her back to fight again another day.' His voice dropped to a whisper. 'And you know those words I just used, the one with the 'F' and the one with the 'B'?' I nodded. 'That's fishing talk, we only ever say those things when we're by the river. Not at home, certainly not at school. But I tell you what,' he grinned, 'that was a bloody good fish and you're going to be a proper bloody fisherman.'

Barada

It's a Family Affair

'Saint Genevieve can hold back the water'
Son Volt, *Tear Stained Eye*

See a small group of people taking part in a leisure activity and often you hear one of the adults – sorry to be sexist, but usually it's the father – offer a dollop of rhubarb, 'I wanted to find something we could do as a family'. Liar. The honest message is, 'I'm obsessed with this nonsense, and I realise I'll be able to indulge my passion only if I drag the kids along as well'. Hence the photos where Dad – in a high tech alpine outfit, shod with the latest carbon fibre skis – smiles smugly; while Mum and the children – in much darned jumpers, with planks of firewood strapped to their feet – bare their teeth as they wonder wistfully how much longer they'll have to keep landing on their arses in wet snow before they can go back to the chalet and the relative delights of peeling potatoes, hoovering, or trigonometry homework. But when my father took up fishing he joined a gang of equally addicted anglers.

Once in a while we'd head out for a short session at the end of his working day, but the marquee event of the week was on Fridays. That was when we piled in the car and drove across the desert to the dam at Jebel Aulia. At the time this seemed like a major journey but I think it took less than an hour. We kept ourselves busy on the way by eating our breakfast. The gourmet treat was sausage sandwiches. In hindsight I can say that these were pretty vile. Nowadays buying bangers from even a modest butcher's shop involves a catechism of trick questions: caramelised onion, Cumberland seasoning, chorizo-style, outdoor bred, organic, gluten-free, whatever. Not when I was a nipper. Khartoum was in the Muslim part of the Sudan, hence the Friday holiday, and no pork products were made locally. One of the import houses sometimes sold sausages in a tin. They were almost square in section, they came packed in a lump of lard, and I reckon they contained more rusk – or maybe sawdust – than meat, more fat than lean. And the lean came from cheap cuts like ear, tail, and rectum. But we loved them, especially Father whose day off was blighted when they were out of stock. We ate sandwiches for lunch as well, often with wormy fingers, and any left at the end of the trip were fried for Saturday breakfast. A Marmite butty browned in beef dripping would be the signature dish if I were to open a restaurant.

Jebel Aulia lies on the White Nile upstream from Khartoum. The dam's a couple of miles long and we'd fish either upstream or downstream. Only one area was off limits, somewhere Father refused to park because his professional predecessor had damaged a company car there. He'd been following a group of camels, leaning on the horn to chivvy them along. I find it annoying when some prat hoots or flashes his headlights at me; camels agree. The laggard of the party stopped dead, waited for the offending vehicle to come close, then kicked in its radiator. Not the cosmetic chrome grille, the whole radiator, clouds of steam and a banjaxed engine. Camels look slow-witted, don't be fooled. You make your stupid noises up their backsides, they'll leave you stranded on the roadside.

Our target was bulti. It was possible to spin for tigerfish in the sluice below the dam but, as little people, we weren't allowed that close to the torrent that came over the spillway. There were stories of people trolling for Nile perch (*Lates niloticus*) in the reservoir as well but I don't remember seeing this happen. Our fishing followed a strict pattern, we were like squaddies at a military tattoo. We'd wade in line abreast formation to a sunken wall, on with a worm, then fish it three or four feet under a float. That was what the experts did, we followed suit. The Nile was full of fish and we did well enough. But sixty years later I wonder if we didn't miss a trick or two. Most of my best bulti came from reed islands, tumps of grass, tangles of roots, but we always set ourselves up in open water. In Botswana I chased tilapia with a Mepps spinner, in the Sudan we always used worms. What might we have caught if we'd tried something different?

A broader idea: anglers tend to be conservative. Not that we vote for the Tories or dress like our parents – mine never wore waders or Goretex. But we choose our baits, flies, lures, and methods based on what's considered normal. When I was a child visiting Cornwall bass fishers

Nile perch

stood on beaches after storms. They used lugworm or ragworm, four or six ounce lead weights. Anything else would have been daft, my handsome. Like businesspeople we find it easier to be wrong in a crowd than to risk branding ourselves as oddities. (I once had a performance review that read, 'He thinks creatively but otherwise his work is excellent.' OK it was in an accounting company, but Cornish beach fishers were as stuck in the mud as any financial wonk.) Nobody thought of using plugs on rocky shores, freelining a mackerel on a calm day, or casting streamers and maggoty flies through the shallows. Anglers nearly always copy the locals, we assume they know what they're doing. Often that's right, but when I moved to the Gambia, shore fishing meant a beach-caster and a fish bait. The rocky headlands were deserted, spinning gear was rarer than an honest election manifesto. But once I started using lures on the surface my results shot up like a zip fastener on a frosty riverbank.

This herd mentality's hard to explain, it's as if we're afraid someone might ask, 'Are you crazy?' Only one thing I could say to that: 'This thing in my hand, it's a fishing rod. Of course I'm crazy. What's your point?'

A Dutch Treat

'I got your message in Amsterdam'
Van Morrison, *Rare Heavy Connection*

I must have been eight when we had a family trip to the Netherlands. Father at this stage was general manager at the Sudanese power utility and a Dutch company wanted to flog him some big ticket item: generators, maybe substations. Anyway the vendors were like scruffpot lads at the first meeting with the girlfriend's family, keen to make a good impression. They put us up in a five star hotel with grounds running down to the Amstel river, paradise for three boys who thought fishing was a biological need running a close second to eating. We'd leave our lines in the water over breakfast, running down between courses to reel in eels.

They swept Father off on an endless round of factory tours, meetings with business leaders, and lunches washed down with the finest wines available to humanity. They also assigned us a minder, Henrik, a young chap from head office who was tasked with driving the rest of the family around in a Mercedes, taking us to see whatever sights tickled our fancy. I imagine they picked Henrik for his perfect English and his familiarity with the Rembrandt museum, the tulip market, and the mouse who lived in a windmill. Little did they know. Mother might have fancied a spot of local culture but three outvotes one, and by this stage she was no mean angler herself. We filed into the Mercedes in our wellies, stowed our rods in the boot, and asked to be taken somewhere with bream and rudd, preferably big ones. Nowadays that would be a piece of cake, out with the tablet, a few google searches, on with the satnav, Bob's your uncle. But poor Henrik spent half an hour and all his pocket money on a payphone, blagged a map from a filling station, and chauffeured us off into the hinterland. And the next day, when I'm sure he was hoping we might fancy a trip to an Edam cheese creamery or a traditional clog-making workshop, he had to do it all again, this time for pike and perch.

On our third and final day he suggested a museum, maybe the zoo. It was tipping rain, forecast to keep it up all day. But fishing nuts are made of sterner and dafter stuff than he reckoned, so on with the plastic macs and where could we fish for carp? At the end of what may have been the longest and soggiest day of Henrik's professional life he dropped us back at our digs. We pludged across the burgundy lobby carpet. Outside the lounge bar we paused to see if Father might be having a beer with his hosts and Mick slipped out of his mac. He gave it a shake, from the sleeve emerged a large, lively lobworm, landing with a soft plop. An elegant lady going into the lounge squeaked like a mouse in a helium bath, Mother looked mortified, and Mick bent to pick up the escapee. But before he could lay a hand on his spare bait a chap in crimson and gold hotel uniform came down like the wolf on the fold, dustpan in hand, and the worm was gone. Then he offered us a warm smile and a pot of cocoa. And that's why I'm so sure it was a five star hotel.

The Allure of the Exotic

'I never knew still waters'
Violent Femmes, *Country Death Song*

Some anglers want to bag as many different species as they can. My older brother Peter's one; as I write he's on a trip to Mongolia and Japan in pursuit of a few of the game fish he's never caught. A chap I run into on a surf beach marks significant birthdays by jetting off to distant lands that offer interesting sport and some sightseeing to keep his partner entertained – his last holiday was in Mexico for marlin, roosterfish, and a tour of Mazatlán. And the fishing magazines run pieces about 'species hunting', running through as many of the UK's sea creatures as possible, mostly using tiny jigs. I understand the urge to complete a set, whatever its elements, though I resent it when language is used to foster bias: coin lovers are numismatists, stamp junkies are philatelists, how come it's OK to call someone who writes down railway numbers an anorak? Anyway there are people who collect fish, good for them, whatever waterproof tops they wear. One of Peter's Japanese targets is the local seabass or suzuki (*Lateolabrax japonicus*). A lot of the lures we use in Europe are designed for suzuki, which seem to behave like our own bass, feeding best in a stirred up wave. In UK waters I was amazed to find there are five or six different types of goby to be caught. The British Marine Life Study Society reckons they're hard to identify because more than half the photographs in books attach the wrong name to the wrong tiddler. It's not just Wikipedia that needs to be taken with a pinch of salt.

Now I have no time for people who claim their branch of our sport's better than any other. Lure purists and whopper hunters can do as they please. But the one who picks on an angler with a squid bait or a mini-outfit for rock-pools strikes me as a bigoted eejit who needs to shut up, grow up, and get a life. However you fish – as long as it's legal – is fine, you're my brother or sister of the rod and line. And I'm not interested in chasing species I've never caught before but I'm glad some of my comrades do just that. We may learn new Japanese wrinkles that help us catch bigger UK bass, we may find different types of goby – or at least get better at identifying the ones that are known already. But what I enjoy isn't the exotic, it's making the familiar increasingly familiar, becoming more knowledgeable about bass. Maybe that makes me boring, but I'm the same way with birdwatching. I see camouflage coated twitchers with telescopes scurrying about to catch a glimpse of a rare American bagel bunting or hamburger hawk that's been blown off its migration path by a storm. Fine, but I'd rather sit in the garden with a mug of tea and see how a robin hunts worms through the kale plants, how a thrush chooses the material for its nest – like a really difficult customer in a hardware shop, rejecting twig after twig until it finds the one that looks just like the picture in *Ideal Thrush Home*. That's what I enjoy so that's what I do. Peter travels the world for his sport, I'll drive no more than twenty miles for mine. Neither of us is right or wrong, we're just different.

But there was a time when I was desperate to go after something new. I must have been about eight, almost all my fishing had been in the Nile for bulti, and someone gave me *A Boy Goes Trouting* by G.P.R. Balfour-Kinnear. It was published in 1959 so I had an early copy. The date also explains why the book was aimed only at boys, today I'm sure he'd have written for a gender-neutral youngster. Either way Mr. Balfour-Kinnear quickly replaced Biggles and Fred Trueman as my idol. I'd seen little streams when my parents were on home leave in the UK, the idea of fishing them was thrilling. The Nile in Khartoum's a massive water, it could be used as a location for a film of Huckleberry Finn or Heart of Darkness. It's also muddy, Mother said the shade Eau de Nil had been invented by a dye maker who never left the confines of the Coats factory on the Clyde. Casting into crystal pools and shallow riffles, that was a weird and wonderful idea. My only tackle was a spinning rod so I focused most of my attention on Mr. Balfour-Kinnear's advice about clear water worming. Some day I might have a split cane fly rod, but one step at a time.

Then came the news that we were to spend part of our summer holiday on the Isle of Man, staying in an old coaching inn at Injebreck. It belonged to a branch of my mother's family and had been converted into a regular house when the motorcar made it possible to travel from end to end of the island, thirty-odd miles, without stopping off for dinner, a few ales, a kip, and a change of horses. And it was within an easy walk of several streams.

When we arrived on the island my mother's uncle Tom marked our cards. I'm sure there was practical advice about the generator and the oil lamps but I cared only for the fishing stuff. Early mornings were best, ideally after overnight rain to give the water the colour of weak tea. This matched up with what I'd read so I nodded sagely, an eight year old veteran trout man. An eight inch specimen was a keeper, Tom told us, the streams were acidic, good for breeding, poor for feeding, the population needed to be thinned out.

On our first morning I woke at dawn, grubbed up a few worms, and tramped through the dew-soaked bracken to the water's edge. Allowing for the way time makes things seem larger, the biggest pool was the size of a generous washbasin, maybe a Belfast sink. The water was clearer than Mr. Balfour-Kinnear and I might have wished, only the stingiest host – or a north American – would serve such anaemic tea. Also his typical small water had pools and rapids, this one had pots and vertical cascades. I adapted his advice, flicking my worm into a waterfall and letting it work around the swirls of the bowl below. After a couple of dibbles I moved upstream and repeated the dose. The sun was lighting the tops of the heather-purple hills when I saw a flash of yellow in the dark water, followed by a tug on the line. You don't really play a fish in something as small as a jam making pan so I swung my trout onto the grass. Nine inches, a keeper, I wrapped it in ferns and fished on.

That holiday was a revelation. Perhaps not up there with Saul on the road to Damascus, but an eye opener for all that. I discovered the joy that comes from seeing something move to your bait, a thrill that led me into the dry fly, dapping, the skating bob, and surface lures for bass. And I learned how important it is to think about the fish and their chance of finding food, to scan a stretch of water for signs of life before either giving it a go or moving on to a likelier spot.

I'm sure G.P.R. Balfour-Kinnear is no longer with us but I owe him my thanks. He taught me that angling – unlike the football they made us play at school – doesn't depend on speed, strength, or natural talent. It's a sport for people who like to scratch their heads and ponder. By the way *A Boy Goes Trouting* sells on the internet for twenty quid. That seems like a bargain, especially if you have young relatives you'd like to turn into the sort of twits who stand around on riverbanks in the foulest of weather.

Watching a Float

'No sorrow in sight'
Hank Williams, *I Saw The Light*

I've never been a tackle buff. When a catalogue comes in the post I take a glance in case my regular braid's on special offer. I flap the new products pages of the odd angling paper to see if anyone's come up with a way of patching waders so they actually stay patched. And by the way it's a shame when they wrap magazines in polythene, damaging the environment and denying me a free read as well. I realise the sleeve's meant to make me put my hand in my pocket and buy the thing. It doesn't work, I just grumble and I do that anyway, it's age-related. I'd never look lustfully at reviews of top of the line rods and reels, I'm happy with what I have. In fact I'm not much of a consumer at all. I volunteer in a couple of charity shops, they take care of my clothes, books, and CDs. I buy old cars and run them until the mechanic tells me they wouldn't pass the MOT even if we found a bent inspector and stuffed the glove box with used tenners. I don't collect anything expensive, no art, wine cellar, antiques, postage stamps. I've always thought of possessions as burdens more than pleasures. When I left the Gambia in my late twenties all my worldly goods were in a carry-on grip and a rod tube. I had to take the shotgun out of the bag and give it to the pilot for safe keeping, but there was plenty of room for it among the shirts and underpants.

In the Sudan I was seven or eight when I outgrew my greenheart rod. I graduated to a pale blue solid glass one with an Intrepid reel. This was a simple bit of engineering, I took it apart with a Meccano screwdriver and oiled it if I was bored, always managing to put it back together without difficulty. It was a very well lubricated machine, I was bored whenever I was supposed to be taking a nap. But the tackle I loved was floats. The standard model locally was a white celluloid cylinder the size of a stumpy pencil with a red tip instead of a rubber. This was a functional bit of kit, not in the least attractive, so I made enough alternative designs to last several lifetimes. Some of my creations involved corks from wine bottles fitted to wooden skewers, shaped with a craft knife and sandpaper, then painted in discreet blues and greens below water level, bright yellows and oranges on top. My favourites were quills. Our house was next door to Khartoum zoo, we fed Mother's baking failures to the elephants over the garden fence.

In the same enclosure were the porcupines, they change their hairstyles as often as catwalk models or New Romantic pop stars, you could pick up quills by the bucket load. I liked them about nine inches long. A loop on the bottom made from fuse wire and whipped on with thread from Mother's sewing basket, a jaunty striped colour scheme for the bit that sat above the water, a few coats of oil-based varnish, you had a thing of beauty that caught fish as well.

Sixty years on my childhood enthusiasm makes perfect sense. When you fish with a float it's the link between the world we know with its sunshine, rain, and Marmite sandwiches; and the mysterious realm where the fish might or might not be waiting. It's a tiny, not fully transparent window into the unknown. Peering at a brightly coloured speck on the surface of the water captures the anticipation of fishing, the curiosity about what's going on down there, the internal debate about whether to be patient or to up sticks and have a try somewhere else. It grabs your attention and doesn't let go. Like a zen exercise it banishes anything else you might be worrying about: climate change, religious bigotry, or cabbage whites on the kale. What's more it's impossible to be gloomy when you're watching a float. It's an emblem of the optimistic fancy that something exciting's about to happen, a physical symbol of the attitude that makes 'one last cast' mean 'I promise I'll go home some time this week'.

The Impossible Dream

'I've always been crazy'
Waylon Jennings, *I've Always Been Crazy*

It goes without saying that anglers are optimists. We'll hit the beach when the websites are rammed with reports of a nightly diet of tiny whiting, persuading ourselves there are bound to be monster cod or bass preying on the plagues of bait-pinching tiddlers. The boat brigade parade on the docks at dawn when skippers are saying sport's been slow but steady, which means parties of eight rods have been seeing four bites a day spaced at more or less two hour intervals. Chucking a buzzer nymph into a five hundred acre lake or a mackerel into the Atlantic calls for a cheery disposition, I've always thought National Hunt jockeys are naturals to follow in Izaak Walton's footsteps. Ask a rider in the paddock for a forecast and you'll hear something like, 'She's in good heart, she'll love the ground, no reason we shouldn't run into a place at least'. This when a glance at the form book suggests, 'She's a recalcitrant jade likely to refuse at the first obstacle, but if I fall into a patch of mud I might survive without breaking many bones'.

There's one area where a rod in the hand pushes us across the line that divides optimism from delusion, and that's our imagined ability to land extraordinary fish on very ordinary tackle. If we competed in motorsport we'd enter the Monaco Grand Prix with glad hearts in our ten year old Ford Fiestas. Then we'd agonise for years over our failure to manage a podium finish. Job asked, 'Canst thou draw out Leviathan with an hook?' The average angler would tell him, 'No worries, it's a sharp size sixteen hook, my leader's made of two pound fluorocarbon, the water's full of razor-sharp boulders, a three foot pike doesn't stand a bloody chance.'

This struck me like the hoof of a camel on a family trip to Port Sudan on the Red Sea. I was nine or ten years old, Father had some business meetings, and we all went along for the jolly. Mother's enthusiasm for the trip had something to do with birdwatching and she was excited that we'd be fed Hadendowa mutton. The Hadendowa are a desert people and they cook their meat by slicing it thinly and laying it over rocks heated in a bonfire. Personally I've never rated food as theatre, I'd rather it were just shoved on a plate. And in the event the low tech cremation didn't come to pass, something to do with a broken-down car or a donkey with duff suspension.

For my brothers and myself the jaunt was a rare chance to fish in salt water and we latched on like puppies chewing up a sofa. We used our normal gear from the Nile, spinning rods with fixed spool reels and twelve pound line, and mostly we fished scraps of sardine from the piers and breakwaters. I don't remember what we caught, likely a bunch of reef fish, but I know we produced a lunch to replace the missing mutton. What I do recall is peering into the crystal waters of the Red Sea as half a dozen enormous shapes nosed their way into the harbour. Even allowing for the magnification wrought by the passage of sixty years they were four or five feet long. Father was convinced they were tuna. He may have been right but in retrospect I'd go with giant trevally, they didn't move quite like tuna. A sensible crew would have scurried off in search of a camera, maybe alerted some of the local professionals – they had harpoons and industrial strength handlines. But no, in typically hare brained fashion we tried to dangle our little bits of sardine in front of the monsters, no thought as to what we'd do if one were to latch on. A hard fighting two hundred pounder on fifty yards of cheap twelve pound line was a possibility I suppose; just like there's a chance that email saying you've inherited an Australian opal mine, send five thousand quid to cover administration costs, is on the up and up.

Over the years I must have tried my luck with dozens of uncatchable whoppers: a shark cruising at the foot of a fifty foot vertical cliff face, a four or five foot ray flapping along the sand when I was using ultralight gear for snappers, a pike as thick as a prop forward's neck as I flicked size eighteen midges into a Lancashire reservoir. And all that damned fool endeavour hasn't put out the flame of stupidity, just dimmed it a little. Only two years back I was wandering along a steep Cornish beach around high water. The sea was glassy, the tide small, and a decent bass seemed about as likely as an alien invasion led by the cast of Coronation Street. I was flicking a flying condom into the millpond when I landed a fat mackerel.

Supper for one, I needed another. I scanned the water for signs of whitebait. Thirty or forty yards out there was a ruffled patch. Half a dozen mackerel flew from the surface followed by a disturbance that looked as if a helicopter had dropped a depth charge strapped to a pissed off rhinoceros. A massive tuna broke the ripple, then another, and another. I've seen a few tuna in my time and I'm sure some of the shoal ran to a thousand pounds. I'd bet an arm, a leg, and the internal organ of your choice that none was under four hundred. My backpack was unzipped ready to dig out a wedge or a German sprat before common sense took over from adrenaline-induced idiocy. If one of these giants should happen to grab my lure the best I could hope was that it would empty the reel before snapping me off and carrying on munching its way through the all-you-can-eat mackerel buffet. Two hundred yards of almost new braid would be added to the non-biodegradable shite in our coastal waters and I'd be out twenty pounds for a refill of my spool. I sat on the sand and watched the feeding frenzy.

I'd like to say it was environmental responsibility that kept my lure in its box but I'm afraid the twenty quid may have been the deciding factor.

First and Last Love

'Feeling good was good enough for me'
Kris Kristofferson, *Me And Bobby McGee*

My father's job in Khartoum carried annual leave of three months. Hard to imagine these days, we've all been laid low by the American virus that means even long-serving employees are allowed just a few days off. One of my bosses in New York in the 1990s gave me a promotion and told me I now had four weeks of vacation but I should never expect to take it. He also said I must check for voicemails at least twice a day while I was away. In other words I was to keep my nose to the grindstone of organisational bollix even when I wasn't working. Luckily our house in Cornwall had an old telephone with a dial. I went away and left a recording on the office system: 'I won't have any digital access, if it's urgent please press zero for my assistant.' Nobody ever did. The content of most business communication has nothing to do with what's said. It's just a bleat into the corporate void: 'I'm still on the payroll here, please don't forget me at bonus time.'

But back to Father and most years we'd stay a month or so with my mother's family in west Cornwall. They lived half a mile from the beach and we spent hours on the rocks at either end of the strand. We used sliding floats with worm baits, limpets at a pinch, catching small pollack and wrasse. And when bites were slow we'd dabble in the rock-pools for shrimps. For some reason we were convinced these had to be cooked in sea water, we'd walk up the lane like the Amazing Blondel on an off day, teetering laboriously as we tried not to spill our buckets. I have to wonder why we thought this was such a good idea. Rock-pools are peed in all the time by seagulls, dogs, and children; and a pail of shellfish must build up a fair concentration of prawn poo. But we just did what the old wives told us, ours not to reason why.

Now I've always been solitary by nature. Maybe I need peace and quiet to think great thoughts, maybe I'm an antisocial weirdo, take your pick. So one afternoon I left my parents and brothers watching their floats while I headed off in search of new rock-pools. The silky green seaweed was my happiest hunting ground and I found a gully full of the stuff. Dragging my net along the walls of the pool I scooped up at least a dozen decent shrimps. Then I took a look out to sea. Ten yards away was an area dimpled with fishy splashes, definitely worth a cast. But I had no bait, the worms were with the main family party. Limpet was off limits as well, Father had the only penknife. So I tried a shrimp. Typical of my angling career, I used one of the best rock fishing baits there is, but only because it was all I could find, and I didn't realise what I'd done until much later. As the float settled it bobbed and darted off towards the depths. I tightened into something, played it carefully, then used an ocean wave to slide it into a depression at my feet. It was a bass, it was a little over a pound and a half, and it was a thing of beauty. I don't believe there were size limits or catch restrictions in the early 1960s, we ate everything except wrasse, but this was a fish that had to go back. It was too pretty to bash on the head and take home. I unhooked it gently and slid it into the wave. It wasn't love at first sight, the Hollywood film scene where moonlight flashes in the leading man's eye as the soundtrack swells with violins; but that little bass was a harbinger of an obsession that grips me to this day.

Fresh Air and Fun

'I love that dirty water'
The Standells, *Dirty Water*

My aunt lived outside Liverpool and my brothers and I stayed with her over short breaks from boarding school. And of course we always were on the lookout for the chance to fish. There were canals in the area where stolid types cowered under their giant green umbrellas watching tiny floats and catching even tinier roach and sticklebacks, but we didn't own any coarse gear and it seemed you needed an enormously long rod to be in with a chance – or at least to avoid being laughed at by the experts. The Mersey in the 1960s was a toxic cesspit where the likeliest catches were bicycle wheels, oily rags, dead rats, and cholera. North Wales was rumoured to have good rivers and beaches but you could get to them by public transport only if you had a couple of days to spare and an aptitude for route-planning that would have put Scott of the Antarctic to shame. So we went to Blackpool, a direct bus ride that took only an hour.

Our favourite mark was the end of the North Pier. For all I know this might have been the only spot where fishing was allowed, it had a platform at the end reserved for anglers. So the ladies and gentlemen who sunbathed in deckchairs – often swathed in thick blankets like tartan mummies – were spared the risk of being impaled by a flying rig or put off their chips by the pong of stale bait. The walk to the end of the structure was under half a mile but it took you past a bingo hall and a ghetto of tumbledown kiosks peddling candy floss, fizzy drinks, and ices. There's something in the British psyche that says sitting in a damp gale of icy wind watching whitecaps scud across dirt brown water calls for summery refreshments. Also sun hats, usually worn with woolly jumpers, greatcoats, and knitted mittens. Halfway along the pier was a giant greenhouse where delicate sun seekers could enjoy their ultraviolet rays under cover in a fug of steam from mugs of soup and smoke from Woodbines.

There was a tackle shop as well. No idea why but the standard rig was a wire paternoster with three size eight offset hooks, a four ounce disc-shaped weight, and one inch portions of dried black lugworm. Grown-ups used this contraption on beach-casting rods, slinging their baits away to the horizon. Youngsters with centre pin reels lowered their kit into the khaki waves, looking for the scours around the pilings. Once your gear was in the water you leaned your rod against the railing, clipped a bell to the tip, and stood back to await nibbles. Bites were slow but almost everyone caught small dabs and flounders, the odd silver eel to provide half an hour of fun as you untangled a macramé bollix made of three brass booms, three monofilament snoods, and a dollop of slime. There were rumours of cod but I never saw one, they always seemed to have been landed by the uncle of the brother-in-law of the girlfriend of the mate of the person you were talking to. It's that kind of hearsay evidence that keeps the Loch Ness monster in the news from time to time.

In wild weather the anglers' jetty was closed, grubby waves washing over the planks. We'd fish from a tea shop, sitting in its relative warmth and watching our rods through the spray-spattered windows. The café owner was an understanding sort; as long as you bought something, you could use his gaff as a bivouac for as long as you fancied. But he drew the line at baiting up or unhooking catches on his tables. A pleasant fellow but obviously no fisherman.

Big Boots

'By the cool crystal waters'
Francis McPeake, *Wild Mountain Thyme*

We lived in Dar es Salaam for the second half of the 1960s. My brothers and I were away at boarding school or university but we spent a lot of our holidays with our parents, and when Peter passed his driving test new fishing horizons opened up. Father's company car was off limits but Mother had a Ford Anglia we could borrow for trips into the Tanzanian interior. It wasn't comfortable. In those days UK manufacturers produced special models for export to Africa. All they did was add one or two leaves to make the suspension bone-shakingly firm and remove the heater. Someone in Dagenham must have seen a few pictures and decided the whole continent was criss-crossed by dirt roads and bathed in sweltering sunshine. They were right about the lack of asphalt but the upland regions of East Africa have frost in winter and there are places where the snow never melts.

One chilly expedition was to Mufindi in the Southern Highlands. The area was dotted with tea plantations and some of its waters had been stocked with trout, from Loch Leven I think. Tanganyika became a British colony only after the Great War so the fingerlings must have been shipped off around the twenties. They were well established, bred successfully, and some grew to five pounds.

Settlers from Blighty often worked hard to recreate the rural UK in their new homes. As well as the fish they'd brought a garden centre full of roses, every tea planter's house had them climbing around the door. Apart from the orange tile roofs they might have been living in one of those Cotswold villages jammed with tour buses and shops peddling rustic pine furniture made in Thailand. If I were in self-imposed exile I dare say I'd miss the land of my fathers but brown trout and roses wouldn't top my list of home comforts to be imported. Maybe a supply of Marmite or a flat pack brewery from Burton-on-Trent. In any event we were glad they'd decided a fly fishery was an essential feature of civilised life in the wilds of East Africa.

There was a guesthouse on the bank of the lake we fished. It had a fireplace to take the nip off the evenings and a leather bound journal for catch reports. The first page of this volume described the fish as 'not free rising'. Given anglers' wild optimism I'd say this meant a trout had been spotted near the surface in about 1949 but it was sunbathing not feeding. The fellow with the most catch reports in the book was a Mr. Niblett and the water-watcher regaled us with tales of his skills. Folk in that part of the world struggle with the sound of the letter 'L' and can't pronounce anything that ends in a consonant, so Niblett morphed into Nibiriti. Nibiriti, we were told, could cast so far that his fly was invisible. He also owned a pair of very big boots – waders – and he could cover the whole water. His rod was long and strong, his line was heavy and it sank to the bottom where he pulled it along at heroic speed. In modern reservoir parlance he was a lure stripper.

I'm not sure where my fly rod came from but it was an old split cane job with an action somewhere between soft and abject. With the benefit of experience I'd say the fibres had started to break down, I imagine it was somebody's hand-me-down. Or maybe it was designed to be rubbish from the get-go, like fast fashion clothes, fast food hamburgers, and customer service from banks. Either way even a champion caster would have struggled to cover more than a dozen yards with it, and I was a clumsy novice. My line had started life as a floater but sections had lost their coating, turning it into a sink-tip, not to mention a sink-middle. But you use what's around. The fishing log said the best flies were Matuka, Peter Ross, and Alexandra. I had an Alexandra, that's what I tried.

If I were to fish that water again I'd use something to suggest a tadpole or a damsel nymph. They can be retrieved more slowly than a lure, my arm wouldn't have been so knackered so quickly. But I kept flogging way with my Alexandra, wishing I had a pair of Nibiriti's big boots so I could reach more water. As my elbow stiffened I tried along the reed beds that lined the bank. By now I was managing just six or seven yards so I could see when a golden flank turned behind my sinking fly. I recovered half a yard of line and hit resistance. It was a slim fish with a kype, a pound and three quarters, and I was smitten. Of the enthusiasms of my early teenage years – they included Vimto, tinned ravioli, Vespa motor scooters, and Françoise Hardy – only fly fishing has stood the test of time. And big boots.

Unnatural Environments

'I don't wanna work in a building downtown'
Arcade Fire, *Television Antichrist Blues*

A lot of anglers tell each other they really don't care whether they catch anything, it's just such a pleasure to be surrounded by nature. Generally this means they haven't had a bite since God was a boy but they want to keep heading out because blanking beats helping the kids with their algebra or fixing the window that's been loose since they moved in. And the oddest bit's that a lot of popular marks are very unnatural, wrecked by hideous human tinkering.

Reservoir trout fans are attracted to ugly dam walls the way politicians are drawn to lobbyists with platinum credit cards. Some waters prohibit access to their dams, anglers see these bans as a challenge and an indication the walls must be fish magnets. I've watched many a fat stockie escape when some fly rod wielding outlaw realises even a telescopic landing net won't reach down fifty feet of concrete blockwork. And fair enough, reservoirs are manmade to begin with, but the bit that looks least like a proper lake is that stonking great structure with the sluice gates in the middle.

Rivers are butchered as well. When I was a teenager my brother Peter had a yen to catch a barbel. He did his research and found the closest hotspot was in Yorkshire. So off we went through the rugged loveliness of the Pennines with hope in our hearts and sandwiches in the boot. The magic mark turned out to be just below a massive weir that had been built fifty-odd years back, lots of steel and rust-stained cement. I don't think we had our barbel, perhaps because of the bait we used. We were told by the locals that a cube of luncheon meat was the best bet, we took them at their word. Looking back I wonder why fish would be hunting lumps of greasy pink pork waste in a clear north country river. Had there been a teashop nearby serving nostalgic snacks from the war years I'd be open to persuasion. 'I'll try the Spam fritter. By gum, it's just as filthy as I remembered, I'm going to chuck it in the river for the fishes.' Groundbait never does any harm.

Sewage outfalls were popular spots in Cornwall when I was a youngster. Mullet, bass, and pollack for the rod fishers, while boatmen surrounded the smelliest coves with their lobster pots. I've never thought much of lobster. Piers and jetties attract attention as well and I've had decent bass from the mouths of harbours as the tide carries their prey in and out through a narrow funnel. And often that's what makes construction projects so fishy: they produce larders where food piles up along with the predators that fancy it. Dam walls trap dead and dying flies and fry, weirs scour out potholes that fill with edible debris, sewage pipes attract crustacea that feed predators and scavengers.

The clearest example of fish adapting to technology was something I saw in Dar es Salaam in the 1960s. The city's harbour was a natural bay with a dozen or so wharves scattered around its margins. Most of the shoreline was muddy, stony, and gently shelving. Someone told me there were red snappers (*Lutjanus gibbus*) in the area and I had a bash. The bottom was too rough to ledger so I freelined a prawn bait. There was easy access by the ferry terminal, I was dropped there and I went for a wander, casting whenever I saw broken coral, structure for prawns to hang out. But it was deadly dour, one missed bite in two hours. Heading back I tried a last cast right beside the terminal, a concrete ramp that ran out into the channel. No sooner had my bait splashed down than the ferry came into view. Dar es Salaam drivers were a spirited gang – they all thought they were competing in the East African Safari Rally – and the ferryboat captain was cut from the same cloth, rushing at the shore as if hell bent on doing as much damage as possible, a maelstrom of swirls from the propellers. Rats, I thought, bound to put the fish off the feed. As I started to reel in I felt a solid yank from a three pound snapper. I fished on, sitting on the edge of the slip. Whenever a ferry arrived or set sail there'd be a few minutes of non-stop bites. When both craft were out in the middle of the passage there was not a nibble. The wash from the screws created whirlpools and eddies that dislodged prawns and crabs from their hidey holes, providing the snappers with an all-you-can-eat-but-you'd-better-be-quick-about-it buffet. When the water was still, the crustaceans tucked themselves safely away and the predators loafed around waiting for the next eruption of treats. Snapper behave a lot like bass, it seems, they're canny opportunists.

Little Works of Art

'Hey good lookin''
Hank Williams, *Hey Good Lookin'*

For the first twenty-five years of my fishing life I was broke. I went from being a schoolboy whose pocket money barely covered essentials like gobstoppers and yoyos to being a teacher living on the faintest whiff of oil on an undersized rag. I'm not sorry. From an early age I learned that you don't need the latest spiffy tackle to make good catches, you just need to spend time by the water. The professionals I met in Khartoum and Dar es Salaam often owned no more than a spool of stout mono, some hooks, and a few knackered sparkplugs for sinkers. They made a living anyway because they knew what they were doing. Their marks were like old friends, one glance and they could feel what was going on in the water, where the fish would be holding, what they'd be chasing. Today I run into anglers, especially youngsters, who tell me they can't afford the kit for bass. Often they've read puffs in magazines, articles about the wonders of a six hundred pound lure fishing reel or a Japanese plug finished by hand and priced like a Savile Row suit. It's my pleasure to show them my gear, none of it's expensive, all of it works just fine.

In my teens and early twenties I made a lot of my equipment. There was a company called McHardys that sold blanks and fittings. The name's interesting. Maybe there was a family called the McHardys, more likely it was a handle invented to send a message: if you can't stump up for Hardy's gear here's the next best thing, brought to you by a frugal Scot with a cheeky sense of humour. Certainly I wound up with a very decent trout rod, salmon spinner, and beach-caster. My efforts never quite looked the business, I hadn't the patience to make two coloured whippings for the rings, I wanted everything put together and down by the drink in double quick time. But the fish can't see what's in your hand until it's too late. I bought something called mill end fly lines as well, usually for between a fifth and a tenth of the top drawer prices. They worked fine, any differences between the full whack efforts and my bargain basement cheapies were lost on me.

Strangely I didn't start tying my own flies till a bit later in life when I was no longer dirt poor, just grubby. I think I was struck by the beauty of the ready-made articles, the precise way they were put together. I must have driven shopkeepers insane, I'd pore for hours over their display boxes eying up the ribs, the tags, the whip finishes. Then I'd buy one Grouse and Claret and one Dunkeld. It was only when I learned about scooping trout, from a weather-beaten Yorkshireman by a stream near Preston, that I began to understand what these tiny sculptures were all about. Peering at the stomach contents of my fish helped me see how many nymphs or emergers it takes to sustain a healthy trout. And I realised a finny eating machine doesn't have time to whip out its loupe and check the evenness of your dubbing or the jaunty angle of your wing. If your offering looks reasonably like the prey species, down it goes.

Nowadays most of my flies are for bass, suggesting little fry, prawns, or weed maggots. And 'suggesting' might be stretching it, more like dropping a vague hint. I don't follow patterns, I just bodge something together and hope for the best. As long as the size is right and the materials bear a passing resemblance to the natural nibble, bass don't seem to be fussy.

I still love a beautifully tied fly, but for artistic reasons, having almost nothing to do with catching fish.

Matching the Hatch

'Many fish bite if you got good bait'
Taj Mahal, *Fishin' Blues*

Trout fishers know about matching the hatch, fish feeding on buzzers take best if you imitate a buzzer, fry feeders go well on little streamers, and so on. I think the principle holds whatever species you target, in freshwater or in the sea. When I chase big bass in the autumn I like mackerel when that's what the day-boats are catching, a squid or a few razor clams when the mackerel have moved away. Although fish don't have human emotions it's an approach that makes sense. If you were to bag a seat at a burger bar then be served a Pavlova you'd do a double take even if you're a champion pudding eater. And why would bass be any different? When they're in a feeding frenzy, gobbling down whitebait like industrial vacuum cleaners, they're more likely to hit something that suggests a whitebait than a fake pollack or ragworm.

But a lot of anglers aren't buying it. The lure brigade are a classic case. I meet people who almost always use the same plug, regardless of the time of year, the state of the wave, the prey species in the water. They tell me, 'It's just such a great shallow diver,' which being translated means, 'It's Japanese, it costs twenty-five quid, and there was a blurb about it on my favourite website.' Fine, Pavlova's from New Zealand, lots of posh ingredients like meringue and berries, and television chefs rave about it. But it's no substitute for a cheeseburger.

Fly fishers fall for the same sort of guff especially around tying materials. When I was a youngster people swore by almost any pattern that included natural jungle cock. I'd say the subconscious analysis was, 'This stuff costs an arm, a leg, and a pancreas, it must work like a charm.' Nowadays there are fads for synthetic materials, often with names that make me think they might be by-products of Sarin gas or Agent Orange. But lots of anglers are converts, they won't tie anything on the end of their line unless it includes the latest fibres from the underwater bunker laboratory of Doctor Fishenstein.

Another excuse for sticking with a particular lure, fly, or bait is, 'It's done the business for me in the past.' Well OK, it's worked under different conditions, what does that tell us? I love bacon and egg rolls but I don't fancy one for dessert after a main course of steak and kidney pudding.

Circumstances matter. Take the chap I met on a reservoir in September. The water was splattered with daddy longlegs and the trout were going wild, leaping through the surface film to grab them. From a distance the fellow looked as if he might be fishing a daddy but he was retrieving a bit swiftly. I like a hearty twitch then a pause, he was stripping line as if it were an Olympic time trial, thirty yards in thirty seconds. As I approached I noticed he was using a fast sinker. Then I saw his fly, a fluorescent pink ball. It's called The Blob, I understand it suggests a clump of daphnia. 'I was here in April,' he told me, 'It was bloody brilliant. So I'm persevering with it.' Bound to say that at any time of year I'd have my doubts about a brightly coloured lump zotting along like a fat tadpole in a high visibility tabard. When the trout are jumping out of the water to grab daddies, colour me highly sceptical.

Scarcity's another bogus basis for fancying a bait. It's the same psychology that makes a Penny Black – a small grubby piece of paper smeared with a stranger's sputum – worth big money. The oddest angling example was something I saw on a party boat in southern California in the 1970s. My brother Peter was living outside Los Angeles, when I visited we went out for yellowtail (*Seriola dorsalis*). They're tasty, hard fighting fish, and as I recall they were in the ten pound range. The fishing style was nifty. The boat was allowed to drift and the crew tried to attract the yellowtail by ladling hundreds, maybe thousands of live anchovies over the side to create a manmade bait ball. Then you'd tie on a light wire size six hook, nick it through a single anchovy, and freeline the little fellow through the feeding area. But here's the odd bit: most anchovies are bluey grey on their backs, one in fifty or a hundred's bright green, and the veterans in our party swore up and down that the green ones were the best baits. They'd spend yonks dipping around in the tank, tossing back anchovy after anchovy until they came up with an emerald beauty. As mad as weapons grade hatters. When predators attack a bait ball they don't target individual tiddlers, they just fling themselves randomly at the whole whirligig like astigmatic boozers in a bar brawl. So faffing around in search of the rare and wonderful greenie was time that would have been spent more wisely drifting any old anchovy among the yellowtail.

When you do match the hatch you can wind up using some odd baits. As children we had a couple of fishing holidays in the south of Ireland. There was a spot in Dungarvan where grey mullet swirled around sucking up the outfall from a creamery, the offering of choice was a bit of cotton wool dunked in sour milk. Not far away was an establishment on the banks of the Suir that made black pudding. There, in the vernacular, a lump of clotted pig blood was your only man, attracting trout, bream, and roach.

But oddest of all was when I lived in Dublin in the late 1960s. Near my lodging house was a canal fed by manicured streams running through a park. Walking beside the canal I'd see big brownies, some over four pounds. But even if the water was buzzing with insects nothing ever moved to a fly. My local barman marked my card: the trout were fish eaters, they took the odd stickleback but the burden of their diet was goldfish. There were sites around the park where travellers set up fairgrounds. The prize for knocking the hats off the gardai or ringing the bell with a lusty blow of the shillelagh was a baby goldfish in a plastic bag. Children would win these prizes. Their parents, not fancying another hungry mouth to feed even with a few pellets, would make them turn their new pets loose into the streams. Goldfish are bigger and slower than sticklebacks, and trout are like bass, quick to tuck into anything nourishing and easy to catch. So they'd adapted to this new food source. Out of a combination of squeamishness and poverty I couldn't bring myself to buy a goldfish from a pet shop. So I set a minnow trap, a bottle with the bottom bashed in and a few worms as bait. Freelined feral goldfish put a couple of good trout onto the bank, the best almost three pounds. Our landlady cooked them in a strong cheese sauce to mask the slightly muddy notes. They tasted OK, especially by the home cooking standards of Ireland sixty years ago, when the Sunday roast went into the oven for cremation at dawn, the vegetables onto the stove on Saturday evening.

A Professional Career

'It's my work, he'd say, and I do it for pay'
Bob Dylan, *Hurricane*

My first full time job was in Dublin. I was between school and university and I worked as a clerk in the accounting office at a factory. My weekly wage was eight pounds but the manager loved to remind us that the benefits were good. We'd a staff canteen for lunch on work days and a card that gave us free bus travel anywhere in the area. My lodging house charged me seven pounds so net disposable income was a quid a week, but entertainment in the city didn't have to cost a lot. There were bars where you could nurse a pint of stout for two or three hours while the top folk musicians of the day wandered in, greeted their pals, and played a few tunes. I never saw the Dubliners perform as a band but individually I watched every one of them in action, often at the next table over. But my office colleagues were young men, we all wanted a social life that went beyond jigs and reels, we wanted to go to the Safari Club where the showbands played. Better still it was rumoured to be full of young women from Canada, they were more liberated than their Irish sisters. As the senior clerk Mike put it, 'Some Canadian girls do it. Dublin girls don't do it. Case fecking closed.' As a matter of record I went to the Safari Club half a dozen times, never met anyone from further afield than Malahide. I reckon the North American dance fans were a fiction put about by the club's owners as a way of persuading Dublin lads to stump up five bob for admission. Women were let in for nothing.

Anyway the fellows in the office were always on the lookout to raise a bit of extra money and one Friday Terry from accounts payable came up with an idea. We should go to Howth, catch fish from the pier, then sell them to the restaurant where his brother worked as a waiter. 'As long as it's fresh the chef doesn't care how much he pays. It's a real fancy place, half the menu's in French, they've candles on the tables and all. And there's gobs of stuff caught in Howth, the sea's alive with whoppers right now. I was walking there a few days ago, loads and loads of big ones.' By the end of our lunch break the motion was passed, we'd meet at eight o'clock next morning at the bus stop outside the factory, all profits to be shared equally, every man to do his duty.

I've always been an early riser, I was there at quarter to eight carrying a salmon spinning rod, a few Tobys and Devon minnows in my pocket. I wasn't sure my outfit would be any use, I'd never seen Howth pier, but the other chaps would have different gear, we'd be covered. Then the other chaps showed up, Mike with sandwiches his mam had made to sustain the professional fishers through their busy day, Terry with a bucket for our catch. Of the five others who'd counted themselves in there was no sight. 'Their loss,' said Mike, 'We'll only have to share the money three ways.' Right you are, I thought, and at least the bus was free, we wouldn't be sharing losses. Eat enough sandwiches and I'd come out ahead even if we blanked.

It was November but warm, I expected the pier to be jammed with anglers, especially as the sea was alive with whoppers right now. But no, just the three of us and two old ladies walking small dogs. 'So where are the big ones?' I asked. 'Last week they were half way along the jetty,' Terry said.

'They'd so many they'd plastic boxes stacked one on top of another. A box of cod, a box of plaice, all sorts.' 'Terry,' I explained, 'those boxes come off trawlers. Nobody caught those fish here, they caught them out at sea. Then they landed them here to sell.' He was so crestfallen that I added, 'But I'm sure there'll be something around.'

An hour later I wasn't so sure, I might as well have been casting my spinner into a bath tub. Mike's mam made a good sandwich, everything else was a total balls-up. Then Terry pointed along the pier. 'Those birds, are they washing their faces or what?' Gulls were whirling, flapping, diving into the wave. I darted along the jetty, chucked my Toby as far as I could and I was fast into a mackerel. It was a good one too, at least a pound and a half. By teatime Terry's bucket was full, twenty-four mackies. The restaurant bought them at three for a quid. None of the chef's regular suppliers had showed up, we'd saved his bacon, or at least his seafood special. He treated us like royalty. Maybe minor royalty, a meat pie to share and a pint of stout each. He also gave us a tip. The Safari Club was a waste of time, he told us, the Zig Zag Lounge was smack on the button, it was full of women from Sweden. We went there. It wasn't.

Explain Yourself

'I'll turn you on sonny to something strong'
Bruce Springsteen, *Blinded By The Light*

From my childhood people have asked why I like fishing. As a lad I didn't care what I said. 'I just do,' was OK with grown-ups, it shut them up and left me to my own devices. With my contemporaries I might raise the subject of bait, little boys enjoy descriptions of lobworms. Then came my teenage years and I needed raise my game, chatting up girls was a priority. I found the best approach was to ask them lots of questions about themselves then look as if you were listening to the answers, sympathetic nods and grunts. But I had to be ready to explain my own interests in return, angling was an obsession too big to hide.

I had fair luck with the old line about loving the great outdoors. In the late 1960s getting back to nature was fashionable in my circle, the virgin wilderness, birdsong. Occasionally I'd chuck in a few riffs from William Wordsworth or The Grateful Dead. If I did this without attribution some young ladies were impressed by my turns of phrase. But I wasn't comfortable talking such total eyewash. Stuff wandering lonely as a cloud, the still, sad music of humanity, and some morning in the sweet by and by, if there were whoppers to be had I knew I'd fish in a concrete pool enveloped by diesel exhaust with jackhammers providing the soundtrack.

Free food's another chestnut but it didn't play with my audience, most of the girls I knew were vegetarian. They were happy to wear Afghan jackets, the ones that smelled like rotting meat whenever it rained, maybe they thought sheep shed their skins like crabs and snakes. But when it came to rations, animal-free blandness was the order of the decade. Older people lashed out at us dirty smelly hippies. Very unfair, we bathed regularly, the pong was because we lived on brown rice, cabbage, and root vegetables. Fibre gives you wind. Putrid lamb outerwear, lots of flatulence, of course we smelled bad.

In the end I decided honesty was the best policy. Or maybe don't talk nonsense unless you're sure you'll remember what you said. I told potential girlfriends I was an angler because I enjoyed trying to work out how my quarry behaved, what it ate, where and when to find it on the feed. It was a hit. The off the cuff reaction was 'You mean you want to think like a fish?' At this point the straitlaced young women would stomp off in disgust. The more adventurous ones, the dopers and wild children, would say, 'Think like a fish. Wow, that's crazy. I've got a little hash in my pocket, should we step outside?'

One even invited me to try some underwater mindreading near her sister's house on the coast south of Dublin. There was a trawler harbour close by and I thought an ebbing tide would empty all sorts of treats into the open sea. We sat on the end of the jetty at sunset, I caught two pollack and a bass, and my young friend thought I was out of sight. In 1969 that was as good as it got.

Miraculous Salvage

'These are the days of miracle and wonder'
Paul Simon, *You Can Call Me Al*

Nowadays the countryside's spotted with still-water trout fisheries like currants in a good saffron bun, but I was in my late teens before I saw one. It was near Wexford, my pal Declan invited me to fish it over a holiday weekend. His uncle had left him some tackle when he emigrated to America and Declan was keen to have a bash, ideally with someone who had a clue about the fly.

We hitchhiked from Dublin to the village where Declan's parents lived. As soon as Mrs. Murphy had us sorted out with tea and sandwiches her husband led the way to the shed where Uncle Liam's gear was laid out on a trestle table. 'My brother only ever buys the best,' he said. 'He's a terrible man for a steak dinner, wouldn't eat an old stew to save his life. So I'm sure this is fierce expensive stuff.' It was. There was a doublehanded salmon rod, custom made, a neat little monogram painted onto the butt section. And there was a Sharpe's trout outfit with a Hardy's reel and two lines, a floater and a sinker. Even Declan, who wouldn't have known impregnated bamboo cane from an expectant disciplinarian, was impressed, running his fingertips delicately over the lacquer finish. And when we went out into the paddock so I could teach him the basics of casting he wouldn't load the rod properly for fear he might snap it. But after an hour catching buttercups and being jeered at by the neighbour's children – 'Janey Mack, he's fishing for a cow' – he was managing fifteen yards or so and the bullwhip cracks of his earliest efforts were behind him. And by the time the sun began to sink I reckoned he was ready to be introduced to the water. Or maybe I was champing at the bit, bored with yelling that he should keep his elbow tucked in, stop stamping his feet and whirling around to watch his back cast, this was fishing not a bloody ceilidh for heaven's sake.

The lake was only about eight acres but even as we arrived I could see rising trout. There were sedges coming off so I went through Uncle Liam's fly boxes for a couple of Wickham's Fancies. I watched Declan make his first tentative chucks. Then I decided he was going to do fine on his own, he hadn't hooked his own arse or flung his rod into the drink, he just needed to build some confidence. So I wandered off on my own. The fish were eejits, never mind a Wickham's, I reckon they'd have hit a bare hook or one of Mrs. Murphy's rock buns (made with real rocks according to Mr. M). They were up to twelve inches and dark backed, beauties. I kept four for breakfast, released as many again. Every so often I glanced across the water to see how my protégé was faring. Still casting away, no sign of broken gear or terrible fankles, he was fine. After perhaps my tenth fish I noticed he was sitting on a tummock, the rod on the ground at his feet. Probably tired, I'd toss him a kind word to keep his spirits up.

As I wandered back to his spot I saw his outfit jump, bounce through the grass, then fly into the lake. Declan was horrified. 'Jesus, Mary, and Joseph, I just put it down for a rest of the old arm. I should have pulled all the line up, I left nothing but a smidget in the water. And now something's after pulling Uncle Liam's fecking Rolls Royce fishing rod away. Dad's going to have my guts for tripes.' I peered into the ripple as Declan carried on predicting a fate worse than the martyrdom of blessed Oliver Plunkett. Twenty yards out I saw a wisp of lurid peach colour, Liam's floating line. A better friend might have dropped his trousers and swum for it but it was a chilly evening. I tied on a big salmon double, waded to the tops of my wellies, and cast as far as I could.

On my third try I felt a drag on the line. I retrieved gingerly, in the bend of my stoat's tail was some dark green braid. I pulled at it and kept pulling. Finally there was resistance, a fair old weight, then the Sharpe's rod broke the surface, the reel cloaked in pondweed. It was empty, all the backing was in coils at my feet. Liam gave thanks to a whole hurling team of saints for this miracle. He started cranking, through the braid, onto the fly line, then he yelped, 'The whole yoke's alive, it's lepping about like there's a mad thing on the end, what do I do?' I stood behind him offering excitable advice as the mad thing ran three or four times.

Finally it tired and Declan drew it into the shallows where I gilled it ashore. It was a four pound brownie, deep flanked and beautiful, the fly wedged in its scissor. 'Sure I'm glad I caught one,' said my pupil. 'I'm never going fishing again as long as God spares me. So it's good to have something to show for the day. I thought standing around with a rod in your hand must be as boring as a Good Friday sermon. But it's too exciting for my blood, I'm a devil for a thrill but I don't need a bloody heart attack.'

Student Foragers

'All you really found was some stems and some seeds'
Loudon Wainwright III, *Samson And The Warden*

I went to Bristol University at the beginning of the 1970s. For the most part the experience was wasted on me because for the most part I was wasted. I spent three years doing enough academic work to scrape passes, all the while holding down part-time jobs to fund my taste for psychotropics. It's not a lifestyle I'd repeat but I never saw much harm from the likes of pot and LSD. The most serious casualties in my circle were a pair of youngsters who went to Snowdonia to hunt for psilocybin mushrooms in the crags. The young woman fell in a stream and sprained a knee ligament, her boyfriend tumbled on a rocky scree and broke his ankle. But they were still keen foragers, a month later they hobbled off to Kew Gardens on the basis of a rumour that you could pinch peyote buds from one of the greenhouses. You couldn't.

An equally dodgy tip-off took me on an autumn trip to the Somerset Levels. The word was that the police dumped impounded cannabis in the corner of a meadow. They contaminated the pot itself with some toxic shite but the seeds had survived intact and viable. Somewhere inland of Weston Super Mare a forest of weed had sprouted and October was the perfect time to harvest it. I wasn't so sure. I'd seen marijuana plants in Tanzania, I couldn't imagine they'd thrive in the sunless south-west, but I owned a car so I was drafted in to provide transport. Nobody knew which meadow held the treasure. We'd a description of the site, but the trouble with levels is that they're level, everything looks the same as everything else.

After half an hour of driving in circles and arguing I decided I wasn't wasting any more petrol, all further exploration would be on foot. I parked by a drainage canal and rolled a smoke. And that was when I saw a swirl in the brown water, a fin waggling in the frothy surface. I always had a rod in the boot so I grabbed it and began searching for bait. The water was too muddy for a spinner, I needed juice and aroma. Under a rock I found a crab four inches across. I skewered it with the biggest hook in my box, squished it slightly, and lobbed it into the creek.

In a matter of moments the rod thumped, and soon enough a two pound bass was at my feet. The free weed was an urban myth but I took home three bass, the best close to five pounds. And in spite of their muddy parish they were delicious. But they were a one off, I tried the same spot three more times for a few flounders and silver eels. The bass must been lost after a wrong turn as they headed up the Bristol Channel. Or maybe they too were looking for dope.

The Jock Told Me

'Somewhere down the road you'll understand'
Steve Earle, *Pilgrim*

Angling writers often tell of their mentors, the wise old rods who initiated them into the sport. A lot of these experts strike me as pains in the arse. They landed fish after fish while their apprentices blanked. They had secret spots that could be shown only to the anointed and in the fullness of time. Their guidance came in the form of gnomic nonsense that added nothing to the sum total of human knowledge. 'One day you'll understand the way of the trout.' 'You catch big bass when you inhabit their view of the water.' 'When nothing takes you can find your soul.' Well thank you very much but if I wanted a guru I'd be on top of a mountain in Nepal looking for a cross-legged geezer with a feral beard. Right now I'd rather someone just told me how to get a bite.

Apart from Mr. Hansome showing me how to fish a float in the Nile I never had a tutor. I read a lot, books are a good way to learn to tie rigs and flies. Nowadays you can watch videos on the internet but I prefer a series of still pictures. Sometimes you want to see exactly what the whole contraption's meant to look like at a stage in its assembly. I find it easier to look at Figure Three than to scramble for the pause button as the instructor rabbits away like an auctioneer with a mouthful of peanuts.

I taught myself to cast a fly by following printed advice as well. My style's old fashioned because it's based on the techniques of the early twentieth century. It can be sloppy too, I blame that on my parents' library. I wanted to wedge a Book of Common Prayer under my right elbow but I had to settle for a paperback copy of the Oxford Dictionary of Quotations. Leslie Moncrieff was my role model for belting a weight out into the surf but I never turned into the sort of chap who can put a bait onto the edge of the continental shelf. No blame should attach to Mr. Moncrieff, I didn't stick at it long enough to acquire the artistry it would take to make up for my skinny build and third rate motor skills.

When it came to finding fish I followed the guidance of a photographer I know. In the days before digital cameras he said the best way to take a good picture was to take a lot of bad ones, snap away long enough and one day you'll hit the spot. I spent hundreds of hours in the blanker's tunnel before seeing glimmers of fishy light. My trouting was limited by my footwear and my poverty. I watched enviously as other anglers waded into rivers and lakes or whipped out their wallets and hired boats. Skint and in wellies I was stuck in the shallows. When you can cover just a small area you study it closely, there's not much else to do. So by default I picked up the knack of finding the features on the bank or the bottom that concentrate nymphs, emergers, tadpoles, terrestrials, and fry.

With bass on the beach I hit my stride through a mixture of ineptitude and idleness. I tried hard to sling my sinker to the third wave. That was what the books said you had to do, along with most of the people I met on the shore. But on a flat strand with a roaring surf the second breaker often was at the limit of my range. Once I'd managed a half decent cast I left it be, no point in reeling in now, the next chuck might be even shorter. And I found an ebbing tide sometimes produced good bites about the time my bait was so close to my boots as to seem plain silly. There might be schoolies in the faraway depths but the better fish feed in one or two feet of foamy mayhem. Another self-taught lesson that's served me well.

A lot of the advice I picked up from veterans didn't change my fishing because it involved illegality, grubby ethics, or both. A grizzled Cornish pixie of a man told me the best way to a basket of bass was with ragworms and a float in the estuaries, he was making mighty slaughters in what now are nursery areas. A gruff northern river watcher told me coloured water called for a fly dressed on a big treble. When I asked him to recommend a pattern he said, 'Anything dark, that way they don't see it coming.' A creaky Irishman whose rod was never straight showed me his nymph, an unusually sparse hare's ear. 'Then you've room to shove a couple of big worms on the bend. And if you see the bailiff you strike like a wild thing, that clears the hook and you won't get in the shite for using bait.'

To this day I gather snippets from just about everyone I meet, a bait to try, a fly pattern I've not used, a lure that does the job without breaking the bank. But just one angling oldie made a lifelong impression, The Jock. There was a small lake I fished not far from Bristol. It wasn't one of the famous ones, Chew or Blagdon, and by now I imagine it's been filled in and turned into a leisure centre or a multi-storey carpark. But it was cheap, if I could come away with two or three trout my ticket was paid for in food. Most people pulled on chesties, puddled as deep as they dared, then slung big lures as far as they were able. The exception was a slim, stooped gentleman in his sixties or seventies. I never knew his real name, he was known as The Jock because of his thick Glaswegian accent. The Jock never put his feet in the water. Using a long floppy rod he'd shuffle along the bank casting four or five yards at most. The fishers with the cutting edge blanks laughed at him, called him a dinosaur. But he caught a lot of fish.

One afternoon he was sitting smoking when I approached him. He'd a reputation for being a man of few words, most of them between frosty and outright hostile. Not a bit of it, once it was clear I wanted to know about his way of fishing he lit up as if I'd offered him a double whisky. 'Loch style, that's what it's called. Or short lining. Normally you do it from a boat on the drift, but as long as you keep moving it works fine from the bank.' 'Right, what are you imitating?' I'd pored over articles about insect life-cycles, I was convinced you had to match something on the water – unless you admitted defeat and went with a streamer. 'You're not so much imitating as suggesting,' he told me as he pointed to his cast, 'and you're not suggesting anything very particular. Your bob fly's big and bushy, when it skitters on the top it just looks like something that might be tasty. And a trout's like a bairn, anything interesting goes in its mouth. Then the dropper and the point, they'll give you a fish that has a look at the bob but doesn't take hold.' For half an hour we chatted as he showed me his fly box and told me about Soldier Palmers and Claret Pennels, bygone days on Loch Leven and Loch Awe.

When we parted I had a new trick in my bag. More important, I had a new insight into the way opportunistic predators behave. If you offer them something not too big, vaguely edible looking, and running away at speed, they may well grab it. On dour reservoir days I've used a leash of traditional wets to good effect. The other anglers have never seen these patterns. They grew up on epoxy buzzers, Boobies, and Cormorants, so an Invicta or a Woodcock and Orange strikes them as exotic. In tough conditions I go for bass with a Toby or a flying condom whipped through the ripple at a rate of knots. I'm not imitating much, just suggesting an appetising nibble that's going to escape if the bass doesn't snap it up in a hurry. It can work when all else fails, and that's thanks to The Jock.

It Ain't Necessarily So

'I need you at the dimming of the day'
Richard & Linda Thompson, *The Dimming Of The Day*

My teacher training was in the north of England and the fishing I remember best was in a reservoir outside Bolton. The dam looked Victorian, the banks were steep and wooded, the bottom criss-crossed by ridges and trenches. It was a spot where anglers in waders often delighted onlookers by toddling smoothly across the mouth of a bay before stepping into an underwater valley and sinking up to the tops of their flat hats. Lancastrians do a good line in cutting commentary. 'Where are your trunks?' 'How about some backstroke then?' 'Empty your boots, lad, we need that water for drinking.'

In daylight you'd have thought you were casting into a relic of the area's industrial past, a spot blighted by decades of pollution from the cotton trade. I never saw a fish move before sunset, and the odd rod with a sunk line had the scowl of a VAT inspector who can't find a single problem with your return. But as the light dropped, especially on a still evening, big brown trout would slurp noisily. It seemed obvious why, there was a hatch of chocolate coloured sedges, fat ones best tied to a size eight or ten hook. I must have spent half a dozen evenings on a blank. Every dry sedge pattern in my box, every nymph, never so much as in inquiry.

Then on one outing I ran into a birdwatcher. 'You're a fishing type, son, what are these bloody big flies called?' I must have looked nonplussed. 'The big ones, they're sitting on top of the water, I'm watching them with my binoculars. Great brown buggers.' 'They're sedges.' 'Aye, well that doesn't sound very nice, does it? Fancy a sedge sandwich, a sedge pie, sedge and dripping? But the fishes don't know they're called sedges. They must just not like the way they taste.' 'What do you mean?' 'Well I can see the trout coming up again and again, eating these tiny little specks on the top of the lake, but they avoid the sedges like they were old black puddings. Here, have a look through my glasses, you'll see.' And sure enough I focused on a plump brown body flapping in the film until at last it took off. All around it were feeding fish, sucking rises to microscopic gnats. So I changed my tune, a three pound leader and a tiddly dark dry or nymph. If the size was right – an eighteen or a twenty – the pattern made almost no difference. Anything tiny and nondescript would take trout. Anything bigger than a size sixteen was ignored. I still can't explain what was going on. Why would good trout – and I had them to three pounds, saw a six pounder at least – turn down a chunky meal and chase dozens of snacks instead? Perhaps Bolton gnats are like those energy bars they give out to marathon runners, massive amounts of calories in tiny packages. Maybe they're full of a chemical that stimulates the pleasure centres in the brain. Maybe they taste fantastic, I should have tried one. The same puzzle crops up with the bass I chase today. They'll take jelly-fry under an inch long when the water's full of plump sandeels, and I don't know why. But it's mysteries that keep us fishing.

Sharing the Wealth

'Who doesn't care about the helpless people'
Lucky Dube, *The Hand That Giveth*

At the end of my teaching course I was invited to a graduation ceremony. It was a three hour gig and you had to rent a mortarboard and an academic gown, a fiver for the day with a ten quid deposit. Even at nursery school I never enjoyed the dressing up box, the chance to flap around in Dracula drag and fork out for the privilege had no appeal. Instead I spent the morning hiking on a scrubby moor somewhere near Derby. It must have been late June, one of the first hot days of the year, but breezy with low cloud cover and the odd gentle shower.

About nine o'clock I felt peckish. There was a little lake just off the main track, flat rocks forming a natural picnic table. As I ate my sandwich and sipped my thermos coffee – that was what we drank before the arrival of the barista and the three page beverage menu, mostly in bogus Italian – I spotted a fly fisher. He was wading waist deep, casting a very long line. He shuffled ashore and sat down, giving me the chance to eye up his gear. A sinking line, a fifteen foot leader, and a large nymph. 'I'm on holiday from Yorkshire,' he told me, 'probably a permanent bloody holiday. I'm a coal miner and they're closing our pit. So I reckoned a day in the hills might put the smile back on my face. The bloke in the tackle shop told me about this spot, he said the fish are down near the bottom. And that's where they're staying, I've been here since first light, not a chuffing wibble.' 'I've seen a few rising,' I told him. 'They're hard against the banks, they seem to be taking little olives.' He squinted at the shoreline. 'Blow me down lad, you're right, that's champion.'

Google tells me the fastest ever Formula One pit stop was just under two seconds. This fellow could have run the Red Bull mechanics pretty close. In the blink of an eye he swapped his spool for one with a floater, attached a new cast, and tied on a small Greenwell's Glory. Then he offered me the rod. 'You spotted them, you told me about the rise, it's obvious you're a trout man, otherwise you'd not have noticed owt. So you shall have the first go.'

The fish were no great size, the best about half a pound, but they were chubby and handsome, black and blood red spots on a deep gold background. We caught and released five or six before the sky cleared and the hatch came to an end. And in those bleak days of economic collapse and the three day week we grinned like toothpaste models at an audition. By the way fifty-odd years later when the fish are dour I still find myself muttering, 'Not a chuffing wibble.' And it still makes me smile.

A Conversion

'We must all stand in the water'
Ozark Mountain Daredevils, *Beauty In The River*

I moved to the Gambia straight from teacher training and soon found myself headmaster of an international primary school. I'd love to say that this post reflected obvious talent but it wouldn't be true. I was the only staff member willing to work full time and the governors picked on the basis of like it or lump it, I was better than nothing. My salary was very modest, pegged to the pocket money earned by volunteers from VSO and the Peace Corps. That meant I was as poor as a church mouse with a gambling problem. Teachers and nurses are underpaid everywhere. A lot of salaries are inversely proportional to usefulness, just look at the amounts paid to young men who kick footballs; and to hedge fund managers, the tapeworms in the digestive system of the market economy. Still it was a lovely school and the Gambia had good shooting and fishing, more than enough to make up for living on the bones of my bottom.

It didn't take long to pick the brains of the local sport fishers and find out that boat trips were the way to catch cobia (*Rachycentron canadum*) and barracuda (*Sphyraena afra*) on the troll, while landlubbers used beach outfits for cassava fish (*Pseudotolithus senegalensis*), threadfin (*Polydactylus quadrifilis*), and a by-catch of spiky catfish. We'd owned a boat in Dar es Salaam, they're holes in the ocean into which you pour money. I had none so I stuck to the beaches where most anglers used six ounce sinkers and 1/0 or 2/0 hooks. Bait was a fillet of bonga (*Ethmalosa fimbriata*), a yellowish herring-like species almost always available in the local markets.

I caught some decent fish. The cassavas and threadfin pulled hard enough and were good eating but there were a few hitches. First, lugging beach-casting gear through soft sand in tropical heat and a hundred percent humidity led not so much to perspiration as outright melting. Second, bonga's a messy bait and I often came home covered with enough scales to go to a costume party as a cross dressing mermaid. Third, catfish were everywhere, omnivorous slimy wretches with mildly poisonous spines. And fourth, the best stretches of sandy shore attracted hordes of noisy and puking drunk tourists, most from Scandinavia. This had a compensating feature: some of the holidaymakers were informal in their choice of beachwear, occasionally I'd watch topless and bottomless blondes when bites were slow. But on the whole I fancied something different.

The trigger for my switch came one autumn evening when my sport was banjaxed by an army of UK-based sun seekers. They were full of beery bonhomie and determined to fling themselves into the waves right in front of my fishing spot. I'd move along the strand, they'd follow, as if the whiff of bonga were the aroma of bacon and I were the Pied Piper of

Barracuda

fry-ups. There wasn't even any payback on the voyeuristic front, they were middle-aged Londoners and they stuck to the British fashion convention that reserves skimpy swimming costumes for people who'd look better in a head to foot bin bag.

I shuffled along to a place where the sand gave way to an outcrop of laterite and basalt, where a reef ran out under the surf. And there in the shallow water I saw little splashes, tiny fish leaping. They were mullet,

Cob

finger mullet if your hands were short and stumpy, two or three inches long. As I watched there were swirls, the odd fin cutting the surface. This was a feeding frenzy. I fancied a closer look but I was barefoot, basalt turns even the most leathery skin into something like steak mince blasted by a water cannon. So I headed home and sorted out some kit for the next evening.

I had an old salmon spinning rod nine or ten feet long. Experience with modern lure outfits tells me it cast between about fifteen and forty grammes. Also a Penn Spinfisher reel loaded with twelve pound mono. I don't think anyone went spinning with braid in the early 1970s, certainly not skint schoolteachers in developing countries. By way of lures I had some Abu Tobys, some German sprats, and a couple of balsawood plugs, gifts from a friend whose shop had received them as trade samples. My waders were a pair of canvas tennies that came up over the ankle – they were sold as basketball shoes in the days before a celebrity endorsement could turn casual footwear into something priced like an old master.

Next evening I was on the reef, again there were baby mullet everywhere. I tied on a Toby and my very first flick led to an almighty swish as something took short. My second cast splashed down and went solid. Snagged on the rocks, the water was only nine inches deep when the wave receded, I waded to retrieve my lure. Clearly anything subsurface wasn't going to do much good. I tried one of the free sample plugs. It was a floater, cigar shaped, about three inches long, finished in glittery white. It had no action whatsoever, a walk the dog retrieve was more like dragging a dead dachshund through the surf by its tail. But it was deadly.

In under an hour I landed three trevally (*Caranx senegallus)* to ten pounds, three cassava fish about the same size. Trevally pull like stink, they run almost as fast as a seatrout or a barracuda, and they're as dogged as a wrasse or a ray. At last light a really good one, maybe twenty pounds, ripped off fifty yards of line before snapping the mono on a sharp lump of rock. It didn't take a genius to realise I was onto something.

Next day I dropped in on my shopkeeper friend and we pored over tackle catalogues. The white cigar thing was made in the USA, the wholesale price was three dollars. Nowadays I see bass fishers flinging Japanese plugs that cost more than my first two motorcars, but it's a fair bet they aren't trying to live on the stipend of a Peace Corps volunteer.

So I went to see a woodworker I knew, armed with a couple of broken broomsticks. Would he be able to cut them into two to three inch lengths then drill an end to end hole in each chunk, in return he'd go onto my list of fish recipients? No problem as long as I kept him in mind for trevally and barracuda, his favourite suppers. I shaped my blanks with a sharp penknife, smoothed them with sandpaper, and poked a length of wire through each with a treble at one end and a loop at the other. Then I screwed in a little eye amidships with a second treble, not so much for better hook ups, more to stop the lure from spinning like a whirling dervish in an aerobics class. The only paint on hand was some white and some red, I dunked each lure body in the white, let it dry, then brushed on a red head. That simple design was the haute couture cat's pyjama suit, never bettered. I experimented over the years – black backs, blue backs, silver bodies, scales – but I always went back to the old red and white effort.

In summer it caught me trevally, cassava, threadfin, and the odd barracuda. In winter the cassavas stuck around, and I'd also land leerfish (*Lichia amia*), cob (*Argyrosomus japonicas*), and a lot more barracuda. And years later I understand why the hours I spent mixing colours and daubing delicate patterns, the air thick with white spirit and profanity, were such a waste of effort. My plugs were zipping along in the surface foam, the predators were a few inches deeper, all they ever saw was a crudely rendered mullet belly against the background of the sky. I could have adorned the backs of my broomstick chunks with gold leaf, high visibility yellow waistcoats, or lifelike impressions of pork sausages, the big fish would have been none the wiser. As long as the size was right to suggest the resident baitfish, nothing else mattered much. And today when I use bass lures I reckon length and profile count for a lot more than design or finish.

I gave my beach rod to a friend. For the six years I stayed in the Gambia I never again had to remove bonga scales from my underpants. I was a lure fisher, only going back to bait in the surf – as one option among many – when I moved home to the UK in my forties and rekindled my love affair with bass.

Leerfish

Ducks, Geese, & Muddy Underwear

'Rise up this morning, smiled with the rising sun'
Bob Marley & The Wailers, *Three Little Birds*

Gambian winters hardly deserved to be called such. Our tourist trade was built on sun seekers from northern Europe visiting West Africa when their own countries were blighted by ice, snow, and four hour intervals of daylight between long, frigid nights. I wet waded all year round, my only concession to the cooler weather was that I'd wear a fleece-lined windbreaker over my shorts and shirt. I owned a supply of these warm tops, I often got them wet and they took an age to dry. Banjul market had stalls flogging cast-off clothing from the USA. It had been rejected by American charity shops, wrapped into bundles, and sold by weight to traders in developing countries. I was on good terms with the stallholders the way city gents are known to their Savile Row tailors, they were my sole source of kit. Not that I was too poor to stump up for a brand new shirt, just that I preferred to save my money for more rewarding stuff like monofilament and cartridges. Anyway the used clothes peddlers knew my size and shape, so short jackets with warm linings were set to one side for me to have a gander.

As well as wrapped up fishing weather, winter brought the wildfowling season. The Gambia's on the migration route for lots of birds and it developed a reputation as a holiday spot for ornithologists, especially from the UK. This must have been a second tourism drive, the first was an approach to the cheap end of the market in the Scandinavian countries where the advertising pitch was a bit different: 'Sun, Sand, Sea, and Sex.' The visitor population became bimodal. You had Swedes and Danes in skimpy bathing suits or birthday suits, drinking themselves senseless on the beaches and copulating at random and in public with anything that didn't get out of the way; and you had late middle aged British twitchers in safari jackets, sunhats, and sensible shoes, buzzing about the rumoured sighting of a lesser mottled teabag warbler. Then the US television drama *Roots* was aired and a third group of foreigners came calling, prosperous African Americans looking for traces of their ancestors. Some of them spread largesse on areas where the villagers were canny enough to claim their parishes were rammed with folk who looked exactly like Alex McGregor from Houston or Marsha Smith from Chicago, bloody uncanny, you just have to be descended from my great great great uncle Mamadou, and wouldn't you like to build a clinic or a school for your newly discovered extended family?

But back to visitors with wings. These included whistling teal (*Dendrocygna bicolo*), small, fast, and delicious; knob billed geese (*Sarkidiornis melanotos*), bigger, even tastier, domesticated in Central America where they're called African Ducks; and spur winged geese (*Plectropterus gambensis*), weighing up to ten or even fifteen kilograms, the spur being a bony spike like a dog claw sticking out from the joint between the wing-bones.

Our shoots were at dawn when the birds flighted into the rice paddies. They were a pest and farmers treated the guns like conquering heroes crossed with disco-dancing superstars. (This was the era of *Saturday Night Fever*, a film I watched to the end, only learning from the credits that there was more than one song in it. I never thought much of disco.) We were fêted wildly when we bagged spur wing. Not only did they eat lots of rice plants, their big bodies flattened growing areas like a Heathrow runway as they came in to land.

Apart from being a half decent shot, the key to a successful wildfowling trip was the same thing that leads to a good bass outing, being in the right spot. You entered the rice paddies by walking along raised bunds, easy footing two or three feet above the ooze and mud. A few fowl would fly over the bunds but the busier air traffic areas were around little reedy islands in the paddies themselves, where there was plenty for the birds to eat. You could reach these natural hides only by plodging thigh deep through the slime. One of our regulars had waders so he always set himself up in a hotspot. For the rest of the party it was a case of weighing comfort and cleanliness against excitement. Some guns stayed on the dry bund and hoped for the best. Polish Joe – in the sense that he was from Poland, not that his shoes were abnormally shiny – wore his heart on his sleeve. He told me, 'I'd love to shoot some geese but my most important criterion is this: a good hunting trip is one when you start and finish with the same dry underpants.' An equally fastidious French fellow bought himself a five shot repeater, he reckoned extra firepower would make up for being away from wildfowl central. It didn't. As the dawn rose I'd hear five reports in quick succession, followed by, *'Merde, bordel alors.'* I was happy to suffer for my art as long as I was dressed for it. I wore one of my American jackets, long trousers, tennis shoes, and thick socks. Folk wisdom has it that snake fangs won't penetrate stoutly knitted wool. I'm not sure this has any basis in science, I suspect it's a myth put about by the New South Wales Merino Breeders' Association or the Guild of Orcadian Stocking Crafters, but I took my chances, even after my brother Mick shot a big cobra at the edge of a paddy field. And the mud, mosquitoes, and risk of venomous reptiles faded to nothing when the first light came up and the skeins of birds began to circle.

Sight fishing provides a quick buzz: see a fish, make a cast, euphoria or gloom. Wildfowling's an adrenaline rush in slow motion: they're half a mile away, they're coming this way, they're veering off, they're back on track, a hundred yards and closing, here they come, no they don't, yes they do. My legs in soggy jeans would feel chilly but my palms would be sweating like sage and onions over a low burner.

At bottom I'm more an angler than a shot, but the best bit of both my sports is the same: work out what your quarry's eating, find a place where that fodder's plentiful, and be ready to change your plan at the drop of a sodden boot sock if things don't work out. Sometimes I'd pick what I thought was the perfect spot, only to have to flounder back into the mud and think again. But I don't believe I ever had a blank day on the wildfowl, flexibility and bloody mindedness always paid off in the end.

None of us owned a gundog. Even if we had we might not have sent a four-legged friend into the rice. Dogs often see snakes as playmates so we used human retrievers, often myself. After all I was lagged with mud anyway, nothing to lose. If one of our more dapper guns dropped a bird he made a mental note of where it came down. When the sky was empty I'd slither away to recover it. Now and then the fowl would be missing in action and I blamed the shooter for lousy sense of direction, failing memory, drunk and incapable, or all three. Then one morning I saw a dead spur wing disappearing through the rice stalks, dragged by a six foot monitor lizard. A better friend might have engaged in hand to claw combat with the goose rustler but I was tired, I let him have his breakfast.

The Stalker

'Das ist gut'
Ian Dury & The Blockheads, *Hit Me With Your Rhythm Stick*

It was autumn, I was casting a plug into a small chop, a couple of cassava fish on my rope. All of a sudden I had the feeling I was being watched. It's something I experience a lot and it's bizarre how often I'm right. I suppose I may be eyed up more than I think – tons of people asking themselves, 'He looks normal enough, why does he smell of squid?' – and it's only when that odd sensation hits that I turn around and notice the bod staring holes in my back. But there was indeed a blond fellow sitting at the foot of the cliff peering in my direction. The cassavas stopped taking so I moved to the next reef. Again when I turned my head there he was.

I know some people routinely fish in front of photographers and video techies, a lot fish with their pals, but I don't enjoy an audience. It's not that I do anything I'm ashamed of, like picking my nose or dropping my bags and flashing the water, just that I like to feel absorbed by my thoughts, no beady eyes to shatter the mood. But blondie was at my third spot too. This was starting to feel creepy, maybe he was an axe murderer waiting for nightfall to whip out his machete and hack me to pieces.

I paddled inshore and wandered over. I wasn't sure how to start the conversation. 'Are you carrying a sharp bladed weapon?' 'Do you have any criminal convictions for crimes of violence against strangers?' I settled for, 'You seem to be following me, can I help you?' He was full of apologies. Yes, he was following me. But nothing personal, just that he loved watching me catch fish. His name was Manfred and he fished when he was at home in Germany. He hadn't brought his tackle on holiday. He'd heard you needed beach gear in the Gambia, if he'd known you could spin he'd have come with his pike outfit. 'I said to my wife that I take five minutes to see what happens with you and the fish. But then I see you have strong takes, good fights, and I cannot leave. My hands are moving as if I turn the reel. But I am sorry I stayed behind you, this was not polite.' 'No worries,' I told him,

Cassava fish

'and why don't you have a go. Don't bother casting too far, they're close in.' 'James,' he said, 'I know this. I've seen the fish you were taking. And thank you, you are so very kind, if I just can succeed with one catch I will be very happy. On the top half of the moon, as they say in football competitions.' We took it in turns until sunset, a cassava apiece then switch positions. When it was dark I offered to drop Manfred back to his hotel. OK, but only if he could treat me to dinner with his wife and their two children. At the table he stood up and raised his beer glass with a little bow. 'This is good, my best holiday. My first love is my family. My second love is my sport. And even when it's in second place I miss it so badly when it's not there. But you are a fisherman, I don't need to tell you this.'

Warthogs, Lizards and Chefs

'Where you goin' with that gun in your hand?'
Jimi Hendrix, *Hey Joe*

At the end of our winter wildfowling sessions we'd stay on in the scrub forest beside the rice paddies to hunt bushpigs or warthogs (*Phachoerus africanus*). The Gambia had a flourishing population of them. It's a densely populated country and the predators that naturally would keep numbers under control had been killed off or displaced. Warthogs are destructive, their favourite fodder's plant roots, a hungry family can turn a field into something that looks like a practise site for an overachieving earthmover operator. The Gambian Agriculture Ministry sometimes invited the Ghanaian army to send a few of its finest on pest control exercises. The Gambia is a Muslim country, species from the pig family weren't eaten locally; but a large number of Ghanaians are Christians, they reckon a cut of bushpig's a treat. The visiting military details would drive through the scrub in heavy lorries shooting with high powered rifles. Then the soldiers

– likely a subset, those whose belt buckles weren't shiny enough to satisfy the Regimental Sergeant Major – would butcher the meat, salt it, and dry it for shipment back to Accra.

We didn't use rifles. Shotgun licenses were easy but a permit for anything more lethal was a major undertaking. I reckon you'd have needed a background check, a letter of recommendation from the president, and character references from Mother Theresa and Sir David Attenborough. But shotguns worked fine as long as you were close enough to your quarry. We all had a horror of wounding a bushpig and being unable to finish it off swiftly, a speculative shot into the distance was cause for contempt. Most of us used double barrelled guns, a rifled slug in the more open barrel, buckshot in the choked barrel. If you could close to within about thirty yards the rifled slug would knock even a big warthog off its feet, then you'd dash up and finish the job with a charge of buckshot to the brain. The challenge was getting into position without spooking your target. As with my great love in later life, bass fishing, this was a case of finding spots where food was thick on the ground, then approaching your quarry stealthily.

Bass mostly are scared off by visual stuff: someone standing outlined against a lightening sky, or wading too close to their feeding areas. Bushpigs are very different, they have the eyesight of a myopic codger with a skinful of beer and a sack over his head, but their hearing's sharp, and their sense of smell's good enough to pick up the aroma of a juicy root across a sandy clearing, the whiff of a sweaty hunter from the next but one county. Some of my pals kitted themselves out from army surplus stores in top to toe camouflage outfits. I always thought this wasn't so much an aid to effective hunting, more a fashion statement – a lot of people enjoy dressing up as Rambo heading out for the singles' bar. More important, you needed to move slowly, watching the ground like a sketchy lawyer checking a contract for loopholes. Step on a twig or in a pile of crunchy leaves and the jig was up. And even more crucial was to approach your warthogs from downwind. Ideal weather for a hunt was a steady breeze, Murphy's Law often gave us almost still conditions, the air moving ever so gently, changing direction all the while. This led to a lot of aborted stalks and a lot of rude words.

But when things came together the effort was repaid in spades, not to mention hot dinners. A big male warthog weighs up to three hundred pounds, that's plenty of meat. I preferred to go for the juveniles, they were less tough and tastier, but even a ninety pounder was a carnivore's delight. The flesh is leaner than farmed pork with a stronger, beefier flavour. Delicious. And we learned to carve up our prizes to waste as little as possible. This came about when Her Majesty's Government funded a job for a British master butcher to train Gambians in the arts of the enormous knife and the cleaver. A decent idea as well, the typical local approach to a carcase – a bullock, a goat, whatever – was simple and none too pure. Using a machete, some well muscled incompetent would start at the head end and whack off two or three inch lumps until he reached the tail. So when you bought meat in the market you'd find your basket had a bit of fillet, a bit of top rump, a bit of shin, some tripe, half a kidney, a few bones, some patches of whiskery hide; and if the machete wielder were clumsy, a scrap or two of his flip-flops and trousers.

Her Majesty's master butcher was one of those chaps destined by his name for his profession, like a fishmonger called Mr. Whiting or Ms. Crook the politician. Mr. Silverside, what other job could he have chosen? We wondered whether he had cousins named Ribeye and Sirloin, if his partner addressed him as Lambchop or Sausage when she felt affectionate, Scrag-End or Chump when he got up her nose. He certainly knew his onions – and his sage I'm sure – when it came to wielding a knife. He showed us how to shave the whiskers from the hide to give crackling without the properties of dental floss: boiling water and a sharp blade, no soap suds, no cologne. Then he had us hang the carcase from a tree, hooks behind the tendons on the hind legs, and separate it into fillet, chops, rump, belly, leg and shoulder joints. A skilled cutter, he reckoned, could leave a skeleton so stripped of meat that it shone in the sunlight. His fee for our lessons was a pittance, he kept a couple of portions for his own kitchen. Even that gave us extra insight into the butcher's art. We'd always reckoned fillet and chops were the prime cuts, but Mr. Silverside preferred shoulder and belly. 'They need slow cooking to break down the connective tissue but that's where the best flavour is.'

On the subject of flavour – though the yarn begins a long way from the table – one of our shooters had a cook and cleaner named Amos. He was a bubbly fellow, brimming with curiosity, and one day he asked if he might come along on an expedition to the bush. He watched from the bund as we splashed through the rice paddies for wildfowl, I'm sure he was taking mental notes so he could tell his chums yarns about loony foreigners removing mud from their ears and leeches from their underpants. He waited by the car during the warthog hunt, it's hard enough for one person to creep silently through the scrub, impossible for two. Then as we were loading a couple of pigs into the boot a large monitor lizard scampered through the clearing. Amos grabbed a stout stick and took off like a scalded cat on roller-skates. About ten minutes later he emerged through the trees, the dead lizard held high in the standard pose of winners of a Wimbledon tennis trophy. 'This is good chop,' he announced, adding the reassuring drivel I've heard on all six inhabited continents, 'It tastes just like chicken.'

A few weeks later Amos' employers had a dinner party. Amos was a first class cook so he was in charge of the menu, a fish starter, followed by poulet au vin blanc. Only after a month or so did the chef let on that his favourite poultry vendor hadn't been in the market that day, the white wine and mushroom sauce had been served over chunks of lizard.

Corrupting the Youth

'So where are the strong and who are the trusted?'
Nick Lowe, *Peace, Love, and Understanding*

When I fished from the beaches around Banjul I often ran into Gambians with hand lines. Once I moved onto the rocks I was on my own. I'm an antisocial so-and-so when there's a rod in my hand, solitude was a side benefit of plugging. Then one summer evening a youngster approached me. He seemed to be about fifteen and shy, looking as much at his tennis shoes as at me. 'Sir,' he said, 'I know you are the headmaster at the international school. Without being impertinent I would like to ask you a question. And my name is Baboucar.' I introduced myself and told him to let rip with his question. How did I catch so many cassavas and how did I avoid the catfish, his mum didn't like them? A pedant would have told him that was two questions but I knew he'd hear more than two answers, start me nattering about fish and there's only one way to shut me up, an orally delivered sandwich. I never talk with my mouth full, Mother brought me up right.

I showed Baboucar one of my broomstick plugs, explained how it suggested a mullet, guessed that bottom feeders like catfish wouldn't go for a surface lure, then illustrated the whole story by lobbing out and hooking a ten pounder. 'Sir,' said Baboucar, 'I would like to ask you a favour. Please don't think me impertinent, but could I try one of your toy tiddlers on my handline?' Casting was no problem, a whirl round his head like a cowboy roping cattle, the red and white lump flew out into the ripple. It was the retrieve that was tough going. If you wanted the plug to make steady progress you were limited to a crawl, the cruising speed of a bone idle mullet swimming through molasses. That left the cassava fish colder than Cornish rain in January. But my apprentice had grit, he wasn't going to chuck in the bonga just yet. Holding the line he swung his arm in a wild arc, a fast bowler warming up for a bouncer. The plug advanced only a yard but it did so at a good clip and Baboucar was into his first lure-caught fish. He missed one more take before darkness fell, but it was hard work, the lad was going to wind up with a desperately stiff shoulder.

Heading off the reef I asked Baboucar where he went to school. I thought I knew the answer, knew his maths teacher as well, a chap who was very fond of the word 'impertinent'. And I was right. 'OK Baboucar,' I told him, 'here's what I think you should do. Tell Mr. Smith you love fishing. Tell him you're helping to feed your family. Tell him you'd catch more if you had a spinning rod and reel. Mr. Smith bought an outfit a few months ago but he can't use it. He's allergic to something in the water, if he wades he comes out in a rash. Play your cards right, do your homework on time, he might help you out.' And he did.

In six years in the Gambia I expanded the school, raised funds, built four classrooms, hired terrific staff, and taught hundreds of children. Another bit of my proud legacy, I turned Baboucar into an angler.

Organic Pest Control

'I am the lizard king'
The Doors, *Celebration Of The Lizard*

Our school in the Gambia didn't pay much but all staff members were entitled to one fish supper per week delivered to their doors by yours truly. A rash promise you might say, that sort of confidence often leads to long blank spells. Cut up the chips before you go to the shore and you'll have not a chuffing wibble. But in six years as headmaster I almost never failed to deliver. It was easy to fill a bag, not so much fishing as catching

For some of the teachers I didn't just have to land the fish, I had to fillet, and skin them as well. Nowadays I laugh at shoppers who think meat grows in little plastic trays with absorbent nappies underneath and cling film on top, but even forty years ago I knew people who'd cook a piece of fish only if it were a rectilinear lump that gave no hint of having come from a living creature. The Year Three teacher, Sue, was a case in point, everything had to look like a giant fish finger. Weirdly this was a woman who'd worked as a trauma nurse; around human bodily messes she was as squeamish as a cannibal black pudding maker. A child with a compound fracture in the playground, a toddler coated in poo after a failure to reach the WC, a reservoir of puke on the staffroom table, no problem, send for Sue. But if I left a shaving of skin on her fillets she'd run from the kitchen in tears of terror and disgust.

One employee who wasn't at all fussy was the school caretaker, Mbacke, a muscular ball of a man who turned his hand to anything. Cleaning, painting, rewiring a classroom, open heart surgery, Mbacke would have a bash. And he loved to eat. In season I gave him ducks, geese, and bushfowl (*Peliperdix albogularis*). He was a Muslim so I asked if he was OK with meat that wasn't halal, having been shot rather than killed with a knife. 'No problem, it's halal. The imam says anything shot by a good chap counts as halal.' 'Mbacke,' I asked, 'did the imam really say that?' 'No. But if I asked him that's what he'd say. Unless he's a bloody fool. And then I don't care what he says.'

He loved fish as well, especially the darker fleshed species that didn't go down as well with most of the staff. Trevally were a special favourite and one winter I caught so many that he decided to salt some and dry them in the sun. Drying fish has a smell as unmistakable as frying bacon but not nearly as pleasant, somewhere between sweaty socks and a seagull with halitosis. So I could tell from a distance that the project was moving along. Then one morning I arrived at school to find Mbacke almost in tears. 'My fish, they are being stolen.' 'Are you sure, who's going to steal your fish?' Maybe someone with a clothes peg on his nose, an oxygen rebreathing set-up on his back? 'It's not who, it's what. Rats. I think they are breeding in the roof space, then coming down at night to feed. They are eating little bites around the edges of my fish, soon there will be none left for me.' 'OK, so we need to get rid of the rats.'

Easy, you might think, even in those dark days before the internet and the smart-phone-for-thick-people. Just look in the yellow pages, find a pest controller, a quick call and off we go. But there was no pest controller in the Gambia. No yellow pages either. The Public Works Department had a chap who'd spray your house for termites, someone from the Ministry of Health dealt with breeding mosquitoes, for rats you were on your own. So we had a cup of tea and hatched a plan: monitor lizards. The school grounds were crawling with them, we'd been trapping them for ages to keep the numbers under control. If we held off on the trapping, the population would increase quickly, and a decent sized lizard views a rat's nest like a Michelin starred eatery with free booze. Better yet one of Mbacke's professional colleagues was caretaker at the hospital, he was trapping monitors as well. If he steered them our way we'd be wall to wall with hungry reptiles, the rats wouldn't stand a chance.

Fast forward a month or two and I was teaching the after-lunch class, a bunch of ten and eleven year olds. After lunch is tough. I'm no biologist but I believe too much energy digesting grub leads to a shortfall of blood flow to the brain. Anyway, the children were in a silly mood and one in particular just wouldn't shut up. Lubabatu, a Nigerian girl, a delightful child, always first to hug a little nipper in tears, always willing to share her snacks. But she was prone to rabbit away like a cross between an auctioneer and a cricket commentator, high speed and stuff-all content.

'Lubabatu,' I said, 'please stop talking or you'll miss the next break.' Silence. Two minutes later she was yakking again. 'Lubabatu, you'll spend afternoon break picking up litter. Now stop talking or you'll miss tomorrow morning's break as well.' Silence, this time for three minutes. 'Lubabatu, for goodness sake be quiet or …' I racked my brain, I wasn't much good at punishing the children, '… or … or … or something really bad will happen.' A piss poor threat, two minutes later I could hear her back at it, a cheerful torrent of maximum velocity nonsense. I wheeled around and glared like a malevolent laser.

Before I could open my mouth to bellow there was a scratching sound from the softboard over our heads. A few flakes of white paint drifted down as the scratching grew louder. Then a dusty lump of ceiling crashed onto Lubabatu's work table, followed by a four foot monitor lizard which landed right in front of the girl. It looked straight at her, its forked tongue flickering, a few inches of twitching rat tail poking through its lips.

Lubabatu won the prize for best behaved pupil for two weeks in a row, and Mbacke's fish drying enterprise was a great success.

One Man and his Dog, One Man and his Rat

'You ain't nothing but a hound dog'
Elvis Presley, *Hound Dog*

During the Gambian summer we shot francolin, tasty chaps with meaty breasts, a single bird satisfies all but the piggiest appetite. We used their creole name, bushfowl, and they were enough of a test to be fun, not so tricky as to leave us hungry or frustrated. Guineafowl (*Numida meleagris*) were another story, scurrying noisily through the scrub but always breaking cover at a range of about a hundred yards. They gave us an all-round exercise session, a stiff walk through the undergrowth followed by an upper body workout as we shook our fists and bellowed expletives at flapping specks on the horizon.

But back to bushfowl. It was walked up shooting, tramping through the groundnut fields as the sun sank. Farmers were happy to see us because bushfowl ate their groundnut crops so we were pest controllers, daft-headed mobile scarecrows. A small gang of scarecrows would head out after work once or twice a week, usually coming home with supper.

Then came a season when one of our regulars, Alun, told us he wouldn't be joining us this year. His mongrel bitch Rosie had given him some hint she might be trainable as a gundog. 'Pointing, retrieving, I'd say she's going to be an all-rounder.' As I write those words I can hear his singsong north Wales accent and the note of almost parental pride. 'So I'm going to spend the whole season giving her lessons. If we came with you lot it just wouldn't be fair. She'd be distracted, she'll probably misbehave to begin with, and that might spoil your shooting.'

Now I thought Rosie was a lovely little thing, as friendly as a rock groupie on her third spliff, and about as bright as a mollusc with a hangover. But every time I ran into Alun he sounded like an anxious teacher on parents' day. 'She's just born for it, pointing, stands like a bloody statue.' 'She hasn't the mouth of a retriever, but goodness me boy, she's learning to compensate for it.' And by the end of the season, 'She's cracked it.'

Through the winter we went wildfowling and hunting warthogs, but come opening day of the next bushfowl season Alun and Rosie were on parade, new boots for one, a new collar for the other. We spread out across a field and started our slow walk over the furrowed ground. I was at the left end of the line, Alun at the right, but after a few steps I heard a bellow: 'Rosie, Rosie, no, no, no.' Twenty more paces over the scrub then, 'Rosie, no, stand, stay.' Then, 'Rosie, you bugger, I'll shoot you. Come here, stand still. You little bugger.' Away to my right I could see a black and white figure criss-crossing the field like a slalom water skier after a dozen double brandies, bushfowl scattering in her bow wave. Rosie's winter had been like a hard partying gap year, she'd forgotten everything she ever learned. I broke my gun and took out the cartridges. It's one of the rarely mentioned rules of shooting safety: never hold a loaded weapon when you're laughing so hard that your spectacles are dripping with tears.

On another trip we were joined by Michel, a Frenchman who only turned out once in a while. He was next to me in the line and as we shuffled across the first field I saw a giant cane rat (*Thryonomys swinderianus*), nearly two feet long without its tail, scamper from behind a stand of tall grass. To my surprise Michel swung through and it dropped like a sack of spuds. I confess I had thoughts of continental yahoos who shoot everything in sight, reported massacres of ortolans and swifts. So at the end of the session I collared Michel and made a few inquiries. Cane rats, he told me, were prized for the pot. He didn't eat them himself but he'd run into the Chief Justice of the Gambia in town recently. This legal bigwig had asked him to bag one next time he was in the field. Now it happened that I'd volunteered a couple of bushfowl to a friend who lived not far from the Chief Justice so I offered to drop him his rat on my way home. They say no good deed goes unpunished. Not this time, the judge and his other half greeted me with open arms and a brew. Then they said they recognised me.

While they enjoyed their sundowners they often watched me fish on the point in front of their house. 'You seem to catch a lot too,' said his worshipful whatever-my-jig, 'Where do you park when you're fishing?' I told him and he snorted. 'That's ridiculous, bloody miles away, especially when you're lugging a big bag of fish. Park here, young fellow. Then it's a skip and a jump and you're on the water. And we've got a copper in the sentry box so nobody's going to nick your hubcaps either.' Of course you don't become a Chief Justice without being a canny bird, he realised I'd pay for my parking.

And sure enough he'd greet me often as I loaded my catch into the car. 'Wow, that's a beauty, did it fight much? What lure were you on?' At which point it would have been churlish not to offer him his chosen whopper. Besides you never know when you might be glad to have the head of the judiciary in your corner. And when you think about it there's no reason why a giant cane rat shouldn't make a tasty treat. They're vegetarian, mostly eating grass, groundnut plants, and a bit of sugar cane when they find it. So the ingredients of a peanut butter cookie. But I bet they taste like chicken.

Money Can't Buy you Bites

'Some is rich and some is poor'
The Clash, *Bank Robber*

In the Gambia I always fished with my homemade surface lures. They worked, they were almost free, and my bank account was a sorry affair. They say you should keep three months' worth of spending money at all times. My goal was to have three days' worth, assuming a diet of fish, rice, and vegetables from the garden. Now and then friends in the import-export companies gave me catalogues from American tackle brokers. They meant well but it was like showing someone the menu from a gourmet restaurant then dropping a stale cheese sandwich from a railway buffet onto the table. I'd pore lustfully over the illustrations, wondering what I'd be able to catch if only I could afford a supply of Creek Chub Knuckle-Heads or Heddon Superspooks. Then one day I ran into a chap with a box full of these crackers. His name was Mike and he worked at the US Embassy. I met him on a rock mark and he introduced himself. He'd seen me catching fish from a colleague's garden overlooking the rocks, he'd asked around and found out that I used floating plugs.

Things may have changed but in those days American diplomats could order anything they fancied from back home. Their government would air freight it out for nothing and it was exempt from import duty as well. Some of the embassy staff took the piss. Fair enough that an expatriate might miss a favourite chocolate bar or a brand of bourbon, but I heard of people having soap and lavatory paper delivered – and I can assure you most Gambians washed regularly and wiped their bottoms as necessary using products from the local shops.

Mike had bought himself a spinning outfit and about a dozen plugs, some poppers, some sliders. They were gorgeous, beautifully finished, designed to fly through the air like javelins hurled by drug fuelled Soviet Bloc athletes. I couldn't wait to see one in action so I sat on a lump of laterite and watched Mike fish. The lure he picked to start with was a humdinger, a shimmery whitish colour and an action that wiggled seductively over the surface, the tinsel on the aft treble adding one more layer of come hither attraction. But half a dozen casts turned into a dozen, not a sniff. I suggested we hike over to the next little outcrop where we repeated the whole performance. Not a swirl, not a wibble. 'Maybe around the point,' I suggested. Mike decided to try a different slider. As he was putting it on I had one cast into the foam and immediately I was into a cassava fish of ten pounds or so. 'Jesus Christ on a pogo stick, that was right where I've been fishing. I'm going to have another go in the same spot.' I eyed him up carefully. His cast was great, maybe a whisker longer than mine. His retrieve looked spot-on, the plug skating like a helpless mullet through the breakers. And nothing even looked at the lure. I tried again as Mike switched to a third selection. My first cast led to a tug and a miss, my second to another cassava, this one close to fifteen pounds. After an hour, five different American plugs, and some creatively rude words Mike asked if he might try a broomstick special. Second cast he had a cassava, third cast another.

I don't think our experience really proved anything. Never mind a double blind test, we didn't even try one of Mike's lures on my rod, I might have been catching left and right with a Gibbs Wave-Walker or a Jobo Junior Pencil. He offered me a plug but I took a pass, when your daily diet's bread and dripping you can't start getting used to fillet steak. Besides my cheap stuff did the job just fine. Nowadays I fish mostly for bass and I still don't fill my tackle bag with stuff that costs eye-watering amounts. As long as the size and shape of my lure pretty well match what's on offer in the wave, I do just fine. I'll use a twenty quid Japanese effort when I find one on a reef at low tide, snagged up by someone else, but I'm not going to spend that kind of money myself. Old habits die hard.

Jiggery Pokery

'I'll fly by the seat of my pants'
King Creosote, *I'll Fly By The Seat Of My Pants*

Gambian winters were never very cold. On even the briskest days the beaches were crowded with scantily dressed European holidaymakers, a few who thought swimsuits were a symbol of repression worn only by bootlicking lackeys, freedom is the freedom to say that I'm bollock naked and you might as well get used to it. But now and again there'd be a sharp wind out of the north. It came from the Sahara bearing clouds of dust and it was called the Harmattan.

These wind storms led to a lot of days off work. People claimed the desert air was full of germs, but the principal symptom of Harmattan sickness seemed to be a feeling of general lassitude, a notion that riding a bike to the office in this shit appeals a whole lot less than wrapping up in a blanket and drinking gallons of tea. There was another spike in absenteeism when the first of the Mali mango crop arrived in the market. Mali mangoes were enormous and very sweet with a creamy texture. Sufferers from Mali-mango-malaise tended to be gannets who'd overindulged, their systems were overloaded with dietary fibre and they were incapable of going more than twenty yards from a loo. Not that I'm accusing your average Gambian of opportunistic hypochondria, I've seen that in its purest form, the good people of Banjul were a million miles away. The proper job lead-swingers were Dubliners I ran into in the late 1960s. I cut myself on a filing cabinet in the office, the wound became infected, so I popped down to the surgery to see about a penicillin shot. In the hallway of the medical building was a desk staffed by a large nurse with a loud, clear voice. As I approached she bellowed, 'If you're after needing to see a doctor, waiting room to my right. If it's a sick note so you can go to the All Ireland Hurling, benches to my left.'

But back to the desert wind and one winter I fancied a change from standing up to my knees in water, the breeze whipping at my soggy shorts. As it happened a pal who worked for one of the big trading companies had just given me a bag of free tackle samples. The customs manifest said they were artificial baits but they were like no lures I'd ever seen, white painted lead lozenges with oddly shaped hooks poking through the metal, the whole things clad in white deer hair. Some were packed with a slice

Dotted bass

of bacon rind, presumably steeped in preservatives, to be impaled on the hook as an added attractor. They were bucktails, a staple of American fishing for freshwater bass, striped bass, and almost anything with fins and a tail. Today's European angler would recognise the hook and weight gizmo as a jig-head. With a plastic shad body, we'd use confidently for bass, cod, pollack, and so on. And today's shopper who ran into a strange lure would pore over the packaging, type the brand name into google, and learn how to fish it in fresh or salt water, how to adapt it for a range of species and conditions, and how to use it to decorate a wedding cake or a swimsuit. A bloke in Banjul in the 1970s thought he might look up these weird contraptions in the public library on his next home leave to Blighty. In the meantime he'd have to fly them by the seat of his pants.

Clearly they wouldn't be much good on shallow rock marks, they sank like speculative shares and the hooks and lumpy heads were naturals to jam themselves into nooks and crannies in the sea floor. Also I reckoned they might attract fish best by skipping along a stretch of mud or sand, making little puffs as they touched down. Some were very wee, between quarter of an ounce and a half, and I tried these tiddlers first.

There was a shallow creek three or four miles out of town where the water was clear and the bottom was smooth. Sometimes I'd seen terns diving and small swirls on the surface. With an ultralight spinning rod – maybe an LRF set-up in modern angling lingo – and a few baby jigs I wandered the banks, casting from the bridges that spanned the offcuts. Bouncing the lure over the sand was a dead loss but cranking it in midwater was a hoot, slashing hits galore. The fish looked like the bass I knew from childhood but with spotty flanks and on the small side. As we nibbled a few from his barbeque a French chum told me they were called *bar moucheté* (*Dicentrarchus punctatus*), which more or less translates as dotted bass. The 'Dicentrarchus' bit tells me they're related to Cornish bass, unlike a lot of species with similar names around the world – fishmongers must be short on creativity, everywhere they go they wind up calling something a bass, a bream, or a trout. Dotties are caught in the Mediterranean, and Wikipedia tells me they run up to two kilograms. I only every seemed to land *bar de l'école* – cod French for schoolies – to about a pound and a half. But they were delicious, they could be caught without standing around in damp clothes, and they became part of my winter routine.

The largest of my free sample jigs ran up to two or three ounces, I reckoned they'd fare best in deeper, swirlier water. I tried slinging them from beaches, retrieving with a stop and start routine so they'd jump up and drop to the sand again. This produced a few cassava fish but they were much more fun on plugs; and the beaches were thick with catfish, nasty chaps that eat anything not nailed down, including lumps of leaping white deer hair. Then I thought of a spit where an arm of the mangrove creek emptied into the Atlantic. In the middle of the ebb there was a fair rip. I once saw a tourist try to swim in it, she jumped in and vanished downstream, emerging a hundred yards along the beach and minus the bottom of her bathing costume which had been tugged off by the torrent. I started out casting upstream and cranking steadily as the lure whipped around, almost like spinning for seatrout. But I fared best when I let the jig roll along the bottom, easing out more and more line until I had a hit or could see the metal of the spool. No retrieve, just a hairy lump trundling across the sand, it seemed unlikely to interest a predator. But I'm not a fish, what do I know? I never landed anything big but I had no shortage of flatties up to three or four pounds. They were diamond shaped toothy creatures, like scale models of the halibut folk chase in the north Atlantic, and they were very tasty fried in breadcrumbs. Today with the benefit of google I think I can identify them: spiny turbot (*Psettodes belcheri*).

I had no joy at all with the pork rind. It's possible I wasn't rigging it right, more likely I had no confidence my Gambian predators were on the lookout for a bacon butty. And when you think, 'I might be fishing like a total prat', that still small internal voice creates a self-fulfilling prophecy, you fish like a prat.

Spiny turbot

Humphry Davy Rules OK

'… at the edge of the sea, they thought great thoughts'
Van Morrison, *Take It Where You Find It*

Samuel Johnson described angling as 'a stick and a string, a worm at one end and a fool at the other'. Humphry Davy, a great scientist and a Penzance boy to boot, corrected him: 'a philosopher at the other'. When he wasn't discovering potassium, sodium, barium, strontium, calcium and magnesium, and on a break from tinkering with the miner's safety lamp, lobbying to have women invited to Royal Society lectures, and hanging about with Mary Shelley, I reckon old Humphry landed a few whoppers. Because he knew the most important bit of fishing kit's the organ we keep in our woolly hats, our brains.

These days people bang on about watercraft. Ask them what they mean and it turns out to be not much more than common sense, thinking, and local knowledge. But watercraft sounds mysterious, as if there were arcane lore to be learned. Maybe a secret society of men and women who meet wearing breathable stocking-foot waders, polarised sunglasses, and baseball caps with the logos of expensive tackle companies. Maybe rituals involving Texas-rigged soft plastics, braid clippers, and fronds of bladder wrack. Or maybe I just resent the self-styled watercraft expert who clutters up my in-box with regular emails inviting me to a 'hands-on learning experience workshop', two hundred US dollars for the day, bring your own equipment.

Either way, what makes anglers succeed's their ability to find feeding fish regardless of conditions. Thought and a bit of experience tell us what our quarry's likely to be eating, familiarity with our marks lets us work out where that food's going to be piling up. For most of my Gambian outings question one was a no-brainer: little mullet. And over the years I came to know where the tiddler shoals would be thickest in almost any sort of wind and weather. So maybe I wasn't a full-blown philosopher, but I was better than a fool. And by the way I tire of London after a day or two, but life in west Cornwall never palls.

Playing to the Gallery

'Watch it now, watch it now'
Sam The Sham & The Pharaohs, *Wooly Bully*

I know married couples who run businesses together. Good for them but I can't imagine being with my wife from nine to five and then going home with her. 'How was your day?' 'What d'you mean how was my day, you were right beside me the whole time?' For my money you need bits of your life that are yours alone. Maybe it's just me, I like my solitude more than most. But in most relationships, even mine, there's a brief spell when you pretend to be fascinated with every detail of your partner's existence. Maybe that's cynical, maybe love's young dream has our brains so full of oxytocin and serotonin that we truly want to know exactly how she hit that forehand down the line, what he did to butterfly the bushfowl so neatly. Or in my case how he landed that trophy.

Shelley and I have been married over twenty-five years. So about that long ago she decided she wanted to watch me fishing and she tells the story to this day. I was casting a hawthorn fly into a reservoir in a swirling breeze and I suggested she sit at the top of an embankment thirty yards from the water. That would give her a panoramic view in case the otters showed up. More importantly I wouldn't catch her if a sudden gust whipped my back cast in her direction. In Shelley's telling of the story I told her to go away because she was scaring the trout, in fact I was taking care not to attack my beloved with a sharp size twelve hook. Either way it was our first and last joint fishing trip.

In the Gambia I went out with a woman called Susan. She was a volunteer with VSO and she enjoyed the outdoors, especially sailing. Now sailing has to be the most miserable spectator sport, watching dinghies from afar you can't even tell who's winning, they all wander round in different directions. And if they come in earshot you're none the wiser. 'Lee ho.' 'Give me water.' 'Ready about.' 'Trim the jib.' But I stood on a sandbank dutifully, little triangles crept across my field of view, and I tried to remember whether her boat had the red stripe or the blue circle on its mainsail.

I'd shown willing and Susan was up for a rematch, she'd sit on the cliff and see what my plugging was all about. It was an ill-starred gig from the start. Her race had been in mid-afternoon, the warmth of the December sun a delight. My outing was at dusk on a grey and chilly day, a cutting wind blowing down from the Sahara bearing clouds of dust. Susan sat on a lump of laterite wrapped up in her jersey and one of my fishing jackets. I landed a couple of cassavas and she came down to the water's edge. 'How many do you need before we go and drop them off?' She was smiling but it looked like hard work, closer to a death rictus than a cheery grin. 'OK, just one more cast.' Now that said a lot about the level of my infatuation, the fish were on the feed and I was ready to pack it in. But as my lure splashed down, the water erupted and a barracuda of at least twenty pounds skipped across the wave. What's more it was hooked in the gill which gave it leverage against the bend of my rod. It made half a dozen runs. Every time I turned it I could recover line only slowly, each crank of the reel a hard won victory. 'Can't you just catch this thing before I freeze?' She was shivering now, her lips pale and pinched. I may have been infatuated but I wasn't insanely besotted, it never occurred to me to break the line and put her out of her misery. That level of adoration would be unhealthy, I reckon, more like idolatry than a romantic relationship.

The barracuda took half an hour to land. It weighed twenty-two pounds, a personal record, and on the drive home Susan wore two of my jackets, put a towel over her head, and wrapped her legs in an old tarpaulin from the boot.

At the end of her volunteer stint Susan went back to the UK. I caught up with her a few years later. She'd married her childhood sweetheart and she was radiant, expecting her first baby. Her husband was lovely, amusing, devoted, and a keen trout man. Sometimes he'd skip his fishing to watch her weekend sailing races. 'Like drying paint to tell the truth,' he told me, 'but the yacht club does a fair curry and a very decent bitter.' Did Susan ever return the compliment, I wondered. 'No, that's the funny thing. She'll suggest we go for a hike in a blizzard, her races go on all through the winter, but whenever I go fishing she says it's too cold.'

No Lifeguard on Duty

'The shark, babe, has such teeth dear'
Bobby Darin, *Mack The Knife*

One winter my car broke down. It was a Renault 4, the standard vehicle for Banjul's cab drivers which meant spare parts normally were easy to find. But for some reason the mechanic had to order a few bits and pieces from Dakar and that took a few days. Getting around to run errands was no problem, town taxis would take you anywhere for the equivalent of about twenty-five pence. It wasn't a straightforward A to B service, the cabbie would fill the vehicle, one in the front and three in the back, then drop people off and pick up others in a wildly random manner. Sometimes I managed to bag the front seat and ride straight from the market to school, other times I'd be in the back between two ample ladies with baskets of live chickens or full grown goats in their laps, and we'd wander all over the place. Out of town trips were private hire jobs, I couldn't afford one to take me to my fishing spots after work every day, I had to stay put.

My house was a short walk from a beach, but a river beach, no good for lures, the water brown and muddy. On an ebbing tide it could be smelly as well, the fish market was half a mile upstream and the waves often were spotted with heads, guts, frames, and discarded bait. And this winter it was noisy, some joker had set himself up to give water skiing lessons to holidaymakers. Through the hours of daylight I'd hear the whine of an outboard engine, the laughs and squeals of drunk tourists belly-flopping in its wake. Being stuck at home when I should have been plugging from the rocks was bad enough, a soundtrack that combined motocross, a stand-up routine, and the Texas Chainsaw Massacre was more than flesh and blood could stand. So I came up with a plan, I'd scare them silly. I shared my idea with Mbacke the school caretaker, he agreed to be my wingman as long as he could keep anything we caught.

I'd given my beach rod away so I cobbled together a heavy duty handline. Some stout cord, a wire trace, a couple of spark plugs, a pair of 8/0 hooks, then I tied in a ten gallon oil drum thirty yards from the end. I set up not far from the ski mob, fastened the end of the line to a palm tree, impaled a couple of bonga on my hooks, and lobbed out. Almost at once one of the sun seekers trotted up and asked me what I hoped to catch. Sharks, I told him. I even managed it in Swedish, 'Haj, bloody big ones.' The last bit was beyond my vocabulary so I gesticulated like a man possessed, flapping my arms to indicate massive jaws. The fellow trotted back to his posse a little nervously. Twenty minutes later I felt a tweak on the line. I tightened, called Mbacke over, and we made our bid for spots on the Gambian tug-of-war team. Now I've always been a long thin streak of misery but Mbacke was a solid two hundred pound ball of sinew. Between the pair of us we hauled and heaved, sweating like warthogs in a Turkish bath, gaining inches at a time before our shark lost patience and charged off into the depths, whipping the oil drum off the beach and towing it around in the swirling brown waves. Three or four times the line ran all the way out, stopping only when the palm tree shivered under the tension, the thick cord thrumming like a bass guitar. Twice we saw the dorsal fin as we drew the fish into the shallows, twice it turned and cruised away again. All the while the water sports school was deserted, the students clustered around us with the breathless excitement of election candidates looking for a television camera to smirk at.

It took us about an hour to land our fish. I think it was a lemon shark (*Negaprion brevirostris*), I know it measured six feet and three inches from nose to fork. Mbacke dispatched it with triumphant grin and a three pound hammer. Then he sent a small child to fetch his cousins so they could help carry it home for the pot. Laughing boy from the speedboat, with the breezy confidence of a total moron, asked the assembled company who wanted to stump up for the next ski ride. Nobody thank you very much, not in haj-infested waters, but there was a queue of eager beavers waiting to pose for snapshots with the fish and its captors. We charged a quid a time and we cleaned up.

Lemon shark

Forensic Research with a Filleting Knife

'With an old blade in your hand'
The Slickers, *Johnny Too Bad*

I eat fish, no apology. A lot of people are catch and release, dyed in the eight strand braid, and they have my respect. When conservation trumps the desire for delicious grub they've earned it. I return my seatrout because they strike me as an endangered species, but I'd be hard pressed to justify the time I spend at the water's edge if I didn't come home with a few suppers. What's more some catches aren't worth putting back. Even with big single hooks, even with the famous circle jobs, the odd bait or lure winds up deep in a fishy digestive system. I'm sure there's a television show somewhere about a charming vet who performs surgery on water-dwelling pets owned by D-list celebrities. If not there soon will be, and I want a royalty when 'There's a Tiffany earring in my rare breed koi' takes to the late night airwaves. But I'm a clumsy type with no background in anatomy, if I needed to use a disgorger my fish would be at the fat bloody chance end of the critical list. So I bang it on the head and take it home.

Now and then catch reports describe waterside operations and end with 'She swam away vigorously.' Hardly surprising and not altogether encouraging, if some ham-fisted oaf shoved a spanner down my gullet and a spatula up my nose I'd run like an Olympic sprinter crossed with a human cannonball, though I'm not sure I'd make it through the night. But some people enjoy fiddly procedures on living patients. I even saw a chap scooping trout before returning them. I suggested there might be a reason his marrow spoon had a priest at the blunt end but he was having none of it. Only when he whipped out his mobile telephone for a google search did he agree that ramming a blunt instrument down a brownie's throat was a something you really want to do only to a fish you plan to eat. And that's the spinoff benefit of keeping a few of your catches, you can find out what they've been feeding on.

Once in a while a bass or a trout spits out a recent meal as you unhook it, but this happens mostly when the prey species is obvious anyway. In summer the reservoirs can be full of rudd fry, the coves rammed with whitebait. No surprise when I beach a predator spitting up tiddlers like a late night drunk losing a greasy kebab into the gutter. But sometimes there's more mystery and it's only my filleting knife that tells me the deceased's last meal was a fistful of tadpoles or bloodworms, a couple of squid or razor clams.

In Banjul I cleaned a ton of fish, most for the school's teachers. Normally my rough and ready autopsies told me little I didn't know already. The shallows looked like mullet soup for someone on a high protein diet, the stomachs of my trevally and cassava fish were stuffed with nothing else. But one autumn evening I foul-hooked a pompano (*Alectis alexandrines*) on a floating plug. It fought like stink and it was delicious, a firm texture and a flavour somewhere between prawns and crayfish. My then girlfriend asked – no, she told me – I should bring more of these home for our suppers. Most people said they went best to a couple of big shrimps or prawns, but mine had a gut full of fiddler crabs (*Uca tangeri*). Anyway prawns were expensive and the mangroves around town were full of fiddlers, I reckoned I could catch a few by hand. But they're speedy little creatures with a nasty nip so I baited them with the frame of a cassava fish, harvesting them when they were picking at the bones like French butchers cleaning a rack of lamb. I thought about removing their fighting claws to avoid being pinched but they looked meaty and appetising so I left them on and took my chances.

Then I pondered where to fish. Pompano could swim right into the shallows around the mangrove roots to be sure of a tasty takeaway menu, but their deep bodies would be awkward in just a few inches of water, like the idiotic oversized Chelsea tractors that get stuck in narrow Cornish lanes. So I found a channel, on a dropping tide crabs should be swept into it creating a conveyor belt of treats. I reckoned there'd be catfish around – not a masterstroke of watercraft, if it was wet there were catfish – and I didn't want to cast my pearl-like crustaceans before slimy swine, so I used one of my topwater plug blanks as a float to keep my bait off the bottom.

On my fourth or fifth cast the gear wobbled down-current, stopped in an eddy, then darted away as fast as a personal injury lawyer chasing an accident victim. But the fight was dour and dogged, a five pound threadfin, a decent fish but not what my lady friend wanted. I tried fishing closer to the bank and the tangles of roots. Another take, this time the plug stopped dead. I tightened and something took off downstream, the reel whining like the same lawyer negotiating a fee. To keep the line out of the tree roots I waded deeper and deeper into the channel, up to my bellybutton, up to my neck, my tennis shoes sticking in the gluey mud. Every time I had the

Pompano

fish close it would turn and zip away again, it was almost dark before I beached it. An eight pound pompano, mission accomplished.

I drove home ready to be crowned with laurels, serenaded with anthems of triumph, at least given a brew while I took care of the filleting. Fat chance. 'That's nice, but how come you got so muddy? Aren't the fish supposed to be in the water while you stay on dry land?'

The Plural of Anecdote is not Data

'Numbers add up to nothing'
Neil Young, *Powderfinger*

I hardly ever ran into other people while I was plugging on the rocks around Banjul, but one summer's evening there was a fellow on the next shelf fifty yards away. As the sun slipped below the horizon it began to rain. Not the rain we often see in Cornwall, a soft mist as if you're standing in a cloud, this was a downpour. The drops were as big as bantam's eggs, they stung when they landed on bare skin, visibility was twenty yards. But it was warm so I carried on fishing, ending my session with some decent cassava fish.

Heading back to my car I ran into the chap from along the shore. 'That was more fun than skinny dipping in a vat of Guinness.' Up close I recognised him, he worked at the Catholic mission. 'I had a fish on every fifth cast or so. As soon as the rain started. It's always that way when it starts tipping. This time of year I stare at the sky like a nun at an orgy, if I see a dark cloud I get myself down here again.' By the time we reached our cars he'd outlined a grand unifying theory of cassava fish behaviour. The splashes of the raindrops made vibrations in the water, these sounded like baitfish trying to escape, the predators came screaming in to attack the tiddlers.

He seemed a pleasant type so I didn't want to tell him his brainwave was as thick as a ditch digger's sandwich. But it was. We'd caught our fish within twenty yards of the shore, the storm had pelted a few square miles of ocean. So had there been a feeding frenzy as far as the eye could see, could we have walked into the middle of the sea on the backs of cassavas looking for mullet? What's more heavy rainfall normally began in the evening, wasn't it just as likely that the time of day was the feeding trigger? Or maybe the change in barometric pressure had something to do with it, or the swirling wind that usually accompanied a storm. It's easy to confuse correlation with causation. Take a course in introductory statistics and they often make you plot ice cream consumption by month against deaths by drowning. The relationship's close but it isn't licking Cornettos that leads to watery graves. Ice cream sales boom in hot weather, that's when people hurl themselves into the briny and wind up in difficulty. When it's chilly, hot soup conditions, there aren't many swimmers in the waves, and you're unlikely to drown when you're sitting on a radiator in a beachfront café nursing your mug of minestrone.

We also look for causality when there is none, because we want to find signal in a world of random noise. When I was consulting I had a client who peddled advice on financial markets. If bonds moved up or down a smidge their guru – and by the way Peter Drucker famously said businesspeople use the word 'guru' because it's shorter than 'charlatan' – would be on the television. Using as much longwinded jargon as possible he'd explain why this had happened. The head of the central bank had made an encouraging remark about yield curve concavity, that led the rise in valuations. Next day's drop was because analysts decided the bank boffin had ignored the impact of heteroscedasticity, or he'd been seen drinking nine double caipirinhas before his press conference. Over a coffee I asked the market maven whether he really believed the theories he spouted. 'Of course not. Stuff goes up and stuff goes down, that's what stuff does, no special reason. But you can't justify charging people a management fee unless they think you know why. In days gone by I'd have chucked chicken bones on the ground and analysed the way they landed, or peered at the entrails of pigeons. I'm a vegetarian so I just come out with theories about things that might influence the capital markets.'

Fishing's a pursuit governed by lots of randomness, catches go up and catches go down, that's what catches do. So it's no surprise that the professionals have developed so many rituals and superstitions. I've never seen a trawler skipper throwing a bag of bones on the deck or tearing the guts from a pigeon, but I've known of plenty who toss coins into the ocean, ban bananas and green clothing onboard, refuse to put to sea on a Friday or allow seafood in the galley, and make a fetish of feeding following gulls.

Anglers have their mumbo jumbo too. A spot that delivered at high water under a full moon becomes our go-to mark for those conditions. A bait that caught a single whopper ten years back turns into our standard big fish attractor. A pool that was full of big fish in the 1970s remains a favourite forever even as the river changes shape. We take anecdotes and treat them as data, often because the real data are too complex to grasp. We don't know what made that high tide mark so brilliant: the moon, the wave, the water temperature, the barometric pressure, the wind direction, the weed maggots from last week's storm, the mackerel spilled from an inshore ring net, or some combination of all these things and a whole lot more we'd never even imagine. Marine creatures go where there's plenty for them to eat and where their food's easy to grab, that's about all we can say for sure. I know anglers who keep catch logs, faithfully noting up to a dozen variables defining conditions and how they fished them. And they're not so much as scratching the surface. There are more things in heaven and earth than are dreamed of in your recording methodology. Write down what you like, know what you can, you'll be surprised anyway, especially by bass, my most mercurial targets.

And the next time I crossed paths with my Irishman the rain had coloured the water with laterite. It was like lobster bisque and the fishing was shite. I had a small barracuda and he blanked.

Not Cut Out to be a Guide

'Take this job and shove it'
Johnny Paycheck, *Take This Job And Shove it*

During my sixth and final year in the Gambia Her Majesty's Government decided I was providing a vital service to the local and expatriate communities and it topped up my salary to the tune of eight thousand quid a year paid into my UK account. Unfortunately nobody bothered to let me know. Back in Cornwall I called on my bank to make the annual apology, sorry about the overdraft, I'll come good one day, keep the faith for the times they are a'changing. The manager was a mousy looking fellow – pale grey suit, tie, hair, and complexion – so I was taken aback when he thumped his fist on the desk and raised his voice. 'What are you thinking, you've got seven thousand six hundred and fifty pounds in your current account. Put it on deposit, get some interest.'

But earnings only make you feel rich when you know they're rolling in so I was always scrambling to raise a few extra quid, enough to pay for luxuries like treble hooks and reel lube. One venture was becoming a very part time manufacturer's representative. A couple of my shooting pals worked for import-export companies and the trade samples they were sent made my mouth water: rods, reels, lures, game bags, their offices looked like one of the catalogues that came in *The Field* or *Shooting Times*. So I wrote letters to half a dozen American export brokers asking if I could peddle their wares to Banjul retailers. I told them I had a special aptitude for products related to shooting and fishing. To mask my real objective, scrounging free tackle, I also boasted of expertise in men's fashion and crockery. This claim stretched my integrity like a rubber band round a warthog – I owned one pair of respectable long trousers and I ate from a couple of enamel bowls donated by an ex-girlfriend – but I reckoned a salesperson was expected to have a tenuous relationship with the truth. I also boasted of connections to the great and the good of Banjul society. This was more honest as the town was small and everyone knew everyone else. And several government ministers and civil service bigwigs sent children to our school, so I chatted them up on parents' evenings and arm twisted them to donate prizes for the fête. Bullshit baffles brains as they say, three of the US companies signed me up.

The fishing samples were disappointing. I was sent a few odd lures for large-mouth bass, things like Christmas trees with rubber frogs and dangling spinner blades that didn't seem likely to interest predators feeding on mullet. Hooks and wire, while always useful, were so cheap that I'd have been happy to pay for them. And massive trolling plugs designed for marlin and bluefin tuna didn't butter many cassava fish. The only really useful free kit was a bulk bucket of soft plastic worms which came with an assortment of hooks with kinked shanks. These were effective for barracuda and trevally, which to be honest would strike at a Cornish pasty as long as it was cranked along the top of the water. More importantly the worms came with instructions on how to rig lures in the styles of Texas, Carolina, and all points west of Timbuktu. So when soft plastics hit the UK bass scene I was one small step ahead of the crowd.

The most significant payback from my repping career didn't accrue for thirty-some years, during which I became an accountant then a management consultant specialising in sales effectiveness. Most of my competitors were fresh faced youngsters with sharp business togs, PhDs in industrial psychology, and MBAs from prestigious American universities. So when clients asked them down to earth questions, like how should you respond when a prospect tells you to piss off and shove your samples where the sun doesn't shine, they were clueless. In the vernacular of the pompous corporate prat I was differentiated by a core competency. I'd heard those words many times, in English, French, and Wolof. I knew the appropriate reply was to say, 'Thank you for that advice,' only adding the parenthetic 'arsehole' when safely out of earshot.

My other moneymaking wheeze was taking tourists on guided angling trips. Some of my pals had asked me to show them the ropes – maybe the monofilaments – of catching stuff on lures. When we caught fish one chum told me I should be charging the equivalent of ten quid an hour for my time and expertise. I put the word out to a few people who worked in the tourist hotels and before long I had my first assignments. Guiding's not a job I'd do again, not as long as there's alternative employment cleaning out the grease traps at fast food restaurants or hand sorting the output of sewage farms. To be sure I had some wonderful outings. An elderly Danish couple asked me to demonstrate my technique, copied it in faithful detail, even scratching their bottoms before casting, caught a trevally apiece, then announced that I was a 'plinking genius' and insisted on taking me back to their hotel for the all you can eat buffet. A Swedish taxi driver who'd never fished before landed a twenty pound cassava fish by cheerfully following my every instruction. Actually not quite every instruction: when a small dog started yapping around our ankles I snarled, 'Bugger off,' to which my cabbie replied, 'OK, I will, but first can we catch this big fish.'

A few of my clients were twenty-two carat shits, the sort of people who reckon they're paying you so you should do everything they want and smile while you're at it. Maybe I was wrong but I never felt my guiding fee covered carrying children and crates of cold beer or wiping dripping noses; and if you want someone to appreciate your desperate jokes, get a recording of a studio laugh track. A few more were unreasonable gits. One German fellow told me he wanted a barracuda. I suggested he was too early in the season for this to be realistic, how about trevally? OK, he booked a trip for trevally and paid a deposit. And as soon as we had a couple he was back to his leitmotif, I want a barracuda, I want a barracuda, and if you don't find me a barracuda I'm not going to pay the rest of your fee. I'd picked him up in the car, we must have been ten miles from his hotel, so I gave him both barrels. 'Fine, you'll catch your bloody barracuda. Just stay here for the next thirty days and I guarantee it.' Then I drove off and left him.

A lot of my victims – clients, I mean – were pleasant enough but incapable of following advice, even when it was costing them a tenner an hour. Cloth eared, obstinate, thick as yesterday's porridge, I don't know, but it drove me to distraction. 'The water's shallow, use a floating lure,' followed by six casts with German sprats, six German sprats consigned to Davy Jones' sprattery. 'I can see the fish, ten metres, just a lob cast,' then a shattered rod tip when laughing boy tries to fling his tackle to the Cape Verde Islands. 'Let it run,' and your man jams the drag as tight as a tick's sphincter, pops the line, and whinges about shoddy workmanship.

I managed one winter season as a guide. Then I jacked it in, my marbles depleted but not totally lost I hope.

Stir it Up

'Put the load right on me'
The Band, *The Weight*

There are days that stick in your fishing memory even as the passing years make you unable to find your spectacles (on your head), your car keys (left in the ignition in a busy carpark), and the remote control for the television (flung across the sofa in disgust at the fifty odd channels of drivel available for your viewing pleasure). This was one of those days.

I needed a good bag. The staff of our school expected to be supplied with fillets and I hadn't been on the rocks for over a week. Through the summer holiday we were building two new classrooms and I was the financial controller, project manager, and unskilled factotum sent off to the shops when we ran out of nails, glue, or biscuits for the construction crew's endless tea breaks.

Most of the funding came from the US State Department. We provided places to children of American diplomats and aid workers so I called on the consul to ask if he could stump up some government cash. In return I offered to guarantee spots for the families of anyone who might join his team. With the subtlety of a tractor driver wielding a four pound hammer I let on that the new classrooms were the only way to be sure embassy parents weren't stuck at home all day while their youngsters' names languished on a waiting list as long as a prog-rock keyboard solo. The consul nodded and handed me an application form. 'The important thing's to fill in every blank. You may need to make some estimates, we call them SWAGs, Sweet Wild Ass Guesses. That's OK, the people in Washington have no idea how things work in the Gambia. Just don't leave any questions unanswered, they'll notice that.' I scurried off with the paperwork and got stuck in, only to find the third box an unfathomable brainteaser.

The first two were fine, 'Family name' and 'Given name', but then came 'Middle initial'. I don't have one, to qualify for Uncle Sam's greenbacks it seemed I needed one. Could I present myself to the Chief Justice and add to my legal monicker by deed poll? What if the consul had to check the request for aid against my passport? I learned later that I should have written 'NMN', no middle name, but at the time I was as stumped as a navvy offered two shovels and told to take his pick. A deep breath and I stuck in a 'D'. Then I made a note in the school calendar so I wouldn't forget my new handle. It was hard to decide what the D stood for, Duane and Dwight sounded like clean cut American names, Dylan and Dante were more artistic, Duncan and Douglas gave a nod to my Scots heritage.

In the end I plumped for Harry S Truman's approach. He didn't put a full stop after the S because it wasn't an abbreviation, it just meant S. With some heroic estimates – SWAGs as I now called them – the rest of the application was easy enough and the dosh came through in time for us to break ground at the beginning of the long holiday. But the deadline was tight and we often worked till sunset, too late swap my tape measure and clipboard for a rod and a lure bag.

At last came a day when we finished a course of blockwork in the late afternoon, plenty of time to be on the mark for the gathering gloom of evening. There was a breeze and the water had an attractive ruffle but my first half dozen casts might as well have been into a swimming pool – literally, no hits, no follows, all I caught was a bikini bottom that would have fit a retired American football player gone to seed. I moved fifty yards along the sandpapery basalt to a little gully. In cowboy parlance, as Zane Grey would have said, it was a box canyon, the deeper water leading in to a vertical barrier of rock. Mullet sometimes were herded against this natural dam and marmalised by predators.

Even as I cast I could see swirls and my first short lob produced a cassava fish of about eight pounds. I bonked it on the head, passed a rope through its gills, and tied it to my belt. After less than half an hour I had four more on my stringer. I gave it a heft, not too bad and the car was only quarter of a mile away, I could carry one more without causing a back strain, a hernia, or a belly-flop on the way up the cliff.

After two or three chucks I saw a monstrous swirl behind my broomstick plug, a crater in the water like the aftermath of a mucked up swan dive by a well built elephant. A twitch, two cranks of the reel, and a strike that almost yanked the rod from my hand. The fish ran doggedly half a dozen times. As soon as it was close enough to give me a glimpse of its deep flank it would turn and charge back into the depths, slow and steady thumps from the beating of its tail.

The sun was setting by the time I could slide a tired cassava into the shallows and gill it ashore. The biggest I ever had, a friend later stuck it on his spring balance, thirty-five pounds. I sat down for a smoke and a ponder. No way could I scramble up the steep laterite to the car with nearly eighty pounds of deadweight. Equally I didn't fancy two trips, leaving half my load at the bottom of the escarpment. There were a couple of local lads fifty yards away. They'd greeted me politely, they seemed pleasant youngsters, I didn't want to tempt them to go on a stealing-by-finding spree.

I called them over and struck a deal: one would lug the monster to the top, one would carry four smaller ones, and when we were done and dusted I'd reward them with an eight pounder apiece. They huffed and puffed all the way up as loudly as water buffaloes with bronchitis – maybe they weren't too fit, more likely they were showing how richly they deserved their payment – but as soon as we set down our burdens beside the car they perked up. As they sauntered out onto the road, each swinging a cassava fish like a sergeant major's swagger-stick, I heard them telling their pals that their new friend the thin schoolmaster-man had landed a leviathan, he was the Bob Marley of fishing. It took over an hour to drive around distributing my catch to the staff, I was starving by the time I made it home. But I was singing Wailers tunes.

Ignorance isn't Bliss, It's an Opportunity

'I don't claim to be an A student'
Sam Cooke, *Wonderful World*

Most years I went on home leave over the school summer holiday. My parents had retired to Cornwall so I had a handy bolthole, rent free and three square meals a day. There were foods I missed in Banjul, notably cheese. You could buy Camembert and Brie from a French import company but it was shipped in refrigerated containers and it cost a lot more than my budget would stand. When I was back in the UK, Mother stocked up on Stilton, Lancashire, and strong Cheddar. Another thing I yearned for was parsley. It's a taste I love and it never grew in my Banjul garden. They say it does well only if you've a nagging partner in the house and I had a few of them in rapid succession. Maybe none of my girlfriends stuck around long enough to benefit the herb patch.

It also was thought good for your health to spend a few weeks of each year in a cool climate. The Gambia was rife with disease and parasites, once a year you went to the clinic to be wormed. A systemic drug killed the little rotters in your skin and guts, then you took a heroic dose of Epsom salts to blast the corpses and unhatched eggs from your digestive tract. This was best performed over a weekend with plenty of reading matter at hand, twelve hours in or near the thunderbox.

Of course I fished in Cornwall, bass from the beaches and trout in the reservoirs and streams. The great pleasure of these outings was being a self-confessed novice. On Gambian rock marks I was the local expert, people came to me for guidance when they were starting out, ideas if they were blanking. In Britain I was a chap who could cast a fly or dump a weight into the surf, that was as far as it went. So I picked brains shamelessly. I was like a modern politician, the sort of moral and intellectual vacuum whose speeches all come from a polling exercise or a focus group. 'The voters like to hear about family values, fine. I'm the candidate of family values, vote for me if you have a family; or values; or if you'd like a family; or some values. And now will someone please tell me what to talk about next.'

Anyway I remember a drizzly morning on a reservoir, olives speckling the surface and trout sucking them down like chips after a night on the beer. Then the sun burned through the cloud and the whole place went flat. I sat down for a smoke and a head scratch, maybe something else would start hatching. Quarter of a mile away I saw an elderly fellow wading beside a bed of reeds, his rod bending. A quick chinwag, the fish were on damsel nymphs, grabbing them in the shallows as they climbed the stalks. He gave me a pattern of his own tying, instructions on how to make my own, advice as to which local tackle shop had the best marabou, and a crash course on the life-cycles of damsel and dragon flies. I gave him half the fruitcake I had in my pocket, I'd say we were equally chuffed with the exchange. Mother's fruitcake was excellent.

One evening I was lobbing lugworms into a storm-lashed surf when a chap from the village came along the sand. 'Little baits are good for the babies,' he told me, 'but the big ones are on fish at this time of year. The day-boats and ring netters catch a lot, they lose a few too. And some people clean their catch at sea, head and guts over the side. A big bass can't turn up her nose at a crippled pilchard or the front end of a decent mackerel. Big hooks mind, even bigger than what you're using.' Of course he was spot-on, the next night my smallest fish was a six pounder.

Now I've always felt a duty to pass on tips. It's how the world works, or should work at least. The folk with the know-how share it with the relative novices, they repeat the dose with the total punters, keep going until we achieve universal enlightenment. What surprised me, and still does, is how many anglers stop up their ears like Ulysses when they hear the siren song of a different way of fishing. 'Stuff damsel nymphs, I'm sticking with my Jersey Herd, it's always done me proud.' 'I use worms, I did it yesterday, I'm doing it now, and I'll do it again tomorrow. Bass love worms.' Then when they don't catch much they accuse the more successful rods of being jammy bastards

Fair enough that most of us have preferences, some have obsessions. I met a woman who only ever goes trouting with a four weight rod and a fly of size eighteen or smaller. Sometimes a lot smaller, I couldn't even see her midges without my readers, never mind tie one to a tippet like spider webbing. I ran into one lure fan who refuses to use anything but topwater plugs, another who's a soft plastic junkie. But these people don't think their methods lead to better catches, they just love fishing in their chosen ways. That makes sense, we all have personal tastes, a few of us have strange ones. There's a market for underpants with a strand of fabric at the back, there have to be men and women who enjoy pulling string from the cracks in their bottoms. So it's no surprise to run into an angler wedded to Patagonian cedar wood centrepin reels or bass popping flies tied with sausage skins and fronds of dill. What's bizarre is the person who desperately wants to catch more or bigger fish and refuses to try anything different, the one who huffs, 'I've been at it for twenty years, I know what I'm doing.' John Habgood was a liberal bishop. Margaret Thatcher didn't appreciate his comments about political and social issues, she told him he should be providing moral certainty. 'But have you thought', he asked her, 'that moral certainty might be a sin?' Being certain about fish isn't a sin, it won't consign you to whatever hell you believe in, but it can lead to a lot of disappointing sessions; especially if those fish are bass, their behaviour changes from hour to hour, even minute to minute.

Silver Kings in Brown Water

'In the big muddy'
Pete Seeger, *Waist Deep In The Big Muddy*

The Gambia was home to plenty of tarpon. If you read fishing magazines you might imagine flats of brilliant white sand, elegantly turned out anglers in shallow draft skiffs casting streamer flies to shadowy outlines in the distance. Then read the fine print and you'd realise a guided trip for the silver kings would cost about the same as a new car. So either you'd fish your local beach or you'd start sending emails from Estonian state lottery winners in the hope that one day your well-heeled halfwit would come.

It was different in Banjul, no money changed hands and no boats were involved either. We did catch a lot of small tarpon on the fly – that's coming later – but the bigger ones were in deeper water and they were suckers for a live mullet. There's a point where the muddy drift of the river delta meets the blue Atlantic, where in autumn and winter you could see tarpon rolling, usually a few yards into the clear water. If that sounds idyllic let me drop a fat hornet into your ointment: the point was home to a tourist hotel, one which attracted the most drunken and dissolute winter visitors. Fishing it in daylight wasn't much fun unless you enjoyed being puked on by boozed up halfwits or propositioned for a quickie by total strangers who bore a passing resemblance to your great aunt Annie or your great uncle Arthur. So my trips were at dawn when the drunkards were sleeping off their binges and the rumpomaniac pensioners were in their bedrooms with whichever boy or girl they'd managed to drag into their sweaty embraces.

The tarpon ran between thirty-odd pounds and over a hundred. The biggest I ever caught was just over eighty-five on a rather rusty spring balance. That's a fair fish on a salmon spinning rod but you didn't need heavy gear, just lots of line. A hooked tarpon would run like a cheetah with its arse on fire, sometimes as far as a hundred yards. Then it would leap again and again, often clearing the water by a few feet and landing tail first. And then it was exhausted, ready to be led in to the shore. Once in a while a big one would make a second run, a second cycle of jumps, but basically the fish played themselves, all I had to do was avoid getting in my own way and let them tire themselves out. Of course not everyone can manage that trick.

I took a couple of Danish tourists to the point – this was when I was guiding – and they couldn't see line streaming from their reels without jamming their drags tight and acting like members of a tug of war team crossed with a Morris dancing side, heaving like mad, then skipping down the shore as their fish carried on moving away. Between them they broke three stout rods and a big toe, this when its owner was dragged over a boulder in the shallows. With all their gear out of commission I tried a couple of casts myself, beaching and releasing a forty pounder. They'd paid in advance for their outing, I wasn't expecting a tip, and they were know-it-all boors with more money than manners. Unkind, perhaps, but I enjoyed rubbing their noses in it.

The tarpon hung around the point because the delta water was heaving with mullet eight or nine inches long. Hunting them down in the silty gunge would have been tough but as soon as they crossed the line into the clearer ocean they were easy meals. The big challenge was finding live mullet in the hours before dawn. Once it was light, local commercial fishermen would show up with their cast nets, but they seemed to need their beauty sleep, I never spotted one before sunrise. I bought a net and tried to learn the knack of flinging it, but it is a knack, and I was no knacker. The professionals' gear would touch down in a perfect circle, mine would splosh down in a dirty great tangle and a torrent of rude vocabulary. I wound up buying a few baits the evening before and keeping them alive in a big bucket with a manual aeration pump from a broken medical ventilator. If I didn't fancy lugging the bucket they went almost as well on surface plugs. The hook holds were less secure with trebles than with big single hooks. A fair few fish would take, leap, then hurl the lure miles into the air, but that didn't worry me. The real fun was seeing them flinging themselves out of the water.

My other tarpon area was a filthy canal behind the bund in downtown Banjul. The water was fairly clear – the tide flowed in and out – but underfoot conditions were between rank and toxic. Black oozy mud was sprinkled with waste paper and plastic, rusty barbed wire gave a hint of the squalor of a trench in Flanders field, and judging by the smell local residents used the area as an outdoor privy. I've no idea what took me to the edge of the canal in the first place, I might have been following a feeding osprey, that led me into some odd spots. Anyway one winter's evening there I was, breathing shallowly on account of the whiff of turds, and watching the water. It was alive with silvery bodies twisting as they chased fry to the surface. They were no size, the biggest looked about fifteen pounds, but I had to give them a bash. The canal was only two feet deep so I reckoned a fly might be my best bet. I dashed home, grabbed an old trout rod with a floating line, tied on leader of twelve pound mono and a Badger Terror, and was back behind the bund as the last of the light was leaving the sky. My second cast produced a ten pound tarpon which dashed hither and yon, jumping a dozen times before it was tired enough to unhook and release. This had potential.

On my way home I dropped in on Ian, the chairman of our school's board. I knew he'd been a keen fly fisher back in the UK so I filled him in on my new mark. 'Wizard, old fellow, let's have a go tomorrow. Five-thirty behind the pumping station.' I should explain by way of background that Ian was the quintessential British toff. I believe he was of Anglo-Irish heritage and his speech and mannerisms were at the golden brown edge of the upper crust. If you sent to central casting for someone to play Bertie Wooster or Lord Peter Wimsey, Ian would have showed up for the first audition.

An American friend ran into him at a boozy party, next morning she couldn't wait to give me the details. 'He even talks like that when he's drunk,' she squealed, 'I was convinced he was putting on an act. I mean, nobody speaks that way in real life, only in Alec Guinness movies.' Ian did.

Next evening at half past five I pulled in behind the old pump house. I'd seen the underfoot conditions, I wore shorts and plastic Chinese sandals so I could sluice myself down with a bucket before going into the house. In my hand was a fibreglass rod, home made to a blank from McHardy's and fitted with an Intrepid Rimfly reel. In my pocket was a spool of monofilament and a small tin of old seatrout flies. Ian's car pulled up and he emerged, cavalry twill trousers and a beautifully cut tweed jacket. He was carrying a bespoke split cane rod with a Hardy reel. 'You've been here before, old man. I'm a new boy. So I thought I should show the fish a bit of respect.' We had several evenings on the canal and we never blanked. Our most productive trip delivered eighteen tarpon and we had to pack in early because we'd lost all our flies in snags. Our biggest fish was an eighteen pounder. And after his first trip Ian switched to shorts.

Firearm Safety

'Come as you are'
Nirvana, *Come As You Are*

My teaching job in the Gambia was poorly paid but I was treated very well by the school. Teachers and parents invited me for meals on a regular basis. OK, you might say, I was giving them a steady supply of fish, bushfowl, wildfowl, and warthog meat, some reward was only fair. But I never saw it that way. I fished and hunted because I'm a fisher and a shot, that's what I do. They cooked for me in spite of the fact that they preferred to birdwatch, build model nuclear reactors, or translate the works of the Lakeland poets into Amharic. The governors were kind as well, they sorted me out with a house a short walk from the school. It was a small affair – a bedroom, a kitchen, a bathroom, and a sitting room – but it was close to the beach. It was built on stilts which meant it caught any waft of breeze on offer, great in a hot and humid climate. And the space underneath was handy for parking my car.

The only snag was that it was made of wood which made it a soft touch for petty thieves. In two years I was burgled eleven times, always exactly the same modus operandi: kick down the front door, pinch my Russian-made shortwave radio, run like hell. Besides my radios the only thing I owned worth stealing was my shotgun and that was well secured. My bed had a steel frame and I screwed it to the floor, running the bolts through holes drilled in the I-beam that held the house together. Then I passed a length of anchor chain through the trigger guard and around the bedstead, securing it with a padlock. And of course it was unloaded, I kept my cartridges four hundred yards away in the little safe in the school office.

The vanishing radios were cheap, ten quid or so, and I think they were subsidised by the Brezhnev government in the hope their owners would lap up Moscow propaganda. If so I took the Soviet so-and-sos for a ride: I listened to the BBC World Service for news, quiz shows, and major events in the racing calendar, US Armed Forces Radio for jazz and the blues, Radio Sénégal to improve my French, and that was that. But even at a tenner a time I claimed my burglaries on the school's insurance. Then the underwriter refused to renew our policy unless we hired round the clock guards. The day shift was a piece of cake. The school caretaker's sister took in laundry so we set up her tubs and washing lines around the house and bought her a baseball cap that said 'Security, Access All Areas'. For the hours of darkness we had to pay and we were faced with a choice. You could hire a walking watchman who patrolled the property more or less nonstop. For slightly less than half the money you could go with a sleeping watchman – a contradiction in terms on a par with business ethics – who'd doss down in a strategic site and raise the alarm if anything happened.

We went with Plan B. I interviewed three candidates for the job, picking a small and wizened chap with a gammy leg – the other two seemed modestly employable but I didn't think anyone besides a soft eejit like myself ever would hire old hopalong. Alhaji was his name, he was the sweetest fellow you could hope to meet. If he'd come with a guard dog it wouldn't have been a snarling Alsatian or Rottweiler, something more like a Labrador puppy in a fleecy jumper. I sorted out a mattress for Alhaji who kipped under the house, and when the cool weather arrived I told him to sleep in my car. It was only a Renault 4 but the wee fellow could stretch himself right out across the back seat.

One winter's night at about one in the morning I heard a clank from under my bedroom, then a crunch and a whispered grunt. I undid the padlock on my improvised gun-safe, grabbed my weapon, wrapped a loincloth around my middle, and crept down the stairway. Peering through the window at ground level I could see two stout figures fiddling with my car. They'd lifted it up, set it on blocks, removed three of the wheels, and were grappling with the nuts on the fourth. Of Alhaji there was no sight. I flung open the door, gun in hand, and stood with my legs splayed in the manner of Dirty Harry. I bellowed the standard salutation in such circumstances, 'Freeze motherfuckers.' They did as they were told – everyone in the Gambia had seen enough films to know that you don't mess with Clint Eastwood – and then the nearside rear door of the car creaked open. Alhaji emerged rubbing the sleep from his eyes. I sent him down the road to the State House where there was a twenty-four hour police patrol. In five minutes he was back, two coppers in tow, and one of the officers switched on his torch. And that was when I discovered that my loincloth had snagged on the downstairs door handle. I was standing with my legs apart, a shotgun in my hands, in my birthday suit.

Things may have changed over the years but the Gambian police force in the 1970s was a fine institution. The constables never batted an eyelid, they behaved as if a naked expatriate brandishing a deadly weapon were part of the daily detail, on a par with a taxi parking in the wrong spot or a cyclist making a sloppy hand signal when turning left at a crossroads. I brewed a pot of tea and the Peelers slurped cheerfully as they supervised the reassembly of my car. Then they took the thieves away to the other side of town. 'They can both swim, we'll dump them in the pond behind the bund. They're under age, charging them would be a big fat waste of time. But if they arrive home covered in turds and diesel oil, then their mothers will kick their bottoms good and proper.'

Handicraft for the not very Handy

'Well the first time you try it you're gonna cuss and shout'
Hoyt Axton, *Roll Your Own*

One year on leave in the UK I picked up a fly tying vice. It wasn't a clever one, you couldn't rotate the head or clip on a lamp or a magnifying lens. I think it cost four pounds. I use it to this day, but when I bought it I wasn't sure I'd take to tying. And if you must own a white elephant, I thought, at least let it be a cheap one. After all a bargain's something you don't want at a price you can't resist. My plan was that on the rare summer evenings we had electric power in Banjul I'd knock up a few trout patterns. Sometimes in stinking hot weather I pined for babbling brooks, windswept lochans, and days when you didn't feel like dropping your bags and wringing the sweat out of your underpants every half hour. As I sat at my vice turning out Dunkelds, and Invictas I'd imagine a breeze rippling the water and cooling my clammy limbs.

In the event I didn't get round to trout patterns for a while. I spent many an evening fishing for small tarpon in the canal behind the town. My partner on these trips was Ian, the chairman of the school board, and we both started out with plenty of seatrout flies. But the water was shallow and the bottom was a tangle of discarded rope, wire, tree branches, and unidentifiable slimy lumps that might have been rotting weed or the turds of a lost race of Gambian giants. We weren't fastidious, we were waving our fly rods in a miasma of sewage scented gunge, but we didn't fancy wading, anything that snagged up stayed snagged up. Pop the leader, on with another Blue Zulu or Blae and Black. And before long our boxes were nearly empty.

So one rainy Saturday afternoon I sat down at my vice and scratched my head. These days Google would tell me in a trice exactly how to make a Kate McLaren. It would try to flog me a bunch of materials as well, along with a guided steelhead trip to Oregon, membership in the highland malt whisky drinkers association, and the chance to meet a mail order bride from Uzbekistan. But there were no PCs in the mid 1970s. Even if there had been they'd have run on alternating current from a plug in the wall, our plugs were ornamental, power cuts averaged twenty-three hours a day. So I started with a few Black Pennells, golden pheasant tippets, black floss body, silver rib. The hackle's supposed to be black as well but I fancied something more exuberant for the canal, a combination of orange and white. On our next outing I gave Ian a couple of my creations. He peered like a chap who asked for a sausage roll and was served curried snails in kimchi but his manners kept him from saying anything. And my Colour-Blind Pennells caught fish, lots of fish. After that I stopped trying to recall exactly how to dress a Jock Scott or a Teal and Green, I just stuck a hook in the vice and cobbled up something with a bit of shiny stuff, a bit of wobbly stuff, and a vaguely fishy profile. As far as I'm concerned that's the secret of lures and streamers. Unless you want a very specific feature like the dumbbell eyes on a Clouser you can make it up as you go along. Look at the fry in the water, see what lurks among your materials, have a bash.

I thought proper fly fishing – for trout feeding on specific insects – would be a different story. I still think so. Bodgers like myself can be trusted to produce a usable Black and Peacock Spider, Gold-Ribbed Hare's Ear, or Pheasant Tail. My shuttlecocks are effective, epoxy buzzers are a piece of cake, and it's not hard to suggest a daddy longlegs. For anything more complicated I'm going shopping. Once I tried my hand at a Parachute Adams. It kept me out of mischief for a couple of hours, that's all that can be said for the venture. The end product was something that might perhaps catch a small and very inexperienced trout if I weren't too ashamed to tie it onto my cast. But I have my pride.

Look Out for the Edge

'I'm like a flashing laser'
Peter Tosh, *Steppin' Razor*

Jerome K. Jerome wrote, 'I like work: it fascinates me. I can sit and look at it for hours.' I'm industrious by nature, I find it difficult to stand by while someone else sweats like an anxious pig. But there's one job I love to watch, that of a good fishmonger. These people are magicians. 'In my left hand I have a perfectly normal plaice, in my right hand I have a knife with a red plastic handle. Hocus pocus, open sesame, perfect portions on the slab and a spotless frame in the cat food bucket.' The speed of the blade's enough to make you wonder how many fingers have been slashed or amputated over the years, whether top filleters have developed an adaptive mutation, bone hard carapace covering their hands. But the experts never use those chain mail gloves you see in the fishing catalogues, they just know what they're about. Equally amazing are professional netters who clean their catches at sea. I can't imagine gutting a cod when my extremities are numb and the deck's jumping up and down like a crosspatch monkey on a trampoline. I can't begin to imagine doing it at speed, but a half decent crew member has a freshly caught fish ready for the slush ice in fractions of a second.

Luckily I don't deal with industrial-sized catches. I've never been dexterous, in woodworking class the other children crafted dovetail jointed marquetry tea trays while I made marble alleys and swept up sawdust. But I butchered a lot of fish for my staff in Banjul and that taught me a couple of things. First's not to strive for perfection. In a Michelin starred kitchen every chunk has to be the same size and shape, otherwise it won't sit properly on the plate between the diver scallop, the artisanal Old Spot black pudding, and the hand-foraged borage blossoms. Regular eaters just need a lump that'll fit in a pan. And the odd tiny bone's not going to kill anyone, it lets them know they're eating something natural, not a fish finger made by gluing together scraps from a gutting room floor.

Second and most important is to use a good knife. People who butcher fish for a living use stiff blades; I prefer mine to bend easily. The rigid ones are good if you really know what you're doing, if the skeletal shape of a turbot or a barracuda's something that lives in your short term memory and the only question's how fast you can separate flesh from bone. The flexible jobs help the more tentative filleter, you can feel your

Cobia

way around the spines and the rib cage. A few more minutes of faffing but less waste. But regardless of its style the knife must be really sharp. The blades in most people's kitchens are fit for moulding butter or plastering the walls. My benchmark's an old style barber-surgeon's razor, something to snip an errant whisker with the lightest of touches. And although I've cut myself hundreds if not thousands of times – with everything from bread saws and fins to secateurs and tins – I've never had so much as a scratch from a filleting knife. When you know it's a deadly weapon you treat it like a gun, with exaggerated respect. In Banjul I kept a knife and a steel in the car and I'd touch up the edge between fish, even between sides of the same fish. Some people like sharpeners, the sort where you pull the blade through a V-shaped gap between two grinding wheels. I find them as useful as a landing net in a supermarket, they produce a dull and sometimes jagged edge. A stone's OK if it's really fine grained but a steel is best. What's more they show up in charity shops all the time, usually for just a couple of quid. Once you've invested in a steel and learned how to use it you keep everything sharp. It's like a hook file, when you're at a loose end you can teach the dog to bark the national anthem or you can make sure your lures have the sort of points that bury themselves deep in a clumsy finger. And the dog's tone deaf anyway, better off doing some basic tackle and blade maintenance. Even my penknife could be used for microsurgery but for the fact that it's coated with scales and it smells of old bait. And one day that came in handy.

I was plugging for cassava fish, a couple dangling from my rope, when I felt an odd take. Most predators hit a lure as if they think it's doing a runner, bash the little chap as hard as you can before it vanishes. This seemed more like a fish cruising along in its own sweet time, picking up snacks the way you might browse the free nibbles at a food festival. Just a slow, gently sucking pull, then solid resistance as if I'd snagged a rock. The rock swam away powerfully but steadily, no screaming run, more like the purposeful walk of someone who carries a pedometer and shows the day's mileage to random strangers. It took fifty yards of line, I recovered it, then away it went again. This was a species I'd never caught before. I was patient, no aggressive pumping. Some of the boats had been landing tuna but surely they'd be faster. Maybe just a cassava but foul hooked, that would give it extra purchase as it cruised away. Or could it be a cobia, there were plenty of them offshore, maybe one had come in after the mullet? Cobia are delicious, I'd caught them in Tanzania, sweet white meat and pleasantly firm. Egg and breadcrumbs on a thick steak, hard to beat. And it looked like a cobia, dark and wide across the head, my mouth was watering. But you shouldn't mush your peas before your fillet's in the pan. After the best part of an hour I had the mystery fish in the shallows: a shark about five feet long, between portly and obese. I think it was a blacktip (*Carcharhinus limbatus*) but I wouldn't bet on that with counterfeit money. It was almost completely dark. Our school caretaker loved shark meat but there was no way I could carry this great lump back to the car. I didn't fancy unhooking it, nasty looking teeth. I didn't want to lose my plug either, some of my broomstick chunks worked better than others, this one was a paragon of catchiness. I ran my penknife around the outside of the bend of the hook, a bit of pressure and the shark was free. It lay stranded in nine inches of water for a minute staring at me, then a wave washed it clear and it swam like hell for the horizon. Back at the car I gave the penknife a quick buff. Sharkskin's tough.

Blacktip shark

Poverty, Abstinence, Wildfowl

'I was high as a bird in the sky'
Little Village, *Fool Who Knows*

When I lived in the Gambia I didn't drink alcohol. It wasn't for moral, religious, or health reasons, I just couldn't afford it. When I ate with friends they'd offer me a beer or a glass of wine but I always said no. If I chugged down other people's booze I'd have felt obliged to lay in a supply for when they dropped in at my place, and my budget wouldn't take the strain. Only once did I fall off the wagon and that was by accident. A shooting pal brewed a batch of ginger beer and offered me a glass. In my experience ginger beer was a soft drink peddled by Corona, the Famous Five had lashings of the stuff then went off catching crooks. It was a hot day so I swigged a pint, swiftly followed by another. Then I felt a bit dizzy and fell asleep under a tree, a ninety minute siesta. Proper ginger beer's up to about eleven percent alcohol. The unpublished sequel: *Five Get Absolutely Faceless*.

One year my teetotal habit looked as if it might leave me at a loose end on Boxing Day. I fancied a wildfowling trip but all the regular guns cried off citing the hangovers they were sure they'd have. I scratched my head. We always went to the rice paddies mob handed, sometimes the car stuck in sand or mud, you needed one to drive and three to push. But I had a little Renault 4, a tinny box so light I could bounce it out of the soft stuff by myself. What the hell, I'd shoot alone.

It felt odd walking along the bund with no companions. Normally we'd chat quietly, deciding who'd go where, speculating about flight paths. There's something about darkness that inclines people to whisper, so even with no one to talk to I found myself muttering softly. Which way was the breeze blowing, could I hear the distant beating of wings? Looking to the weak gleam in the east I saw a knob billed goose coming straight at me hardly ten feet in the air. I loaded quickly, fired, and the bird stopped flapping and carried on gliding. It landed with a thump at my feet. Oh boy, I thought, Polish Joe should have come today, it's the first time I've bagged one without getting my underpants wet. Whether you're fishing or shooting there's something liberating about breaking the blank. That first success doesn't make you smug but it bucks you up, it helps you focus and feel alive in the moment. The rod or gun seems comfortable, almost as if you were born with it in your hands. And you smile, that relaxes you even more.

Scanning the horizon I could see flocks of fowl taking to the sky over the river. Then I peered at the rice. There was a block twenty yards across that stood out from the rest of the field, like the square in the middle of a cricket field. Recently planted, I thought, just the spot for a gourmet goose get-together. Of course Murphy's Law decreed that it was three hundred yards away and on the far side of a channel nearly six feet deep. But it really did look like a wildfowl magnet and there were two or three little islands to the river side of the new seedlings, long grass for a bit of a hide.

Stuff it, I'd go for it. I'd be off my rocker if I didn't and then watched bird after bird circling where I might have been. And if I wound up cold I could always head home, no need to wait around for any chums. I took off my jacket and shirt, wrapped them and my cartridge bag around the gun, then through the mud to the flowing drain. I didn't really swim across the creek, more of a pogo action with a bit of forward thrust, bouncing along the spodgy bottom on my tiptoes, my chin wet but my specs and woolly hat clear of the water, the gun and gear above my head in a two handed death grip. I slithered out onto a grassy tummock, dried my upper body with the shirt, and slipped back into the fleecy top. Fair enough, chilly but not actually shivering, and now the sky was stippled with incoming birds. On most of our wildfowling expeditions you shot whatever came in range. A decent bag was a couple of birds, four was a red letter day. And generally we'd take home a mixture of whistling teal, knob bill, and spur wing. My belated Christmas present from the Gambia river was skein after skein after skein. I didn't fire a shot at a teal, they were tasty but small. I took a pass on the spur wing as well, heavy to cart back to the car and sometimes tough. I went home with six plump knob bill. And as much as I liked my regular shooting chums, I loved being alone in the swamp, free to go where I pleased, all decisions off my own bat. It was just like fishing.

Mbacke helped me pluck the fowl. Then we made a charcoal fire, skewered them on two pieces of reinforcing steel, and spit roasted them above the flames. Mbacke was a Muslim so he didn't drink either. We made a huge pot of tea and we had one hell of a Boxing Day party.

A Gourmet by the Water

'Heaven on earth with an onion slice'
Jimmy Buffet, *Cheeseburger In Paradise*

They say that if you give a person a fish you provide food for a day. It's more complicated than that. Often you create an expectation that there are plenty more where that came from, any time I'm peckish you'll top up my larder. One chap didn't just want more, he told me the species and size, as if my Renault were one of those internet sites where you can find out of print Japanese import CDs and size fourteen Claret Bumbles tied by left-handed Basque speakers. I'd been plugging when I foul-hooked a four pound snapper. I'm not sure of the species, there are a ton of similar looking snappers, but it was pinky grey with a beaky mouth. I dropped it off with a friend who worked for the Medical Research Council. I owed him a favour, he'd taken care of me when I fell ill in an outbreak of infective hepatitis, the fish was a very small gesture of thanks. I ran into him a few days later and he told me the snapper was the most delicious thing he'd ever put in his mouth, the perfect size to cook whole for his family. If I ever landed another he'd be chuffed to have it. My first thought was that this was one choosy so-and-so, next he'd be telling me I must catch his fish between four and five o'clock on a Wednesday while standing on one leg and singing the national anthem. But maybe he reckoned I'd enjoy the challenge of an unusual target. He knew my twisted sense of curiosity. When I was sick it had been fifty-fifty whether I'd make it, he'd cheered me up, 'The medical profession recognises two versions of hepatitis, type A and type B. This is a new one and they've just named it. They had a committee to come up with a designation. James, you'll enjoy this, I bet you're thinking type C. Not a bit, epidemiologists have more imagination than that. They're calling it type Non-A-Non-B.'

So how to catch smallish snappers. Bigger ones were a common by-catch when I was after tarpon but the tiddler had been a fluke on a par with finding a hoard of Viking treasure in a supermarket carpark in Accra. I asked my doctor pal if he'd noticed the stomach contents. As a researcher of course he had, the shells and heads of prawns. 'And I'm sure that's why it was so tasty, it had been eating like a politician on an expenses-paid junket.' Now I wasn't about to stump up for seafood from the market so the first hurdle was bait. At school I found a plastic crate and wrapped it in odds and ends of chicken wire. The spaces in the mesh were on the large side but I wanted big prawns. I used fencing cable to fashion an entry chute inspired by a Cornish lobster pot. Then I field tested my handiwork in a creek just outside town. With a bonga head for bait I caught a dozen whoppers in a couple of hours. This was just a proof of concept so I ate them with garlic and chillies.

Next day I set my pot at the edge of a tangle of mangrove roots. I had one prawn left from my test haul – it had died before the water boiled – and I lobbed it out on a size two hook. As it sank it was snaffled by a catfish, so I tied in a plug blank as a float to keep my gear off the bottom. By the time I'd landed three snappers in the right size range I had twenty surplus prawns in my basket. They went really well with snapper. Or anything else come to that. Give someone a fish and you can wind up with a whole new source of food for yourself.

The Tales we Tell

'He's a liar and I'm not sure about you'
Kirsty MacColl, *There's A Guy Works Down The Chip Shop*

In popular culture a fisherman's story means a lie. Maybe so but I reckon my brother and sister anglers are honest most of the time. When we bring our catches home for the table it's hard to tell tall tales. The pollack that makes a not very fishy fish pie with bolstering from a packet of supermarket prawns and a leftover chunk of finnan haddie clearly wasn't a six pounder. The trout that fits neatly across a ten inch plate may have shrunk under the grill but nobody's going to think it was a foot long when you caught it.

The chance to be creative comes up when we let fish go, and it's not so much telling porkies as time-adjusted truth. When you feel something pick up your bait in the surf you hope for a sequence that involves tightening, bringing your catch ashore, removing the hook, and waving goodbye to a handsome bass. Sometimes the middle section goes missing, you strike too soon or too late. Things go straight from the first nibble to the fare-thee-well. Strictly you may not have landed your trophy but the opening gambit and the end result were the same, she bit and she swam away.

So only a pedant would deny you your victory, it was a long-range release. And when you return an eleven inch brownie you do it in hope she'll thrive, next year you might run into her again after she's grown a bit. So calling her a thirteen incher, that's not a lie, it's just using the fast forward button on the facts. You're not telling it like it is, you're telling it like it's going to be. With a bit of luck. Or a lot of luck.

The time we stretch the boundaries isn't when we brag, it's when we talk down our successes. We're not daft, we know better than to tell everyone a favourite spot's heaving with monsters. Let that catfish out of the bag and you'll come back to find the shore looks like the pavement outside Harrods before the big sale and some scumbag's set an illegal net. So when a busybody in a carpark asks if you've had any luck a canny angler mutters something vaguely off-putting. 'Slow.' 'Not as good as I'd expected.' 'It was better twenty years ago.'

And that last one's a beauty. Immanuel Kant said that lying's always wrong, even if a murderer asks where the potential victim's hiding, you must tell the truth. Harsh, but he left a get-out clause. You can say something honest but adding nothing to what's known already; factual but useless. The twenty years ago malarkey ticks that box perfectly. Face it, a lot of things were better twenty years ago. Beer was cheaper, my joints didn't creak, fish stocks were in healthier nick.

When it comes to misleading idle slobs who couldn't be bothered to find their own marks I'm a good Kantian; or in everyday fishing language I'm a bullshitter. Ask me which reach of the stream holds the best trout and I'll tell you I had a one and a half pounder from just below the bridge. I did. It was in 1978 since when I've seen nothing of size within half a mile of the place. Run into me when I'm loading a monster bass into the boot and I'll explain that I've spent endless hours in this cove. Again that's so much on the up and up that it's vertical, it's been a haunt of mine since I was six or seven years old. This morning I had five decent fish in a dozen casts, but that's for me to know and nobody else to find out.

In Banjul there was one so-called sporting type who snuck around all the time trying to find what other anglers were up to. His name was Sven and he worked at one of the hotels. When he made a decent bag he'd hang the fish from a gibbet outside the café and invite holiday visitors to pose for snapshots with him and his brilliant catches. And when the corpses began to smell he'd chuck them in the bin and plan his next outing. Mighty slaughters, total waste, nothing was eaten, nothing was released. In the everyday slang of the angling community Sven was a complete arsehole. And in the technical jargon of environmental science Sven was a complete arsehole (*Rectum absolutum*).

Anyway one weekend morning I went after tarpon. I overslept, only arriving at the point an hour before dawn. On with a live mullet, a gentle lob, and I sat on a rock to await developments. But not for long, I could sense that my bait was stirred up, jigging like a drunk at a ceilidh. Then a solid pull and a screaming run of a hundred yards or so. Tom McGuane wrote that hooking a tarpon's like pushing a Steinway piano off a cliff. I've never pushed any sort of piano off anything but I know what he meant, there's a mixture of wild acceleration and unstoppable power. I'm not sure how a falling Steinway would leap but my fish spent plenty of time in the air as well, hefty splashes in the inky darkness. It was fifty minutes before I could lead it into the shallows. By then the light had come up and I could make a fair guess as to its size: sixty to seventy pounds. It was lightly hooked, a quick release, then I sat down on a boulder to watch the sky turn from red to grey to blue while I had a ciggie.

Heading to the car I ran into Sven, twitching with beady eyed curiosity. 'Did you catch anything?' I gave him a look that said, 'Stuff this for a lark, I'm knackered.' Then a deep sigh, 'I was there well over an hour, just one nibble.' Technically true, totally deceptive, Immanuel Kant would've have been proud of me.

Luck is for Lotteries, Anglers are Astute

'Good luck had just stung me'
The Band, *Up On Cripple Creek*

Land a whopper and some bright spark's going to say you're as jammy as a Women's Institute tea party, 'You were just in the right place at the right time'. There's one word in that sentence that gets up my nose, 'just'. Of course you catch fish by being in the right place at the right time, you'll struggle if you cast into a muddy puddle solidified by an overnight frost or a municipal swimming pool while it's being drained for repairs. And there's always a wee bit of luck. When your fly swims through a favourite trout lie the sipping rise might be from an eight inch tiddler or a thirteen inch trophy. A mackerel bait in a perfect autumn surf could be picked up by a two pound bass or a double figure monster. But how you pick the place and time, that's not blind good fortune.

Time first, and some anglers need their beauty sleep, nothing wrong with that. But if you keep bankers' hours you can't resent the person who out-fishes you before the dawn or at the end of the day. You ply your craft in sunshine with a beer in your hand, of course you don't fare as well as the nutters who stay out all night or roll from their beds at very silly o'clock. Some fish are diurnal, mackerel and wrasse come to mind, most are nocturnal or crepuscular. That's not going to change, get used to it.

When it comes to picking places there are no shortcuts either. The more time you spend by the water the better you understand your spots, especially if you don't spread yourself too thinly. Some people are convinced there's an anglers' Shangri La out there, you just need to find it. These are the types who'll pile in the car and drive hundreds of miles for a day on a lake, the ones who say, 'I've never been there, let's have a try on the next big springs'. Variety may be the spice of life but always fishing new waters means being a permanent novice. Here it is, five hundred acres of reservoir, which bay do we start in? A three mile strand beside a headland battered by Atlantic swells, where do you think we should set up? Ask a local and the chances are you'll be given some advice. 'Try by the yellow hut', which means 'I'm heading for bass central, that's in the opposite direction, I'd appreciate it if you stay as far away from me as possible. And please catch nothing, that way you won't come back.' Stick to just a few areas and you learn how they respond to the weather, the time of year, the state of the tide. You don't just know which beach to try over slack low at the end of an October gale, you've a pretty good idea which bit of that beach might deliver. And that's not luck.

One year in Banjul the rains came late. Normally they started in June but it was mid-July before the first thunderheads built up. As if to make up for their tardiness they were massive, the heavens opened and stayed open, day after day of steady downpours. I loved the wet season, when the first storms broke everyone flung dignity aside and enjoyed the respite from the heat. Children rolled in puddles, old folk danced in their underwear, even the dogs joined in, bounding around like soggy otters. But a week of nonstop precipitation played hell with the fishing. It wasn't a case of being a fair weather sportsman, it was so warm that a sopping shirt was a pleasure. The problem was mud. As the Gambia River swelled, more and more fresh brown water rushed into the ocean. Away from the estuary my rock marks were overlooked by laterite cliffs which washed into the wave. So we had brown Windsor soup flowing into cream of tomato, not a tasty combination. Lures were a waste of time, invisible in the gunge. Even the bait fishers were failing, chucking their bonga into a sea of brackish cocoa. This wasn't funny, the implicit terms of employment at our school included a supply of fillets, blanking wasn't an option.

About fifteen miles from town there was a mangrove creek. It had a stony bottom and mangrove trees often seem to keep the water clear. Maybe they absorb suspended matter, maybe the mud sticks to their roots. I'd caught small snappers in the creek by float fishing a prawn bait. But small snappers weren't going to feed the staff unless I bunked off work and fished an eighteen hour day. That idea had some appeal but I was paid to be head-teacher, strictly speaking the free fishmonger racket was optional. I knew bigger snappers went well to live mullet, I imagined the main channel of the creek would be fairly clean, and I reckoned where there were tiddlers there might also be whoppers. So one afternoon I drove out to the mangrove area. It was a much longer trip than normal, a stretch on my petrol budget, but I couldn't see any alternative. I arrived in time to spot a mullet netter making his last few casts of the day. Half a dozen livebaits went into my bucket. On with a frisky one, a lob into the deeper water, and within ten minutes, line was buzzing from my reel. Six pounds. I finished the session with seven snappers, one bait was stuck in its captor's throat still kicking, it had a second outing. My best was just under twelve pounds. When I stopped on the way home for the first drop-off the teacher looked in the back of the car. 'Wow, there was absolutely no fish in the market this evening, how did you catch so many?' 'I was in the right place at the right time,' I told her. No 'just'.

The Voice of Authority

'Gonna buy five copies for my mother'
Three Dog Night, *Cover Of The Rolling Stone*

Not long before I left Banjul, a Swedish magazine asked to interview me about fishing in the Gambia. Well, it was a magazine if I were putting together the sort of CV where the person who served the boardroom biscuits claims to have played a key role in strategic leadership deliberations and the receptionist directed the ongoing customer value proposition. More accurately it was a gussied up brochure put out by one of the tour operators. But there was a fee involved and as usual my financial situation was as tight as a toreador's Y-fronts, I was game. So one afternoon I sat down with Per and Greta in the bar of a holiday hotel, he was in charge of words, she did the pictures. Both looked too young to drive, buy alcohol, or be sent to the WC without supervision, but they were pleasant enough. And the barman must have reckoned they were eighteen at least, our table was a car crash of beer bottles and empty schnapps glasses.

Per turned on his little tape machine. 'James, people say you are the top fishing guru in the country, the number one authority. Please will you tell us how you achieve your success.' A damned silly introduction, but I was being paid so I played along. Now I'd met enough gillies, bailiffs, and water-watchers to have a pretty good handle on this local expert racket. Rule one's never to make a declarative statement. Say something like 'The predators come in to eat the mullet' and right away you'll hear from a bright spark with a doctorate in marine biology whose dissertation showed that trevally and mullet show up at the same spots not because one's chasing the other, it's just that they're both nibbling chocolate eclairs and listening to Brain of Britain on the BBC World Service.

Rule two's to be Eeyorishly gloomy, reconciled to the fact that the fish'll be dour, the weather crappy, and some poor bastard's going to a watery grave before the day's out. If you promise abject disaster you can claim a triumph when the trip turns out modestly lousy. And rule three's to be meaningless, muttering a mixture of generalisations, zen riddles, and choruses from Celtic folk songs. So I burbled about glorious uncertainty, inhabiting the tragedy of the moment, seizing the power of the wave between your fingers, listening to the noises of the silence, the wearing of the green, labouring by the sea, and following Henry Joy.

Per nodded approvingly. Or maybe he was falling into a stupor. Then Greta asked if we could go somewhere to catch a fish, she wanted scenic panoramas, a lone figure in the sunset, action snaps of a monster of the deep, and a couple more beers to stick in her camera bag. Again I'd run into enough proper authorities to hit the brief. Both angler and tackle have to look as if they've been around the block enough times to be dizzy. You can have a top of the line rod or a budget number, no matter, but it must be battered, lots of sweat stains on the cork grips and reattached rod rings. My gear was spot-on. Your fishing clothes should look as if you've worn them for ten years, bathing and sleeping without stripping off. And above all you have to look politely bored at all times. If the fish don't bite it's the boredom of resignation, the Atlantic's a cruel mistress and a proper angler expects no mercy. When a trophy hits it's the boredom of familiarity, this may be a twenty pound barracuda, it may be running like a ski-jumper who's overdone the amphetamines, but a veteran's seen it countless times, just one more whopper to join the thousands that went before.

Once I'd caught a couple of cassava fish Greta declared herself well pleased and chugged a beer. Per's bottle was empty, he was at a loose end, running a hand idly over my rod. 'So these hooks you use, are they very pointed?' Then a yelp, he'd impaled his thumb on a size four treble. I drove to the hospital where the duty nurse dunked his hand in iodine, yanked out the barb with forceps, and gave the poor fellow a thousand words about public drunkenness, wasting medical resources, and being a broad spectrum twit. Per moaned softly and threw up while Greta paid my fee. She added fifty percent to cover ambulance driving duties, gave me a wobbly kneed hug, and my work was done.

I waited in vain to see the finished article. Before its next brochure came out the tour operator went bankrupt. Maybe businesspeople should learn a lesson: don't hire employees who get legless on company time and assess the sharpness of unfamiliar objects by stabbing themselves.

Top of the Water Silliness

'He came dancing across the water'
Neil Young, *Cortez The Killer*

While I was in the Gambia I qualified as an accountant. I had to keep the books for the school, I wanted to do a decent job, and I knew I'd stick to my studies only if I took tests. My final certification depended on working for a year in an approved practice, and I found a position in Penzance. A trout stream and a reservoir were not far from the office and I often spent an evening at one or the other. I also did some beach fishing, I enjoyed not having to watch tourists spewing their lunches or trying to seduce underage locals. The only annoying thing was people who thought the best aspect of night fishing was fiddling around with Tilley lamps. Nowadays most people wear headlamps. They're fine if you have the discipline to turn them off before facing the sea, dire if you wade into the wave like a Home Guard squaddie hunting U-boats. But a light that glares nonstop's a total disaster. Luckily in the late 1970s there were enough bass that even Cornwall's answer to the Blackpool Illuminations didn't scare them all away. I caught my first double figure fish during my Cornish year. It took half a mackerel in a wild surf after a late summer storm.

Sometimes I scrambled out on the rocks and fished for mackerel and pollack with a Toby or a German sprat. And that was what I fancied one September evening. I'd had a long day trying to make sense of a farming couple's financial records. That makes it sound as if they wrote things down or filed bits of paper. Not a bit of it, they just had a large cardboard box marked 'Accounts' where they chucked invoices, bank statements, wedding invitations, parking tickets, veterinary prescriptions, spare parts from defunct agricultural machinery, out of date discount vouchers for the supermarket, and half eaten pasties. They were amazed speeding fines weren't allowable business costs – 'My handsome, we've got so much work on that we have to drive like shit off a shovel' – furious that payments to the beauty salon and the drycleaner were classified as personal expenses – 'If I get pulled through a hedge backwards by a heifer and covered in slurry the taxman reckons I should just lump it, that's not fair.' Accounting principles and tax rules are arcane at the best of times. With clients who think the cat's mange is a financially significant event they're really heavy going. So a bit of peace and quiet was in order, out on the point watching the sun sink silently into the sea.

Fat chance, there must have been half a dozen youngsters scattered around my spot hurling spinners and obscenities in all directions. I wandered along the shore until they were out of earshot. By now I was in a tiny cove, the water rock-strewn and weedy. It was too shallow for a metal lure so I rummaged through my bag, coming up with a little popper from the days when I was repping for tackle companies in Banjul. I gave it a chuck, started to retrieve, and almost laughed out loud. American bass, I thought, must be eejits. A pink and silver cone zotting along the top, jumping like a frog in a steeplechase, spewing spray like a water cannon with a banjaxed gasket, and some halfwit fish is going to try and eat it. Why not pull the other one, it's got fluorescent rubber dangly bits on? And that was when my ridiculous lump of balsa wood disappeared into a vortex and a three pound bass started a thumping run.

I'm sure I'd have done a bit more experimenting with bloody silly lures if I'd had the chance. But the next day my Achilles tendon popped like a string on a bass fiddle and I was in plaster until I left Cornwall for Botswana.

Wildlife with Missing Biscuits

'Where the highway ends and the desert breaks'
Bruce Springsteen, *The Price You Pay*

Through the first half of the 1980s I lived in Gaborone. If you're a geographer – or have a map to hand – you'll not be surprised that most of my fishing involved a few hours behind the wheel. Botswana's landlocked and short on rainfall and rivers, most of it's covered by the Kgalagadi Desert. Water's a treasured resource, the name of the currency and the Tswana greeting for a notable are 'Pula', meaning rain. Drip and wet, I imagine, must be terms of affection and respect; while only a total monster would have a sunny disposition or a dry wit.

The first time I saw the great grey-green greasy Limpopo was in a winter drought, it was a stagnant silty puddle and the fever trees were dying from boredom. But there are a couple of larger, permanent rivers in the north, the Chobe and the Okavango. The Okavango rises in Angola, disappears underground, then pops back up in Botswana; by which time it's been filtered through hundreds of miles of sand so its delta is gin clear. And did you ever wonder how gin came to be the benchmark of water clarity? I reckon anglers coined the phrase when the fish were hard to tempt and their thoughts drifted to a lunchtime tipple with tonic, ice, and a slice of lemon.

Anyway I spent time in the Okavango delta doing accounting work for luxury safari camps. Drifting along the channels you could watch hippos faffing around like chubby scuba divers in wrinkly wetsuits, crocodiles lying in wait for their prey with the quiet menace of people selling breakdown insurance in supermarket carparks. There were tigerfish and tilapia as well. Most days I'd wet a line before or after work, sitting on a camp dock with a Mepps spinner, and I caught my fair share of tilapia, mostly to three or four pounds. They were good eating, none of the notes of earth and farmyard manure you find in specimens from muddy waters. But generally I fished as a way to watch the animals and to keep myself out of the camp bars. In my younger days I had a hollow leg but there was no way I could keep pace with the safari guides, they were hollow from toenail to tonsil, slurping scotch in industrial quantities without noticeable impairment.

On long weekends I sometimes drove up the delta for some do-it-yourself camping. This was nothing like the five star experience of staying

Tigerfish

in the tourist set-ups, just two or three four wheel drive vehicles, tents, an icebox full of meat to cook on the campfire, heroic amounts of beer, and a lot of spare wheels. The thorns were hell on inner tubes and you could expect a couple of punctures a day. We patched our tyres in the evenings, but you needed to be set up for quick wheel changes if you didn't want to miss the prime game viewing times.

A lot of people were nervous about camping in areas where lions were as common as lawyers round an accident victim, but the experts said you were safe as long as you kept your tent zipped up. It seems big cats find the touch of fabric terrifying. I don't see the logic, but then again people are frightened of worms, who knows? Certainly tourists who slept in open tents – tempting when the weather was stinking hot and a waft of breeze brought a little relief – ran a risk. Most years there'd be reports of one or two who'd been dragged off into the bush and scoffed.

The other animals with healthy appetites were the monkeys. They'd learned to recognise odd canvas shapes and folding chairs as sources of grub. As soon as a tent went up they'd be in the trees above, watching us unpack and chattering like restaurant critics waiting to see today's menu. 'I wonder if they'll have tomatoes. Look, ginger biscuits, that's my pudding order sorted.' And anything on the camp table would be gone in a flash, furry kleptomaniacs swooping down to grab it, then scarpering back aloft and sneering as they laid into your rations.

Everyone had a theory on how to deter monkeys, none of them were worth a damn. A boom box playing disco music worked for about ten minutes, after which the campers were heartily sick of the BeeGees and Donna Summer while the monkeys boogied as they looted. Slow drying adhesive on the table top deterred about two thieves in a dozen, the other ten munching away regardless and smearing the glue over everything else in camp. Tupperware didn't help, you lost your snacks and your plastic boxes as well. One fellow swore by a stash of oranges, each injected with a shot of vodka – the idea had come about when his pals were smuggling alcohol into teetotal South African rugby grounds. The notion was that a well oiled monkey would toddle off for a snooze and leave you in peace. The only chap I knew who tried this trick wasn't impressed. The first monkey to snitch an orange climbed up to a handy perch, ate its treat, then fell from the tree branch in a drunken stupor. It landed in the breakfast platter, squealing softly and emptying its bowels into the scrambled eggs.

Tournament Tactics

'We have victory, a famous victory in our sights'
Ballboy, *A Relatively Famous Victory*

Competitive fishing's a contradiction as far as I'm concerned. One of the loveliest attributes of my brethren and sistren of the rod and line's our willingness to help one another out of a jam. Bump into someone who's run out of bait or lost a fly box, every instinct tells us to chip in with some squid or a few examples of the pattern that's been doing the job. See an angler with the look of a long term blanker – it's what you'd expect from a constipated undertaker with a hangover – and we're driven to offer words of advice or encouragement that might lead to success. Of course there are a few who disagree. Once I casually asked what fly a fellow was using. I wasn't interested, it was the trout fishing equivalent of, 'What do you think of this weather?' But his reaction was to snap, 'Why would I tell you that?', his hand racing to cover the end of his leader. I even heard two chaps on a beach arguing because one wouldn't give the other a side of mackerel. But these are outliers. The general population includes people who want to be drug dealers, even tabloid hacks and hedge fund managers; any sporting subset's bound to produce its tiny quota of sociopaths. The vast majority like to cooperate.

That said I once took part in an angling match. I didn't sign up so much as give in to the economic realities of the luxury hospitality industry. I was staying at a very high-end safari camp in northern Botswana while I worked on the owners' tax returns. The only other guests had booked the whole place. They were an extended family group headed by an American couple who'd founded a technology company. Over dinner one of the women of the party remarked that she'd watched me fishing from the dock, I seemed to do rather well. At this the son of the tech millionaires announced that I couldn't hold a candle to his skills with rod and line, we should have a contest to show what was what. His name was Bradley, he was about twenty-five, and depending how charitable you were he was either a bit brash and insecure or a self-absorbed little shit. No matter what was said or done he always had to show he knew best. If someone proposed compliments to the chef Bradley would give a five minute blether on the best way to season a beef fillet. Show him a brilliant photograph of a lion and he'd tell you it would have been better with slower film or a wider aperture. I thought he was struggling with the fact that he was filthy rich as a result of an accident of birth, a lucky sperm keen to prove he was the sort of genius who'd have made millions under his own steam even if he'd grown up in a beer crate in the middle of the Kgalagadi desert. Be that as it may he issued his challenge and the owner of the camp said, 'That sounds like fun, Bradley against James, five till six thirty tomorrow evening, biggest tilapia wins.' I was committed.

Then we came to the rules. Because his family had booked out the whole camp Bradley put dibs on the mobile pontoon as his platform, the small motorboat to carry his cousins who'd watch him fish and record his triumph with their video cameras. That left me with the dock in front of the main lodge. He'd be guided around the delta to all the best fishing spots, I'd chuck my lure into an area twenty yards square. And at first I didn't give a hoot. My clients were making fifteen hundred dollars a day from this young man, plus his bar bill. If that fee covered victory in a race between his Formula One Ferrari team and a bloke on a second hand push-bike, so bloody be it. But as the evening wore on Bradley crowed like a bantam cockerel auditioning for the lead in the Rocky Horror Picture Show, he was going to kick my butt, whack me like a piñata. By bedtime my mind was made up, I'd give him a run for his money. Make that his parents' money.

The way we caught tilapia in the Okavango was simple. A bar spoon – I liked a black Mepps with yellow spots – fished on a steady retrieve in areas where there was deep water and plenty of cover. Delta tilapia seem to be ambush feeders, they sit hidden in roots or reeds until a tiddler comes too close then pounce on it. There's really no way to target the bigger fish, you just pull your lure through the likely areas and hope for the best. My normal approach was to try for a basket of table-sized fish, two or three pounders, releasing a fair few little ones along the way. And that led to my competitive tactic, I'd avoid the babies. Next morning I took three spinners to the camp workshop, borrowed a pair of pliers, and replaced the size eight trebles with single two-zero hooks. The less time I spent unhooking nippers the more chance of a stonker. I stuffed the modified lures in my pocket, this was a secret weapon.

At five o'clock Bradley set off in the pontoon, yelling to the bar staff to put the champagne on ice ready for his triumphant return. His relatives had the good grace to look as sheepish as a flock of Herdwicks as they zipped away in the motorboat, and I waited for the dock to stop leaping about in the propeller wash. Then I started casting to the reed clumps along the bank, a slower than normal retrieve to drop the lure a little deeper. About one chuck in four led to a sharp knock but nothing was hooking itself. At five thirty the bar waiter trotted down to offer me a beer. Bradley was on the radio-telephone providing live commentary, so far he'd had two three pounders and a lot of smaller ones. I soldiered on through endless wriggly hits until just after six fifteen when I had a solid take. It was a lovely pink-tinged fish and I reckoned it was close to three and a half. But no sooner had I put in in the bag for the kitchen than a fresh beer brought an update from the pontoon: four pounds three ounces. I swigged the beer and pondered. It would be ill-mannered to give up early, if someone's going to win he should have the satisfaction of knowing you kept punching till the final bell. And a gratifying victory would have Bradley holding forth in the bar until the small hours, vintage Moet by the bucketful, my clients would make a packet. I shuffled across the decking, a chuck here and a chuck there, more nibbles along the way. At six twenty-five I thought I could hear the putt-putt of the pontoon's engine, soon Bradley would be in earshot with enough snotty remarks to foul a whole box of paper hankies. I tried a cast to the edge of an underwater mound. Everything went solid, I must have let the spoon sink too deep. Then wild thumps as line ran from my reel. With my big hook there was no need to play the fish gently, I had it on the bank in short order. It was at least a five pounder.

In came the pontoon and the motorboat. I sat on the dock nursing my beer as Bradley stood over me posing for his cousins' cameras. 'Four pounds, three and a half ounces, that's a real tilapia.' He held his fish high. 'Should we head for the bar? My treat.' The waiter fixed him with an innocent smile. 'I think, sir, the drinks are on Mister James.' He pulled my fish from the bag. 'This is what we call a tilapia around here. Five and a quarter on the dot.'

I conducted myself with as much good grace as I could muster. Mostly luck, you never really know what's going to grab your lure, it's just chuck it and chance it. I never mentioned my stroke of genius with the two-zero hook, or the way fate so often frowns on the arrogant tosspot. I knew

I'd have enjoyed my whopper a lot more if I'd been fishing for my own amusement, not to score cheap points against a bumptious prat I'd never meet again. And in the forty-odd years since I've tried to avoid anything like a competition.

Lions, Bass Fishers, and Local knowledge

'Bring it to me'
Sam Cooke, *Bring It On Home To Me*

Wildlife films often show sequences where a lion prowls through the scrub then sprints across an open plain before leaping onto a gazelle. It's a terrific spectacle, hats off to the camera crews, but I'm not sure it's typical behaviour. I must have seen half a dozen lion kills, either the act itself or the aftermath. None involved long hunts or dashes through the savannah, all were ambushes. In the dry season the best place to find predators was a pool that stayed damp even in a drought. A lion would tuck up in some cover. Watching from our vehicles we'd have no idea where it was hiding, if it was there at all. But when a wildebeest started grubbing in the mud a massive tawny streak would flash from the trees, deliver a hammer blow with a paw, and rip out its prey's throat to be on the safe side. Once I spent an hour watching a lioness training her cubs to catch their own food. They were stalking a family of warthogs, lying low and letting the pigs draw closer. Every time an excited youngster started to sprint towards its prey old Mum reached out and gave it a no nonsense smack. No son, that's not the way it's done, minimum effort is the order of the day, sit on your bottom and wait for your meal to be delivered.

Humans must be the only animals that take exercise routinely and voluntarily. Even when a dog chases a ball it's following an instinctual trigger that tells it to hunt down that round bouncy rabbit, it'll be delicious. But we jog in circles, sweat in gyms, cycle for miles just so we can wear lycra outfits and look like prats. Of course we're the species with an obesity epidemic, we've become so good at producing stuff to eat that we can afford wasted exertion. That's why even our pointless workouts often have a nutritional payback: 'My FitBit says I burned six hundred calories, anyone for a cheeseburger and a few pints?'

Fish certainly don't work any harder for their meals than they have to. I watch bass from the cliffs in calm weather, once you find a big one it tends to stick around for a while. There's no restless cruising but a lot of hanging about in a spot that's sheltered from the wave or the current. Trout are the same. In fry season I'll see them lurking behind a tree root or a sunken wall, springing into action only when a shoal of tiny rudd comes within a foot or two. The things I love to catch by and large are static. At a familiar spot I know where to find them, where to set my ambush. But nobody's going to mistake me for a lion. Male pattern baldness took away my mane.

Assume the Fishing Position

'There's a man with a gun over there'
Buffalo Springfield, *For What It's Worth*

I was in New York City for fifteen years beginning in the mid-1980s. I had less outdoor entertainment in those fifteen years than in a typical month in most places I've lived. I even became a marathon runner, not one of the freaks who cross the tape in a couple of hours, a hacker who'd get to the end through bloody mindedness rather than fitness or athletic ability. The finish was my only goal, never mind how long it took. I'd stop after twenty-one miles and scrounge a cigarette to gee myself up for the final push, then go home on the subway, hoping there'd still be enough strength in my legs to walk up the steps at my local stop. Apart from running, every other kind of sport involved hours of travel, and I hate sitting in trains or buses. I detest cars even more than public transport. If there's a hell I suspect it looks like the M25 over a bank holiday.

Sheepshead Bay wasn't too far away and it had party boats fishing for flounder (*Pleuronectes americanus*) in the spring, fluke (*Paralichthys dentatus*) in the summer, and blackfish or tautog (*Tautoga onitis*) in the autumn. But these outings were more about putting fresh fillets in the deep-freeze than sport. I didn't care much for my boat fishing. All the skill came from the captain, who put his craft in the right spot if he was competent, anywhere wet if he was oafish, drunk, or bone idle. As an angler you just had to lower your line without an overrun, detect a bite, and reel in when there was something on the end. If a skipper was any good his boat would be jammed. You'd be shoulder to shoulder on the rail, hoping you wouldn't snag the gear of your twenty-five stone neighbour, the one with 'Hate' and 'HATE' tattooed on the fingers of his left and right hands, with a knife in his belt and a half bottle of cheap bourbon never far from his lips.

But even if the company's delightful I loathe fishing in a crowd. Solitude plays a starring role in my sessions, the knowledge that it's just me, the water, and the fish. That's one reason I love my bass. At four in the morning I think they'll be on the go, and I know most anglers will be tucked up in bed. Lots of people take the opposite view. They head out first for a bit of craic, second for some beer and sandwiches in the great outdoors, the fishing itself being a distant third and an optional extra. I like a natter in the pub or the charity shop but down by the water I'm a standoffish so-and-so. And focused.

Tautog

I did manage to find one reasonably deserted shore fishing spot in Brooklyn. I noticed it on a trip back into the city from JFK airport when my taxi driver took us on a series of byways. With the cynical attitude of a New Yorker I guessed he was driving the scenic route to run up the meter, but he ferried me home for the expected fare, he may have been avoiding the worst of the traffic. Anyway we were held up at a stoplight when I saw a fast-flowing creek. JFK was built on reclaimed land and there's a spider web of canals and ditches draining away the water. This was a big one, twenty yards across. There were terns diving, splashy swirls everywhere. I asked the driver whether he knew what kind of fish there were in the area. 'Coney Island whitefish, I guess.' That's the local term for a floating condom, but I suspected striped bass (*Morone saxtilis*) or bluefish (*Pomatomus saltatrix*). I made a mental note of the spot and wrote down the name of the nearest station.

It was a long subway ride to the creek but I had a few good sessions there. The water was shallow, the bottom very snaggy. British yobs push supermarket trolleys into ponds and rivers. Their American opposite numbers are more ambitious, they prefer old cars, and I often snagged my gear on rusty Buicks and Chevrolets. But I used bucktail jigs so I wasn't snapping off anything too expensive. And all around the underwater breaker's yard I'd catch striped bass up to three or four pounds. The water was too grubby for me to take them home, I thought they might glow in the dark or be so full of diesel as to catch fire in a hot oven, but they were fun on light gear. And sometimes shoals of bluefish would stream down the canal, baitfish scattering, birds skimming the water with the air of a springboard diver spotting a turd in the pool. Bluefish were worth keeping for the pot. They spent most of their time in the cleaner water of Long Island Sound, only braving the polluted slime when the shoals of tiddlers led them inshore.

One Sunday afternoon I was whipping my jig along, a couple of bluefish in the bag, when I heard a bellow. 'What the hell are youse doing there?' Two police officers were looking down from the bridge, a large white fellow and an even larger black man. There's something about being yelled at by an armed copper that makes you feel guilty. Did I need a permit, was it private land owned by the Federal Aviation Authority, was angling banned on the sabbath? 'Fishing for bluefish, officer.' I went with honesty, politeness, and an extravagantly British accent, something by Derek Jacobi out of Maggie Smith. Being an obvious foreigner sometimes helps in a scrape, you can plead well-meaning ignorance. 'I've had a couple as a matter of fact.' 'Get the hell outta here,' this was the black policeman, 'There ain't no fish in that dirty ditch.' As he spoke my rod hooped over and the reel buzzed. 'You just caught a Chrysler.' I beached my fish and gave it a whack on the head – bluefish have nasty teeth. Then the officers strode down the bank for a closer look. They inspected my tackle, wondered about bucktail jigs versus metal lures or chunks of mossbunker, asked if I ever caught striped bass. It was curiosity, these blokes didn't want to bang me up in a police cell, they were anglers themselves. Then the white one said, 'If I give you ten bucks, will you give me one of them fish? Only we've been here

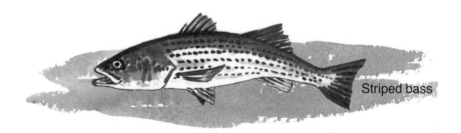

Striped bass

fifteen minutes watching you and talking shit, the sergeant's going to ask why our patrol car was stopped so long. He's got some computer deal that tells him how fast we're going, where we are, all that stuff. And when we're pulled over for a quarter of an hour he's going to say we musta stopped in a tavern for a beer. But if I gotta a fish I can prove where we've been.' They left with a bluefish apiece against the promise each would make a contribution to the charity of his choice. And I went back to the solitary angling that makes me happy.

Stay Out of Trouble

'Everything's broken and no one speaks English'
Tom Waits, *Tom Traubert's Blues*

Boat trips generally don't give me lasting memories, but one stands out. It was a triumph, a comedy adventure with a bizarre soundtrack. I was in Seattle for a family shindig, I had a day at liberty and I booked a morning after salmon. I chatted up the skipper the evening before. We'd troll with cut herring on downriggers, but if we found a bait ball we'd cast lures into the action. So at first light I clambered aboard full of anticipation and porridge, only to learn of a change of plan. The overnight breeze had stirred up a nasty chop, the salmon marks were off limits, we'd have to stick to bottom fishing with jigs. While we waited for the rest of the party, the mate rigged up, stiff rods, multiplier reels, and great lumps of chrome-plated steel that must have weighed sixteen ounces apiece and looked as if they'd been pinched from the bonnets of American cars of the 1950s. We'd fish these monsters in tide rips, keeping the boat facing into the wave and dropping our gear from the stern. There was room for five anglers to space themselves across the transom as long as we lowered and retrieved our lines in unison to avoid tangles.

Then my shipmates hove into view, four small figures in dark suits, each carrying a tan Burberry raincoat. They were the management team from a Japanese company on a fact-finding mission to Washington State. One, Reiji, spoke perfect English. With a bow he apologised for their lateness, they'd spent the night in topless bars and karaoke clubs and they'd lost track of the time. I introduced myself as another foreigner and Reiji replied, 'British sir, fantastic, marvellous, jolly good show. We love

Ling cod

your Mister Tom Jones', at which his partners broke into a lusty rendition of Delilah.

American party boats often organise a pool. Everyone chips in an ante, the person with the biggest catch scoops the lot. It's a lottery as much as anything else, betting you'll be the jammy so-and-so who lucks into a whopper. Reiji and his chums thought this was a great idea and suggested fifty dollars per head, the amount they'd been stuffing into the underpants of the waitresses in their watering holes. I was more used to two or five but national honour was at stake, I didn't want to seem like a spoilsport, so I stumped up. I'd already paid forty-five bucks for my spot on the boat, this was getting expensive.

It took twenty minutes to steam to the mark while the mate showed us how to use the tackle and the business types sang Stand By Your Man, fell over, and threw up into the scuppers. Then the engine slowed to an idle and the captain kept the boat nosing into the wave. This cut down on the pitching and rolling but seemed to do nothing to settle the stomachs of the boozers on the rail, their trenchcoats streaked with spray and puke. Our first drop set the pattern for the morning: one bird's nest, one rod over the side, and two lines knitted together in an intricate cable stitch pattern. The skipper took me aside. 'I'm going to refund your payment, there's no way you're having proper sport around these jokers. Besides there's a charge for lost or broken gear, they're going to pay me hundreds of bucks before we get back to port. And you might want to stay away from the mayhem, try your spinning rod with a smaller jig from the bow.'

The tide was whistling along but a heave up-current was enough to let the lure sink to the bottom before it ran into my companions' endless tangles; and the icy water must have been jammed with life, even a few moments in the depths was enough for a strike on every third cast. The fish included greenling and ling cod (*Hexagrammos decagrammus* and *Ophiodon ozymandias*) and the mate told me they were excellent eating.

They pulled hard enough as well, especially as I had to haul them up before they reached the disaster area in the stern. I wound up with six keepers and a dozen nameless reef fish that we released.

The Japanese economy was booming at the time. Back at the dock Reiji cheerily peeled off nine hundred dollars for two lost rods and several dozen metal pirks, another two hundred for my victory in the pool. I split my winnings with the mate, I'm sure he'd never worked so hard in his life as he unpicked balls of mono, tried to free gear snagged in the kelp, and dodged geysers of projectile vomit interspersed with choruses of The Green Green Grass Of Home. Even so I toddled ashore with a bag of fillets, a profit of a hundred dollars, and a new appreciation for Tom Jones and Tammy Wynette. Sung by hackers their tunes are instruments of torture.

The Fish Don't Know When You're Clueless

'Put me in coach, I'm ready to play today'
John Fogerty, *Centerfield*

Here are words that make me wish I could vanish in a puff of bait scented vapour: 'I'd love to learn how to fish, can I come along with you?' Don't get me wrong, I'm all for encouraging youngsters to try our sport. But the people who buttonhole me tend to be my contemporaries, that's another story. In my twenties I taught children, later in life I ran business meetings, I know the difference. Boys and girls are terrific, keep them busy, tell them about interesting stuff, give them the odd bollocking when they faff about, they'll be all ears and delightful. On the other hand grown-ups, especially corporate types, have the attention span of preoccupied fruit flies. They can't hear you say anything without delivering a pompous rant designed to show your idea's half decent but theirs makes Leonardo da Vinci look like an underachieving thicko. And they've perfected the art of pretending to listen – the pained frown, the peer over the reading glasses – while they ignore you in favour of the rude jokes popping up on their mobile telephones.

These days I apply a screening device to my angling student wannabes. 'No worries, meet me in the Tesco carpark at three thirty tomorrow morning and we'll decide where to go.' When my eager beaver finds out we won't be sitting in the afternoon sun with a few cold beers the enthusiasm dries up into a welter of prior commitments. 'Maybe next week, tomorrow's bin day, I've got to spend a few hours jumping up and down on the green waste so I can shut the lid. And it's the dog's birthday, I promised him a long run down the bridle-path.' But in New York my outings were in daylight, it was hard to escape. Maybe it's my mealy-mouthed British manners, I never managed to say what I felt: 'I enjoy your company over a drink or two, but the idea of spending six hours with you on a boat while you ask bloody fool questions and ignore the answers fills me with fear and loathing. Find some other mug.'

So it was that my friend John met me on a Brooklyn dock at six o'clock one October morning. Of all my work colleagues John was the most fun. In management meetings when some stuffed shirt made an inane suggestion one of us would give the other a wink. Then we'd press the levers on our swivel chairs, sinking as one till our eyes were at the level of the boardroom table. Once our boss proposed a spectacularly stupid cost cutting drive: charging the staff for coffee and tea from the communal kitchen, in effect cutting people off from a legal stimulant that keeps them awake and working. John and I developed a presentation with interactive financial models to show the return on investment if we installed coin operated loo rolls as well, five cents a sheet. What's more we made it to the very last slide before we were overcome by fits of hysterical cackles. So if anyone were to be an entertaining angling companion he stood a chance.

We were after blackfish so step one was to show him how to put on a hard crab bait. You poked the hook in one leg socket, out of another, then the little morsel was firmly attached and the point was clear. John had three stabs at this, the last of which literally was a stab, straight into the palm of his left hand. Not one to whinge he dug out a hip flask of bourbon from his bag, dribbled a little over the wound, drank a healthy swig, and yanked the hook clear. The mate provided a sticking plaster, John declared himself fit to play, but now I was in charge of his baiting up.

Once we were at anchor I went through the routine of dropping your gear to the bottom, thumb on the spool for control. I should have smelled a ratty idea, John had the look of someone coming up with a creative solution to a problem that doesn't exist. Sure enough as his sinker went down he announced proudly that taking your thumb off the line had your bait in the feeding area really quickly. Cue a massive bird's nest when the weight hit the bottom, five minutes unpicking crochet work while my own rod lay idle in the cabin. Then he snagged the wreck we were over, that can happen to the best of us. But it's likeliest if you ignore what you pal said and fail to reel in a yard when the gear touches down. I sent him into the galley to buy a new hook and weight but no prizes for guessing who had to assemble the rig. We were on our second anchorage before my line was wet. But worth the wait, a walloping bite, I muscled my fish away from the snags and drew it slowly to the surface. Five pounds if it was an ounce, this was the sort of fish that cleaned up the pool money. I called to the mate for the net as my helpful companion shouted, 'Don't worry, I'll swing it over the rail.' He grabbed my line, gave a lusty heave, and the hook length popped. My trophy lay in the ripple for a moment, you'd have sworn it was mouthing the words 'stupid wanker'. Then it made its unhurried way back into the depths.

By our last drop my spirits were on the mend, I had four decent blacks in my sack, John had one, and I'd topped up with some of his spirits, the ones in the flask. I never was a bourbon man but any port in a storm of frustration. Then came the straw that gave the camel backache, John reeled in a four and half pounder; with my whopper gone this was the day's best. And the straw that led to a fracture just behind the hump, he gave me a cheery smile and said, 'That was fun, when can we do it again?'

Boots and Salmon

'One of these days these boots are gonna walk'
Nancy Sinatra, *These Boots Are Made For Walking*

My first wife Gretchen died about thirty years ago. One of the happiest memories I have of her was a holiday we took to Victoria Island in British Columbia. We were living in Brooklyn so the silence of a temperate rain forest was a welcome change from the city. Make no mistake, I adore New York and New Yorkers, but it's tiring when every day sounds like a pissy football crowd being run over by a motorway pileup. And we loved the people in BC as well. National stereotypes exist for a reason and your modal Canadian is polite: spill your coffee all over him, he'll apologise for being in the way. New Yorkers are more robust with their manners, so some gentility was refreshing. For the sake of balance I ought to say something negative about BC but it's a struggle. The best I can manage is that they missed out on the Boston Tea Party but Canadians share their US neighbours' inability to make a brew-up – they serve a cup of tepid water with a dry teabag cowering in the saucer. Also a café in Vancouver served me a 'Real Cornish Pastie'. I forgave the spelling, but it was full of sweetcorn, peas, and mushrooms and wrapped in puff pastry.

On the island we were very well fed. We stayed in a modest hotel owned by a chef and a skin diver. She'd spend her mornings flippering around in the frigid kelp forests, then he'd turn her catches into tasty meals. And that chilly water was alive with fish. Even as the ferry docked I saw a coho salmon (*Oncorhynchus kisutch*) of about six pounds leaping, and the tackle shops – always an early port of call in a strange area – were buzzing with rumours of big chinook (*Oncorhynchus tschawytscha*). I bought a few metal casting lures, one to two ounce jobs, and studied the map to find an accessible rock mark.

Next morning an hour before sunrise I was chucking my little jig into the Strait of Juan de Fuca and cranking it at speed. As the light began to turn the fish came on. I used a stout salmon spinning rod, they were easy enough to play, but landing them was another story. I had to drag them into a sandy cove, beach them, then scramble down an almost vertical scree to collect them, shuffling like a clumsy mountain goat on the beer. Our hotel couple offered to cut each of my fish in half. They'd serve the front end as steaks for their guests in the restaurant, the tail end would be hot smoked and vacuum packed for us to carry back to New York. So over the week I kept quite a few, all between five and ten pounds.

One day Gretchen decided she'd come along and see what my trips were about. She wasn't a fan of early rising so that gave me pause. To avoid a hubbub of grumbling I went with a late start, just after first light. And the weather was glorious, an orange sun climbing into a clear sky. Gretchen spread a towel at the top of the promontory and rummaged for her book while I scurried down to the edge of the rocks. As I made my first cast I saw a coho leap clear of the wave. 'Salmon, straight out,' I yelled. Gretchen looked up. 'Can't see anything.' Every few minutes it was the same story, by the time she shifted her gaze from the page to the ocean there was stuff-all

Coho salmon

in view. She saw me catch a small salmon, slithering down into the cove to recover it, but she took my fish sitings the way I view the bollix that comes from economists, politicians, and tabloid journalists. 'You fishermen make this stuff up,' she huffed, 'You dream of these things jumping and splashing just so you don't get bored.' I shrugged and headed back to my mark. Immediately saw an enormous splash. Then a pair of killer whales came clear of the water a hundred yards out and heading our way. 'Orcas,' I yelled. But Gretchen's nose was planted in her book. 'Oh sure, more of your imaginary friends.' As she spoke one of the giants broached twenty yards from shore. It slapped the ocean with its tail, a fountain of spray soaked the whole rocky point with icy water. 'Believe me now?' It must have been a migration, or the start of the summer sale at all-you-can-eat Orcaland. For an hour we watched pod after pod of whales move along the strait, leaping as they went.

Towards the end of our stay the weather turned mizzly and the years I've spent chasing other types of fish gave me the optimism of a Cheltenham festival punter with a hot tip and a bucketful of Guinness. If ever the chinook salmon were to show up, surely this would be the trigger. Of course most silver linings are wrapped in clouds, there was a downside in the shape of slippery underfoot conditions. I slithered to my fishing spot on my bottom, a bumpy toboggan ride, and found a barnacled patch of rock to give traction to my trainers. Then a lob to send my jig out into the gloom. After twenty or thirty casts I began to wonder, maybe Pacific salmon don't appreciate dull conditions, maybe they're sun worshippers, spending grey days searching the kelp for underwater tanning salons. Or maybe they were lying deeper.

I tried letting the lure sink, a count of fifty, then a slow retrieve. It stopped dead, fifty was too high, I'd snagged the weed. Then the weed yanked fiercely and line began to stream from the reel. It wasn't a speedy run, nothing like the desperate sprinter's dash of a coho, just a steady, powerful wander in the direction of the US border. Every so often I turned my fish and recovered a few yards of line, then it would dive again and muscle its way back into the depths. After forty-five minutes of this routine the salmon began to tire, I could see it almost on the surface. But how was I going to land it? I reckoned it was a thirty pounder, too bulky to haul into the cove. Besides I couldn't manoeuvre over the rocks, they were like an ice rink ankle deep in WD40. I was close to despair when I heard clanking footsteps. A beefy fellow approached, skipping over the sodden rock with the gobsmacking grace of a tap-dancing hippopotamus. Plaid shirt, ponytail, and a cap proclaiming the rights of First Nation people. All around him like midges on an August evening hung the smell of beer.

'Good chinook,' he said. 'I'd shake your hand, but I figure you need to keep them both on the rod. I'm Sam, eh.' 'James,' I said. 'Good morning. But how am I going to get it ashore? I can hardly walk on these rocks, and I can't pull it up the ledge.' 'Right enough, you don't want to be climbing in those shoes. Here's what you need,' he pointed to his feet. 'Logging boots, titanium steel spikes, grip on logs in an iced-up river, nothing's too slippery for these babies. But here's what we do, you keep the fish close, I'm off to my truck for the gaff. Then I'll pop down and bring her in.'

The gaff hadn't come from a tackle shop by royal appointment. It was a pick handle with a nine inch nail driven at an angle through the thick end of the wood. Using it as an ice axe Sam scurried down the rock face, planting his boots on a patch of kelp. Then showing the confidence of a natural athlete with a dozen beers under his belt he started slashing at my fish. I was more than a bit nervous. Never mind the titanium spikes, Sam looked as if the swinging pick handle might dislodge him from his perch into the swirling grey water. What's more – and I hope this came second – I was afraid his flailing might part the line. I should have had more of the faith that can move rusty nails because his third or fourth swipe was a bullseye. And with my fish firmly skewered through its head Sam scrambled back to my side. 'Thirty pounds easy. That might win you an award. Biggest shore-caught chinook gets you fifty bucks' worth of gear from the outdoor store. Get yourself a pair of proper boots, eh?' I was relieved Sam didn't need to drive home, his cabin was a hundred yards from the point. He slung the gaff into his pickup, we put the salmon in the boot of my hire car, then we headed for the nearest twenty-four hour tavern so I could buy him a beer or three. My fish weighed thirty-four pounds and won me fifty dollars. But I didn't buy logging boots, the only way I'd climb a well lubricated rockface is in a helicopter.

An Act of Belief

'Faith is the key'
Curtis Mayfield, *People Get Ready*

My brother Mick's middle name's John. Mother wanted her children to reflect the sons of Zebedee, Peter, James, and John. She added the Michael when she realised two Battys with the initial J would cause confusion in boarding school laundries. In Luke's gospel the Zebedee boys were blanking when Jesus told them, 'Launch out into the deep, and let down your nets for a draught.' They took his tip and up came a miraculous boatful. The evangelist understood fishing psychology. There's no sign of life in the water, a random stranger offers a tip, of course the lads give it a go. I don't think Luke was a fisherman himself. He doesn't bother to tell us the species of the catch, no mention of size, and he misses the bit where James says, 'Good on you Lord, this one's my personal best, can you draw a picture of me holding it?' But he knew how we think, he'd a perfect grasp of the way optimism merges into idiocy.

I fish still-waters for trout from time to time. I can look at the surface of a lake or reservoir, notice nothing moving, and still go and chuck a quarter inch midge pattern into a hundred acres of the unknown. I chase bass a lot, that means a bait or a lure seeking out a target in the hundred million square kilometres of the Atlantic. And I expect something to take. In Casablanca Rick says, 'Of all the gin joints in all the towns in all the world, she walks into mine'. By rights I should wonder why of all the gallons of water in all the bays in all the ocean a feeding fish should be near my squid. I don't, I just wait for a bite. Sometimes I bunk along the shore and try a different gallon of water but I never reflect on the unlikeliness of making a catch at all.

This might be down to atavistic memory of spectacular hauls. We've read tales of explorers who could barely sail across the St. George's Bank because the cod were too dense to let their ships pass, rivers where you couldn't put your feet into the water in the shad run, employment contracts that banned the boss from serving salmon more than twenty times a week. I take these yarns with a pinch of salt, pepper, and Madras curry powder. Stocks were healthier in bygone days for sure but I don't think they were that healthy except in the yarns of travellers and bullshitters. Anyone who deals with fish walks the line between hyperbole and outright bollix, the truth never gets in the way of a good story. Even more exaggeration comes from our less well-known attribute, our modesty. When some fifteenth century suck-up told John Cabot he'd made a record bag he thought, 'That's because I have the looks of a court favourite, the fine motor skills of the lady in waiting who tatted my ruff, and the intellect of Machiavelli'. But as a typically humble fisher old Cabot said, 'Couldn't miss really, they were jumping in the bloody boat.'

Of course there are times when we don't need belief to know we're covering fish. Trout sipping flies, bass swirling into shoals of tiddlers, sights that tell you they're feeding, this is where to cast, and don't worry that your pulse is thumping. But sometimes there's no sign of activity and we're just as convinced we've found the hotspot.

I was casting into a river at my in-laws' place in Connecticut. It was August and the weather might have been imported from Cornwall, light rain with the odd downpour. The water was coloured and cooler than normal, so I tried a popping fly, maybe some surface splashes would do the trick. No, not so much as a follow. I wandered along, one eye on the water, one on the trees. And then I noticed something that made me sit down and take a deep breath. Go slowly, I told myself, take your time or you'll make a balls-up of it. I nipped off the popper and tied on a Clouser minnow. They're great in snaggy places, the bead eyes make them swim with the hook point up, less chance of fouling bottom. A short cast, a lift of the rod tip, and line was zipping from the reel. It was a two pound small-mouth bass, a good one for the area. I wondered why I'd been so sure I was looking at a fish lie. It was on the outside of a bend where the current was fastest, there was a tree root creating little eddies, and although the water was brown, in my mind's eye helpless minnows were being pushed about by the swirls. Half a mile downriver I came across a similar structure and landed another bass. So what gives us the confidence to think we'll have bites when we can see neither fin nor scale of a fish? Some say it's faith. I think it's the experience of years by the water, experience that seeps into our unconscious minds and crawls to the surface only when we pick up our tackle. Jesus wasn't guessing. His father may have been a carpenter but he was a fisherman.

Vanity of Vanities

'You can zig, you can zag'
Captain Beefheart, *ZigZag Wanderer*

Here's a psychology experiment for you. Stop in a waterside carpark on a filthy day, monsoon rain scudding in on a gale of icy wind. Sooner or later a figure carrying fishing gear's going to come out of the gloom with the look of a pillion passenger in the round Britain underwater motorcycle race. Offer the drowning rodent a greeting. Then suggest that only a nutter would choose to stand around in this shite. You'd expect a defensive reaction. Tell a driver that a right turn into traffic's the mark of a prat and you'll hear excuses, I didn't see your car because it's the same colour as the McDonalds sign, it was an emergency born of a need for a curry. Ask why your chum was goofy enough to show up at a black tie party in shorts and sandals, he thought it was a fancy dress ball, and flip-flops are formal dress on Lundy. But suggest an angler's a few coupons short of a popup toaster and you'll see no embarrassment. The opposite in fact, there may be a few words about a fall of spinners in the rain or a building wave. But the body language tells the real story. Your bedraggled eejit's going to give you a shy grin, as if you'd said 'That sodden hat makes you look like a young Robert Redford' or 'I heard you singing, you must be related to Janis Joplin'. 'You're too daft to come in out of the rain', that's a compliment, at least in the mind of this fruitcake with a rod, a reel, and a meal that would have cost ten quid off a fishmonger's slab. People who fish, we're proud to be wacky.

Americans on boat trips told me they lived in a conformist culture but they were free spirits. Fishing, they said, turns you into a rebel who lives by a different code, we were like outlaw bikers with Penn reels instead of Harley Davidsons. I don't buy it. I take a robust view of some regulations, I'll park wherever I please between the hours of three and six in the morning and I put the recycle bin at the kerb a whole day ahead of the pickup time. But my brother and sister anglers realise you can break the laws of man, you can't defy the laws of nature. Ten degrees of frost chills your fingers, storm force winds pelt you with sand and seaweed, raindrops like golf balls make you wet. We acknowledge rules, we know they apply to us, we just pretend they don't matter. It doesn't work just with the weather. On a spring day with bright sunshine not much hatches on my streams. I'll cast away anyway with a hare's ear or a tiny streamer fly, a trout against the odds is such a delight. I'll try for bass in a tiddly wave on a neap tide because logic says I'm pissing in the wind, I'm going to show logic where it gets off the bus. You could blame this on wild optimism, a hallmark of the angling brain. That's part of the story, but a bigger part's the way we revel in our nuttiness. And that makes me wonder why our genes have survived. How do a few – maybe not such a few – loose screws provide an evolutionary advantage?

I think the answer's that healthy communities need weirdos. When Homo sapiens started to spread from Kenya and Ethiopia, the conformist hunter-gatherers, the ones who lived in semidetached caves and wore pinstriped mammoth skin outfits, kept things on an even keel. They picked berries from the trusted bushes and dug traps along the known migration paths of big herbivores. But the further people wandered, the more things changed, different flora, different fauna. Common sense foragers kept looking for the seed pod that grew along the Omo river, traditional hunters looked for proto-giraffes or zebras. It took an oddball to try that strange purple dangly thing; she discovered grapes and Chateau Grotto 190,000 BC. A lateral thinking freak was first to sling a sharpened rock at an aurochs; he bagged an ancestor of cottage pie and cheeseburgers. In times of transition it's the zigzag mind that helps the group to prosper. And if survival relies on having a few crazies they'd be respected. The attitude wouldn't be 'You're odd', it'd be 'You're odd, that's cool'. The ziggers and zaggers would attract mates, their genes would go on and multiply. So that weather-thrashed halfwit you met in the carpark wears dripping jumpers and gale-matted hair as a signal. The message: 'I am indeed barmy, that's what makes me so sexy. Nuts rule OK.'

Grumpy Middle-aged Men

'That's when a sport was a sport'
John Mellencamp, *Cherry Bomb*

For our last few years in New York I worked for a big US based company and I spent a quarter of my time overseas. With a wife and a little one at home this wasn't ideal but I knew I wanted to strike out on my own, travel was the best way to make the contacts I'd need. My employer was a typical multinational, self-important oafs at the top and some very parochial attitudes. My bosses would tell me to trot off to a faraway land

and make the local employees follow head office policies. When I said this couldn't be done, the legal framework was different, they were amazed. 'Different laws? Why?' One senior fellow was outraged that he couldn't telephone the Paris office at four in the afternoon. 'We've got four time zones in the US, the French could pick any one of the four. But no, they goddamn have to be difficult.' I didn't bother to tell him there are in fact six American time zones, just that the earth's rotation was something he'd have to live with. I joined this company after a year with a start-up. To make sure they wouldn't expect a lackey who wore dark suits and sucked up to vice presidents I interviewed wearing a beard, hair in a ponytail. And the hippie look went down a treat. Some people conflate odd mannerisms with intelligence, the nutty professor thing, and the senior mucky-mucks treated me with exaggerated respect. The support staff referred to me as the Unabomber but I took this as a sign of affection.

One of my regular ports of call was Singapore. Repressive, but there's a fair amount to like about the place, plenty of interesting cuisines, ethnic diversity, and if you need a jacket you can have one made to measure in an afternoon. And our office was a delight, the employees were young, bright, and fun. With one exception, Awang the facility manager, a fifty-ish Malay gent with a bushy beard, beady eyes, and a permanent scowl. One of the youngsters marked my card. 'He never likes people from the UK. I think maybe it's because his father or his grandfather was a communist, killed by the British in the insurgency.' And sure enough I was the frown magnet, I'd see him chatting away, the minute he came into my room he was monosyllabic, a look as if someone had rubbed stale squid into his moustache. Never mind, I told myself, you can't win them all.

One evening I went for a constitutional along a dock. There was a fellow fishing at the end, a long rod and a small fixed spool reel. I stood and watched, hoping I might see some action. For an angling addict even someone else's catch feeds the monkey a bit. Then the figure half turned and shouted, 'Lah, are you watching me back there?' I walked over. 'Yes I am, I'm sorry if that seems rude, it's just that I love fishing myself. I was hoping I'd see you have a bite.' 'I know you love fishing, obvious, otherwise you wouldn't stand there for ten minutes.' It was Awang, the usual sourpuss look. 'I don't mean why are you watching me, I mean why are you watching me from back there. You won't see anything unless you're beside the water. Sit down, you can notice little shrimps around the concrete. You see them? Sometimes the fish come in to eat them, that's what I hope for.' We chatted for almost an hour. On weekends he went on a boat with his friend, they caught barramundi, coral trout, and mangrove jacks. On the jetty he was after small snappers. 'And mostly to look at the water, often there are no fish. You want to try tomorrow? I have a spare outfit, it's only cheap, I bought it for my grandson but he prefers football.' Now he really grimaced, the usual filthy look was a warmup. 'Football, he thinks football is better than fishing. He loves Manchester United. That's what I hate about England, football. I wish Manchester United would stay in bloody Manchester, then I wouldn't have to buy shirts for very high prices. And he'd fish with his grandfather.'

I was in town for three more nights. The area manager invited me for dinner, he was an important business contact, but I said I had a prior engagement. I sat with Awang holding a child's fibre glass rod and twitching a tiny jig among the shrimps. I had two tiddlers, he had five. The best bit was when they came to the surface. He'd point the rod at the fish, tighten the line, then give an almighty hoick to send his snapper flying onto the decking behind us. 'Is that what they call a Singapore Sling?' I asked. He laughed so hard I thought he'd fall in the water. And when I saw him in the office he'd frown and say, 'Do you need anything, maybe a Singapore Sling?' Then his face would crinkle into a crazed grin.

Frying Tonight

'If you'll be my Dixie chicken'
Little Feat, *Dixie Chicken*

In Botswana I met a young woman at a barbeque. She was intriguing so I tried to make a good impression by showing off my manners. Heading to the buffet for a second whack of chicken wings I offered to fetch her a plate as well. 'Heavens no,' she huffed, 'I never eat fried food. My body is a temple.' I didn't think that was anything people said in real life, maybe in a melodrama set in California. But I've spent enough time bored out of my skull in houses of worship to be very clear I don't want to live in a temple. A pub might be good, maybe a blues bar or a greasy spoon diner. But liturgy, sermons, and uncomfortable seating leave me cold. So does an exclusive diet of grains and raw vegetables. Fat makes thing taste good. I read an interview with a famous chef who said the big difference between home cooked food and Michelin starred meals was that the professionals used hotter pans, more salt, and above all more butter.

Living in New York I rarely ordered seafood in restaurants. The city's wholesale fish market was old and inefficient, it stank. People said it was controlled by mobsters who blocked any effort to modernise, and even expensive eateries served swordfish and haddock that smelled as it had been marinated for a few days in shark pee. So I spent plenty of time frying fish I'd caught myself, experimenting in our kitchen. I cracked it in the end. I'm not a fan of batter, too many school memories of searching through greasy dough to find what passed for my piece of cod. I love crumbs and the secret's to have a crunchy outside while the fish inside stays moist. I like fillets about three quarters of an inch thick, much thinner and they dry out. And most people overcook fish, I'd rather err in the opposite direction. When I'm cleaning a bass or a mackerel the cat and I both eat our fill of raw scraps from between the bones, she's nearly seventeen and I'm nearly seventy so we can't be poisoning ourselves too badly.

I've watched television chefs make crumb coating. They talk about one hand for the dry stuff, one for the wet. It's never worked for me, I just make an ambidextrous mess. But you need three bowls anyway. To serve four people I use two tablespoons of plain flour with a teaspoon each of garlic salt and smoked paprika. That's bowl one. Bowl two just has a beaten egg. Bowl three has a dozen Ritz crackers smushed to a powder and about the same volume of finely grated parmesan. If you own a pestle and mortar – and like most people never can find anything sensible to do with it – use it to grind the crackers. If you don't you can just bash them with the heel of your hand. Press your fillets into the flour, dunk them in the egg, then roll them in the cheesy crumbs.

When it comes to cooking you want to heat the pan before the oil goes in, it stops the fish from sticking. I don't know why this makes a difference, it's one of those mysteries, like the fact that hot water in the ice tray freezes faster than cold. I use medium heat, not enough to make the fat smoke, just a healthy sizzle. In goes a tablespoon of vegetable oil and the same amount of butter. Three minutes cooking on each side, job done.

I've eaten a ton of this over the years, fillets of tilapia, snapper, cassava fish, fluke, blackfish, pollack, bass, and who knows what else. My body may not be a temple but it could be a half decent aquarium.

PART TWO

THE UK
MOSTLY BASS

Who Needs Indoor Plumbing?

'There's flies in the kitchen'
John Prine, *Angel From Montgomery*

We moved to Cornwall from New York in 1999, my wife Shelley, myself, and our four year old daughter Bailey. I was working as a management consultant with clients all over the world. No matter where we lived I had to jump on an aeroplane to earn a crust. New York has a very pricey property market and we'd inherited my parents' cottage in the UK so it made sense to return to the land of my fathers. Also we thought it might be easier to find a good school for Bailey if we left the city. Parents in Manhattan start fretting about their children's academic futures when the pregnancy test strip changes colour. If your youngster wins a place at one of the top public schools you've got it made; but the bad ones are frightful dens of ignorance and iniquity. Cornwall was a safer bet.

Apart from Bailey's education not much worked out as planned. Most of my work trips started from Heathrow and I'd forgotten that the train from Penzance to London moves at the speed of a snail with a dodgy work ethic. So I frittered away a lot of time in transit. And my parents' old cottage needed what the real estate mob would call 'sensitive cosmetic restoration' – in other words it was a draughty tip with plumbing installed by builders who thought indoor bathrooms were a passing fad to be indulged as cheaply and bodgingly as possible. When we moved the best shower was something added in an old farmyard shed. Mother used it when she came back from the beach, sluicing off sand and seaweed so she wouldn't track it into the kitchen. It had better water pressure than the upstairs facility and I scrubbed up in it often.

Shelley didn't think much of the old piggery because it was grubby and populated by slugs and spiders. I like spiders and an early morning wallow was an entomologist's treasure hunt, checking a dozen webs to see what insects were on today's menu. Through the summer mosquitoes and houseflies were the seasonal special, the odd moth or bluebottle. Then around early September I'd start to see a few daddy longlegs, first the skinny fellows best suggested by something on a size ten hook, then the great thugs of the crane fly world, long shank eights, even sixes.

There's a small reservoir nearby. It's a lovely spot, the dam was built in the 1950s so it has a natural feel. Until a few years ago it was tree-lined and there was plenty of insect life and often enough breeze to cover the surface with terrestrials. In modern fashion the water's stocked with rainbows, ugly lumps with stumpy tails. But it also holds some handsome native browns which go crazy when the water's speckled with daddies, munching like bass on jelly-fry or Cornish rugby players at a pasty supper. The only trick's knowing when to find them charging about on the top, and my daily showers helped with that. Cleanliness is next to troutliness.

Tackle catalogues offer a range of flies to imitate a daddy longlegs, trailing limbs made from feather fibres, skinny rubber piping, you name it. I don't think subtlety's the order of the day. I tie up a dubbing body to hold oodles of floatant, some legs made from my wife's chestnut gelding's hair, and that's your lot. Justin's a clumsy sort inclined to carry a lot of condition – that's horsey speak for saying he's fat – but he sprouts a magnificent tail, the whiskers are long, strong, and easy to knot, and the old boy's been responsible for a lot of trout. Fishing the daddy's straightforward in my book. Find the edge of a wind lane where insects pile up, chuck out your fly, and give it the odd tug to create a wake. And takes are no nonsense affairs, none of the tweaks you feel when you use nymphs, just a swirling boil as if someone had dropped a brick from a helicopter. The fish hook themselves. Sometimes brown trout fling their whole bodies out of the water, their tails still swimming as they fly through the air. The odd sporting snob – often the one with a fly box the size of a car – can be snooty about daddies. 'A crude approach, too easy to catch.' Rubbish. If you want your fishing to be challenging try casting into a pond full of heavily chlorinated water at a motorway service station. Fishing isn't meant to be difficult every day, it's meant to be fun. Watching a fat trout erupt from the surface with a bushy fly in its scissor certainly fits the bill.

Destiny Calls

When someone on the radio says 'Tell me about your personal journey' I reach for the off button. I can't stand self-indulgent psychobabble from the self-help section of a railway station bookshop. But when we moved back to Cornwall and I took up bass fishing again I had the feeling I'd arrived where I was meant to be. Everything else I'd chased, with a rod or a gun, had been preparation. This was the real thing.

What I like best about my sport is thinking. Some types of angling call for physical skill or endurance, the ability to hurl a weight to the horizon or keep a whole fly-line in the air, the muscles and fitness to bring a thousand pound tuna to the boat. That stuff doesn't interest me much. A good job too, I'm clumsy, uncoordinated, and somewhere between slim and scrawny. But given that I'm a bass fisher, which means I must be somewhat daft, my brain works reasonably well. And I enjoy pondering, trying to work out what the fish are eating and where they're finding it. In this regard trout are a great build-up to bass because both are opportunistic feeders. The range of insect life, in all forms – larva, pupa, and imago – is so broad that the best trout hunters are top notch entomologists. But trout don't stop there, they'll suck down leeches, tadpoles, worms, snails, slugs, and all manner of fry. So one of the most important weapons in a trout hunter's arsenal is the ability to recognise what's on offer in the water. Tie on the right fly and the battle's half won.

Bass are even more catholic in their eating, like trout but turned up a notch. They're the opposite of the eejits who take dietary advice from social media quacks, the ones who give up everything tasty and live on tofu, turnips, and turmeric – then wonder why nobody invites them over for supper. Regularly I find bass feeding on weed maggots, tiny jelly-fry, prawns, lugworm or ragworm, hard and soft crabs, sandeels, whitebait, small mullet, whiting, mackerel, garfish, pilchards, squid, mussels, or razor clams. Cleaning my catches I've come across weevers, rockling, flatties, a small lobster, a rodent of some description, a bird that looked like a wagtail, a baby ray, bootlace congers, the head of a fair sized codling; and once I saw a pork sausage chucked from a pier disappear into a bassy gullet. What's more there tend to be visible clues as to what trout might be scoffing: insects on the surface of the water, terrestrials in the breeze, fry splashing in the shallows. Bass feed best in darkness, and though sandeels, whitebait, and mullet sometimes give themselves away by flipping or jumping, often the bass larder's nearer the bottom than the top. So choosing the right lure or bait and deciding where to fish it comes down to experience and intuition as much as observation. Even more it comes down to being prepared to be surprised, to change your mind and experiment. For me at least, that's fun. And because so much about bass fishing's mental it's easy to share what I've learned with anglers who're struggling. I don't have to teach them difficult skills like pendulum casting or double-hauling, or send them off for an endurance-building session with a personal trainer. Often all they need is an idea or two to set them on their way. And I'm learning all the time as well, that's even more fun.

One May morning I woke at three – a combination of jetlag and a biological need to feel a sea breeze in my face after a week of air-conditioned hotels, airports, and jargon-spouting executives who seemed to have swallowed copies of the Harvard Business Review. There was someone already fishing in my normal starting-out spot, a tiny rocky lump that marks the mouth of a shallow cove. He was a serious bass man too, using his headlamp rarely and only with his back to the ocean. But he wasn't having much joy, just a few suicidally tiddly pollack. 'What are you on?' I asked. A pale six inch shad, it always saw him right when the sandeels were swarming. I tried a long slim shallow diver, then a big fat one. Pollacks to me too. Time for a smoke, and as I propped my bottom against a comfy boulder my boot skidded on the ground. I'd stepped on a little knot of dead whitebait. Off with the big plug, on with a two inch Rapala, and I felt the familiar no nonsense thump of a bass. After a second fish – just to be sure the first wasn't a fluke – I scurried over to the other chap and filled him in. He was a committed soft plastic man so he switched to a tiny silvery shad. Just as good. As long as the lure was the right length, more or less every other cast came up trumps.

Then there was a warm November outing. The day-boats were jigging squid, one of my locals was serving them as a special with garlic and chillies, and I was stuffing myself on a regular basis. So were the bass, every morning I was beaching at least a couple, the best over nine pounds, the smallest about four. But not today, just a mini-conger and a rockling. I had a couple of razors in my pocket but they might as well have stayed there, a long wait and another rockling. As the first light started to show

I took off my bait rig and tied on a wedge. It might have been a flash of brilliant insight, more likely I was bored and fed up with wiping slime from my fingers. The lure was a bit light for the rod and I could chuck it only twenty or thirty yards, but that was enough, in came a ten inch mackerel. Back to a weight and a pair of 4/0 hooks, on with my joey, and an eleven pound bass grabbed hold even as the sinker settled onto the bottom.

If you want a fish that pulls hard, runs fast, or leaps like a marine kangaroo, bass aren't your best bet. They're nothing like as athletic as tarpon, trevally, seatrout, salmon, gilthead bream, wrasse, or garfish. But if you want something that keeps you thinking and guessing, I reckon they're hard to beat. Journey's end.

Smile for Crying Out Loud

'If it's less than this you know I can't approve'
Aztec Camera, *Going Down The Dip*

I don't watch much sport on television, but even news programmes carry interviews with players. The typical set-up's a sombre looking bod – someone who might be a central banker warning of an imminent depression or a cooking show contestant whose soufflé came out like a cowpat. And this unsmiling figure says, 'I just tried to execute the team strategy, I didn't want to let down the supporters or the rest of the side.' Here's a person who just earned ridiculous money for kicking a big ball or whacking a little one with a piece of wood, a lucky bloke who's paid to do what normal folk squeeze into their week after they've spent forty hours at work, ten stuck on a commuter train, and ten more doing odd jobs around the house. And this jammy eejit behaves as if his spaniel choked to death swallowing his toddler's hamster.

If you work in a grim call centre or deal with stroppy customers in a railway station you've every right to scowl. If your profession's to wear a silly outfit and run around in the fresh air, do it with a smile on your face. Sport just isn't that serious. Spill an easy pass yards from the try line, so what, nobody dies. Dropped catches lose matches but they don't cause wars or famines. So I wish these overpaid ninnies would recognise that their role's to entertain. And if you want a spectator to enjoy the performance you might want to stop behaving like a short tempered grave digger with acid reflux.

I'm almost as bemused when I run into a grumpy-guts on the shore. 'It's bloody dire, four hours for one schoolie and a little pollack.' 'Yes,' I want to yell, 'but at least you were fishing. The rain that's seeping down your neck came straight in off the Atlantic, the sand in your pasty has the clean tang of seaweed, and there's a fat seagull over there flamenco dancing with a sandeel in its beak.' Going home empty-handed doesn't mean our families will starve, they'll just have to make do with bangers instead of bass. A banjaxed reel won't bring civilised life to an end, it'll give you a few hours of innocent fun with a screwdriver and some WD-40.

And no, it's not true to say you might as well have stayed at home. Down by the water you don't have to listen to light jazz while someone at your bank eats crunchy biscuits and pretends to find your account details, you're not watching self-important eejits maunder away on TV. So at least look as if you're having a good time.

Watch your Step

'It's a rocky rough road but I don't care'
Jim White, *Ten Miles To Go On A Nine Mile Road*

Some marks develop a reputation for being dangerous. I'm in favour of keeping people away from rocks that are cut off at high water, shingle banks that collapse on spring tides, and headlands where swells wash away tripods and their owners in storms. The RNLI and the search and rescue people are busy enough as it is. They work flat out, often mucking up Darwin's idea about the survival of the fittest: they save people so blindingly stupid that their genetic contribution should come to a full stop. But now and then locals talk up the risk of an area as a way of keeping the crowds away. I don't do it myself, I just don't let on where I fish, but my comrades of the angle are more devious. Or diplomatic, take your pick.

One of my favourite beaches was said to be a death trap. It's flat, rutted with gullies, and I was told they were full of quicksand. What's more, folk wisdom has it that a making tide comes in as fast as a galloping horse. That's something I've heard about strands all over the place. There must be a lot of really slow nags in seaside communities, I've yet to see the tide advance any quicker than a veteran point-to-pointer walking over in heavy ground with three stone overweight and a combine harvester in tow.

The final warning was that sport was deadly dull unless you used a freshly caught live sandeel, casting out your weight and clipping the hook link onto a sort of zip-wire effort. With any other bait you were wasting your time, might as well shove a pasty on the end of your line for all the bites you'd see.

My first outing to this supposed trouble spot was in late spring, an hour before dawn over the last of the ebb in a surf that was small but bubbly. I walked with care and some effort through the dips. Underfoot conditions were midway between soft and spodgy, my footmarks four or five inches deep. Had I been in flip-flops I might have worried I'd lose one, in waders I was fine. The quicksand was on the slow side. And so far from galloping, the water receded at the speed of a slug wriggling its way up a rose bush in a toad-strangling downpour. It took an eternity to reach the shingly area that looked likely to hold sandeels. I dug out my scraping knife and assumed the bait catcher's crouch, welcome to Lumbago-land. But I could see no trace of eel, just a row of razor burrows. I hadn't brought a jar of salt so I used my bait box to slop seawater over the indentations and grab a few clams. In six casts I landed two bass and a gilthead bream.

I've fared well there since with razor and squid in a decent wave, ragworm in a wussy little surf, German sprats and small fry-type flies in a high summer calm. I must have tried live sandeels three or four times, not a chuffing wibble from a bass, just the odd postcard-sized turbot. But one thing to be said for the rumour mill, I almost always have the beach to myself. The only chap I run into lives in the nearby village. He greets me with a grin and a wink: 'I see you managed to avoid sinking into the slough of despond and drowning in the raging flood. Tight lines my beauty.'

Some Dogs Don't Walk

'Nobody here can dance like me'
Jason Isbell & The 400 Unit, *Last Of My Kind*

It's easy to see why lure fishing for bass is so popular, it appeals to a lot of aspects of the angling personality. Like the way we collect stuff, even give in to a bit of hoarding. If you show the slightest trace of that tendency you should warn your dependants now, 'Whenever I hop off the twig, don't expect to inherit any money. Maybe a few hundred Feed Shallows, Sammys, and Patchinkos, maybe some credit card bills, but no money.' And like our love of tinkering, changing the hooks on plugs, fitting internal weights to soft plastics, experimenting with different types of clip, it's fly-tying for people who can't find their reading glasses, cabinet-making for the impatient. And that's a trait lure fans show in bulk spools, impatience. We always like to be doing something, wading, emptying our chesties, moving along the shore, trying a different plug, varying the retrieve.

Mostly that's an asset around bass. If one thing isn't working, get busy doing something else. What's interesting is the way we extend our love of activity to the things we cast into the drink. When I started using lures from the rocks, the Rapala was a popular choice. 'Brilliant action,' people said, 'wiggles like mad.' Which is true. Then videos started showing up on the internet, how to make a popper go wild, walking the dog to achieve as much zigzag motion as possible, the best pumping action to jump a shad about. It looked like fun, but I was sceptical, most of my takes came when I was cranking steadily, maybe a touch of stop and start, but no wild yanks. My lures weren't leaping or slashing from side to side. I thought back to Gambian days, I caught tons of fish off the top and my plugs did nothing at all, no ducking, no diving, no dancing. A two and a half inch piece of broomstick makes a piss poor Fred Astaire, but the cassava fish, trevally, and barracuda would grab it anyway. It was all rather confusing.

Then one summer we had a long calm spell. The fish were hard to find, and most of my lures seemed crude and silly. Something that lands with a splash then zips through the surface, that's fine when there's a wave. In glassy water two feet deep it looks like a device that should be tearing round a model boating pond firing torpedoes at a radio controlled Cutty Sark. So I tried soft plastics. I had a few samples from my brief career as a sales rep in Banjul, American-made 'worm baits' for large-mouth bass. Some looked ridiculous, high visibility yellow, or pink and orange hoops, like mascots for a football team in the Cornwall Colour-Blind League. But others were silvery, white, or pale with black backs. Squeeze your eyes half shut and they might suggest sandeels or baby mullet, so I gave them a bash. I used them first with a cone-shaped lead in front. Tackle shops were selling these special sinkers, presumably anglers liked them, but I found them as helpful as a boy scout when you're already on the right side of the road.

My fishing water was so shallow that any weight at all just meant I was decorating the bottom with snapped off cylinders of latex – bad for the environment, worse for my temper. So I went weightless and weedless. That raised another problem, retrieve at anything like a reasonable lick and my little wormy job came straight to the surface, and predatory fish didn't seem to fancy something that looked like a rubber band in a life jacket with jet propulsion. Now there was just one option, no action at all. Chuck it out, let it sink, twitch the reel handle, let it sink again. And hey bloody presto, I started catching fish. It seemed bizarre, catalogues were trying to flog me a rod that would make my topwater plug career about like a slalom ski racer being chased by a polar bear, the bass were telling me they wanted a floppy pencil shaped lump that wallowed aimlessly in the drink.

Then one morning I was heading back to the carpark when I ran into a twenty-first century rock-pooler. As a child I scooped up creatures with my net, plopped them in a bucket for a closer squizz, then let them go. Nowadays it seems you stick little waterproof cameras in well-chosen spots and record videos. At some stage these wind up on your mobile telephone, and this lad had hours of footage. And guess what a sandeel does most of the time? Not a lot. It lies nearly still in the water, then advances a leisurely foot or two before almost stopping again. It's like a caravan on a Cornish lane, crawling along at the head of a twenty-car tailback while the person in the passenger seat tries to make the satnav realise Land's End's a place, not just a clothing catalogue. A whitebait's more like a learner driver at a roundabout, a very short burst of acceleration before the engine stalls. And a mullet's much the same, a few flicks of the tail, then a long wait while the instructor reassures a weeping student enough to start the motor and have another try. The only baitfish he showed me that seem to be on an NHS-sponsored keep fit programme were mackerel, they're in constant motion. But an awful lot of the things bass eat don't do a lot of wiggling, splashing, or zigzagging across the top of the water. Not quite a mystery solved, but a chink of light to lighten our darkness.

I still use shallow diving plugs, Toby spoons, shads with waggly tails – things that move. I reckon they may suggest wounded baitfish. But I'm just as sold on things that do very little indeed. And for real lure addicts this has to be good news: keep buying those plugs, but you can run a side-line hoarding soft plastics as well.

My Old Pal

'Don't you know the same thing happens each and every day'
Gram Parsons, *The New Soft Shoe*

When we moved to Cornwall lure fishing for bass was taking off, at least locally. People in more fashionable areas may have been doing it for ages, but things move slowly down here. The far west often brings to mind the old joke about New Zealand: 'We're about to land in Auckland. Please extinguish your cigarettes and turn your watches back fifteen years.'

Asking around I found most people used Rapalas, shads, and the odd popper or surface slider. And that made sense. The small Rapalas and shads suggested sandeels, the big Rapalas were OK for mullet, mackerel, and pollack, and the topwater plugs worked like the skittering bob for trout, something that looks vaguely edible and moves at speed. I added wormy soft plastics into the mix, the ones I'd been given as samples in the Gambia. Fished slowly they became my calm weather standard. I fared decently, a few blanks, a few bonanzas, and a lot of days somewhere in between. Then I started to hear tales of miraculous Japanese plugs that cost the same as a pub supper for three total gannets who'd missed their lunches. I wasn't sure I fancied spending that kind of money on something I was going to chuck into weedy, rock-strewn coves, but I had the feeling my tackle bag needed something. Maybe a new lure would catch more bass on the mid-season days when I found them so hard to please.

Then one July morning I ran into a bloke in one of my favourite little bays. He clearly wasn't a leading light on the newly fashionable bass fishing scene, you could tell that from afar. No trouser waders, just a pair of wellies. Not a trace of Gore-Tex, he was wearing yellow plastic waterproofs from the farm supply shop. And no spiffy peaked cap with a tackle company logo, he sported a tweed hat that looked as if he used it also as an oven mitt and a brush for a very hairy dog.

Mackerel

As I approached, his rod started thumping with the unmistakeable rhythm of a bass. It was a three pounder. 'Handsome,' I said, 'what did she take?' 'A Toby, that's all I've got, all I ever use, my beauty. Works for mackerel when they're in, pollack any time, bass in the middle of the summer.' He unhooked his fish, laid it on a rock, and it spat up three whitebait. And wouldn't you know it, they were almost exactly the same size as his spoon. And the middle of the summer, that's the time for whitebait. Eureka. Never mind a twenty quid plug with a name I might not be able to pronounce, I had my new secret weapon. I couldn't find any in our local shops, but an online outfit sold them in lots of a dozen, one pound ninety-nine each. As the old boy said, they're great in July and August. And at other times of the year, if all else fails, I'll sling one out and crank like a maniac, skittering it along in the surface layer. That's a tactic that's saved a few otherwise dour days.

I've tinkered with my local chap's advice. He was using a twenty-eight gramme version, I prefer the twenty, it's even closer to the size to match the hatch. And he'd a range of colour schemes, I like the silver and white one, watch it in the water and it's a dead ringer for a whitebait. Anyway I reckon I've a right to a personal relationship with this lure. It was launched in 1955, the year Shelley was born. So my favourite woman and my favourite blank-buster are contemporaries. And who says anglers aren't romantic?

The International School of Bass

'A thing that I keep in the back of my head'
Paul Simon, *I Know What I Know*

When I started bass fishing again I realised some of my ideas didn't match up with the conventional wisdom. Had I been younger I might have gone with the flow, copying what I saw other people doing, even taking as gospel what tackle companies said about the brilliance of their gizmos. But I doubt it, New Yorkers are sceptical and I'd been there too long to be suckered by commercial puffery. And anglers were doing stuff too bizarre to imitate.

Some – especially the ones who used artificials – plied their craft in bright sunlight, working on their tans as they fished, dehydrating themselves ahead of a lunchtime pint or three. Most swore by particular lures or baits, sticking with them through thick, thin, and modestly chubby.

A lot were always in their cars, shifting from mark to mark in search of the promised land, never spending more than a couple of sessions at any spot. Quite a few fished only when the tide was big and the wave was fizzy. And almost everyone waded to chestie-topping depths as preparation for casting to the horizon; or shuffling back to shore to empty a few gallons of the Atlantic from their boots. But in my forties I didn't ask myself, 'Why do they do it that way?' Instead I told myself, 'That doesn't make sense.' I'd spent years fishing, shooting, and watching wildlife, I had strongly-held views about how creatures behave.

To be clear I don't think of myself as an outdoorsman. I'm not like the chaps on the television who use two flints, a cactus, and a fistful of cockroaches to produce a roast dinner, or build an ocean-going cruise ship from birch twigs and penguin skin. I can't look at a patch of grass and tell you it was stepped on by a dog fox on the way back from McDonald's with a packet of chips and a strawberry milkshake for the cubs. But I'm not an indoorsman either, I don't rely on books, magazines, and websites to tell me how and where to find things on the feed. My hours by the water, in the shooting field, and driving around in search of lions taught me a few lessons, and no amount of catch reports or lure advertisements were going persuade me those lessons were wrong.

First is that nature has a timetable; some species do their thing by day, some by night. I only ever saw tarpon on the surface at dawn and dusk, antelopes and elephants dossed down under thorn trees through the middle of the day, geese flighted for a short period as the sun came up. So when it came to bass it didn't take a leap of faith to become a nocturnal angler, and experience showed me that the end of the night was when I fared best. I have a slight tan, but it comes from burying guts in the garden and standing around in onshore hoolies.

Next, living things often focus their eating on specific sources of nourishment, the way people who've drunk six pints and a few rums always seem to want a greasy kebab. Matching the hatch for trout was solid evidence, but so was the way Gambian geese would turn up their beaks at newly-grown grass once the rice seedlings were planted out, cassava fish would pick up dead bonga from the bottom only until a shoal of mullet pitched up, and Pacific salmon would ignore everything else when the baby herring were in. Almost no matter how tempting the treat, predators and scavengers wouldn't pay it much heed when they were stuffing their faces with something else. That's an insight that's saved a few quid over the years. I might have been snapping off Feed Shallows on the reefs or belting pricey peeler crabs into the surf, but in whitebait season I use Tobys at £1.99, in an autumn surf I tie on joey mackerel I've home-frozen. And I catch more big bass like that as well.

Building on this, natural restaurants can be very little, exclusive bistros rather than giant cafeterias. Warthogs browse in clearings in the scrub, and some of their favourite excavation sites are smaller than a tennis court. Okavango tilapia hang out in snags, ambushing passing tiddlers only when they come within a couple of feet. Snappers are the same, lurking around a mangrove root or a lump of coral. Searching far and wide for a meal, that's a mug's game if your existence depends on stuffing as much grub as possible down your neck and not burning off many calories finding it.

And that leads straight into another observation: mammals, birds, and fish congregate in spots where their meals are easy to pick up. They're like the people who visit drive-through fast food joints: 'Cool, we can get a whole bag of fattening junk without even levering our fat arses from the car seats.' Trevally would herd baitfish into coves and gullies where there was no escape route, yellowtail charged compact bait balls, trout lurked in specific lies and waited for something to drift by. And this showed me that successful bass fishing isn't just about finding the right beach or bay, it's about studying that beach or bay in such detail that I know where to chuck my bait or lure. No petrol-guzzling road trips in search of pastures new, lots of hours wandering around pastures old, in all weathers and at all states of the tide, looking for potholes and gullies in the sand that hold drifting odds and ends, gaps between rocks where baitfish are washed about in the wave and the tide. And easy grazing for a hunter-gatherer fish also means shallow water where tiddlers have nowhere to hide. Most of my cassavas came from places where even a light spoon would snag bottom, and only a floating plug would do the job; while barracuda seemed to go best when their bellies were on the bottom and their dorsal fins were in the air. So my bass hunting begins and ends very close to the shoreline, a depth of two or three feet seems ideal.

When it comes to wave and weather I'm closer to agreeing with my fellow bass fans. A stirred-up sea brings more food into the shallows and knocks the baitfish about, making them easy prey. But again the hundreds of hours I spent on Gambian headlands showed me that a lovely fishing wave was indeed lovely but even a flat calm didn't have to be hideous. As long as there was something to keep things on the move – the tide, the flow of the river water – I'd fare reasonably well. Over the years I've found bass marks where there are swirls and eddies even when the ocean looks like a mirror, and they produce fish.

The last pointer I picked up in all my hours of fishing, shooting, and watching animals was the need to be stealthy. Not ridiculously so. I don't hit the shore like a sniper in top to toe camouflage kit. I reckon a lot of people who do that enjoy dressing up for its own sake, I bet they have Wonder-Woman pyjamas and Davy Crockett hats at home. But it makes sense to avoid doing things that are going to scare the bejesus out of your quarry. Warthogs hightail it when they smell something unfamiliar, like body odour, Brut, or retired heavyweight boxers. A trout scarpers if a shadow crosses its lie. And I've seen bass do a runner when someone stands on a rock, body outlined against the sky. More often I've watched wader-clad anglers shuffling through the shallows, fish scattering in their bow waves. I like to keep a low profile, to stay back from the water's edge when it's calm, and to stomp through the shallows only as a last resort. I wear waders as a matter of course – like Nibiriti I love my big boots – but mostly as a way of proofing myself against splashing breakers, biblical rain, and the lumps of bait that otherwise would wind up on my trousers.

So my approach to bass these days isn't quite in line with what a lot of other people do. When I run into holiday anglers they can be surprised to see me pulling big fish from a couple of feet of surf, or from a flat calm. They're amazed that cheap lures like Tobys lead to takes when their £25 Japanese plugs are coming up blank. When they look at me – squid-smeared hat from a local builders' merchant, stained and much patched waders, well worn rod, jacket mended with duct tape and fluorescent fly-tying thread – I imagine they think I'm a typical local yokel and that my quirky tactics reflect parochial west Cornish know-how. Wrong, I fish the way I do because I'm a sophisticated citizen of the world, the ratty togs and tackle are a disguise.

Under your Nose

'I'll see what I can do'
Pulp, *Common People*

Inshore bass forage close to rocks and beaches. That's isn't an opinion, it's a fact, one that I've proven to myself time and again. But still I can be surprised just how near they sometimes come to feeding on dry land.

One moonlit July morning I took my lure rod for a walk along the coastal footpath, scrambling to the water whenever I saw a likely-looking cove. I meet people in breathable chesties, they look comfy, but I'm not tempted to join them. Slogging through brambles and sliding on my bottom over sharp granite shreds anything short of chain mail or motorcycling leathers, neither of which would suit my stylish angler profile. So I buy cheap trouser waders. And when they're beyond patching I cut off the boots for use in the garden. PVC creates a sauna effect, but sweaty legs are a minor inconvenience for a bloke who dries fishy hands on his woolly hat.

Anyway there were bass about and they were hitting very small sandeel shads. I released three before the light came up. Then I remembered that my wife had promised a fish to a friend. Fine, I'd keep the next one. But pride goeth before a cock-up. On two successive casts I snagged bottom, my only baby shads were gone. I tried a bigger one, no takers. A shallow diving plug, again the bass were unimpressed. A Toby moving fast, my fall-back lure in times of trouble, not a wibble. There was a pool at my feet. It was the size of the basins they put in aeroplane WCs, the ones that make it impossible to wash your hands without slopping soap suds down the front of your trousers and looking as if you had an embarrassing accident.

I ran my fingers through the weed at the bottom. Something wriggled. So a more business-like scoop and out came a prawn. Now I'm a great believer in matching the hatch for bass, offering them something they're feeding on; but I'll make an exception for a live prawn, I reckon they're the equivalent of Yorkshire pudding with gravy, even people who've eaten to the point of groaning indigestion can't resist a nibble. So on with a 2/0, nip it through the tail, and I lobbed out. Within a few minutes line was streaming from the reel, a solid fish, mission accomplished. Until it turned out to be a wrasse of a pound. That's the problem with Yorkshires, everyone loves them. I scratched around for another prawn. This time, I thought, I'll keep my powder dry, I'll cast only when I see a bass swirling. In the meantime I dangled my bait right below the end ring. It was in six inches of water on top of a flat shelf of granite. I tucked the rod under my arm to roll a ciggie. As I licked the gum, whack. There was a whirlpool at my feet as a three pound bass grabbed its treat, made a high speed hairpin turn, and headed back to the deeper reaches of the cove. The rod's a nine footer. Eighteen inches for the part in the crook of my elbow, that's a decent bass at a range of seven and a half feet.

Who's Afraid of the Dark?

'And the sun refused to shine'
Warren Zevon, *Accidentally Like A Martyr*

When people find out I fish at night there are two reactions. Sensible folk wonder whether it's safe to potter around by the sea when you can't see where you're going. Anglers have no such worries, they talk about their headlamps, number of candlepower, time between charge-ups, different colour modes, and so on. One fellow's cost nearly three hundred quid, I'd expect it to come with a case of Islay whisky as your free gift with purchase. And maybe it did, but he never mentioned it, just told me it was waterproof to a depth of two hundred metres. I don't intend to go deep sea diving in my waders so I use a pocket torch, three quid at the petrol station. I find my way around by shuffling carefully, on slippery rocks I use my bottom as a third leg to improve stability. I'm waiting for the fifty metre arse-bounce to be recognised as an Olympic sport, but the television rights might be a problem, it has to be done in total darkness. The only time I need light is when I'm changing a rig, a lure, or a bait. I'm absent minded so I hold the torch in my teeth. That way I remember to turn it off before spinning round to face the water. If it were strapped to my forehead I'm sure I'd forget I was a walking beacon, blast the wave with searchlight beams, and scare the bass away to Devon.

Lure fans sometimes say, 'But even if you're catching fish in the dark, you're missing all the fun. When you see a bass smash your lure, that's as good as it gets.' Well, not quite. One moonless July night I was casting a silvery white soft plastic in a shallow cove. There were sandeels about and before long I was releasing a schoolie. Then I heard a swooshing sound, then another, and another. It was as if a whole class of children with rotten table manners were sucking down giant noodles. I stood still and tried to identify the loudest slurp, aimed my lure at it, and another bass grabbed hold. This was beyond exciting, wondering whether you'd picked the right boil, whether it was a whopper or just an aggressive sandeel-basher. After an hour a holidaymaker showed up with his tackle. I told him what was going on and we fished together until the light came up, five or six bass apiece ranging from babies to a fat four-pounder. My new pal was a professor of statistics. His tentative conclusion: the noisiness with which it eats baitfish is not a reliable predictor of the size of a bass, but the data set's too small for a significant conclusion, further study required.

Another black dark session was in June, and it started out as an exercise in frustration. First there was someone casting across my favourite little bay so I had to bunk further along the shore. Then I couldn't get a take for love, money, or anything in my lure box. A sandeel shad, a shallow diver, a slider, a Toby, a flying condom, a soft plastic stick bait, not a chuffing wibble on anything. The bloke from my regular spot wandered along to see how I was faring. And now there were two blankers in the dark. As I sat down to dig out my tobacco pouch I caught a whiff of something on the breeze. Not that your man had poor personal hygiene, this was coming off the water. It's hard to describe a smell, unless you work for Chanel Number Five I suppose, but I'd say newly mown grass with notes of seaweed and cod liver oil. And I know that scent, you pick it up on beaches when your boots squish tiny jelly-fry into the sand. Soon you'll be able to buy it from your local pharmacy, 'Eau de Leakyboots, Cologne pour la Pêche', a little dab and the seagulls will follow you anywhere. I tied on my newly invented special fry rig, a shiny size six streamer fly on a dropper, a big soft plastic on the point, and I had a bass on my second cast. I sorted out the other fellow with a similar set-up and we managed half a dozen between us, nothing big but plenty of fun.

So who cares if you can't see where you're going? You can listen, you can follow your nose, what else do you need?

He Blinded me with Science

'Einstein can't be classed as witless'
Ian Dury & The Blockheads, *There Ain't Half Been Some Clever Bastards*

Solve a fishing puzzle and it's easy to be smug. I'm never tempted to think I'm a genius, 'not as daft as he looks' is good enough. But I've always been pleased with my approach to jelly-fry. I'd see them in a cove, my divers and shads might as well have been badger turds, even if there were sandeels or mackerel in the water as well. As a trout man I decided the best way to suggest a tiny tiddler on a spinning rod was to stick a glittery fly on a dropper, a weighted lure on the point. Over the years I've shared this tip with dozens of anglers and helped them catch bass. I like to be a good stick so I'm pleased when a long faced blanker turns into a bundle of jelly-frying joy. But I'd be even more delighted if I could say, 'And I came up with that wheeze all by myself'. I can't of course, British reserve. But I can think it. At least I could until I met a real inventor like Alex.

Bass

We were in a cove in early summer, his plug was doing him as much good as a samosa, and I gave him a muddler minnow with a soft plastic to let him cast. He was thrilled with the fish he caught, and I almost blushed as he told me what a brilliant idea I'd cooked up. Then a year later I saw him on the same stretch. OK, I thought, I'll mark his card again, I wonder if he kept the muddler rig. Clearly not, he was belting out something that flew for miles and landed with a heavy splash. Not to worry, I had a spare. Then his rod hooped over with a schoolie. What, I asked, was he using. A smile as he showed me: it was a tiny oval of shiny metal with a single hook astern. 'We had fry on my local marks,' he told me. 'I tried your rig, and it caught fish. The problem was that our water was weedy. Two lures on the leader means twice as many chances to get snagged. So I decided to make a one inch jig that'll cast by itself.' By this stage he was grinning, his cheeks wrinkled like a cat's bottom. 'I had to use lead. Tungsten's twice as dense, but the melting point's too high for a laboratory in the shed. But I got up to twelve grammes for a twenty-two millimetre lure body. A steel shank, lead wire around it, then I melted the wire with my blow-lamp to get a smooth finish. Wrap it in holographic silver tinsel, some epoxy varnish, a single hook, there you are. I brought a few spares in case I ran into you again.' I've used them, they're fantastic. Alex is a man in whom smugness would be excusable. But I'd describe him simply as chuffed.

Spoilt for Choice

'Do it wrong, 'til I do it right'
Johnnie & Jack, *Down South In New Orleans*

Early summer isn't my favourite time of year for bass. Late spring and early winter are when we expect the big storms that bring crashing waves and double figure whoppers onto the beaches. But one great thing about fishing, there's always a way to turn it from plain old fun into hoots of fun.

It was June and the general synopsis bit of the shipping forecast was the same for days, high pressure static over Iceland. The sea was so flat that the only surfers were the ones who stand up on their boards and paddle along with giant wooden spoons, like gondoliers who've lost their tourists. People were bounding off the Isles of Scilly ferry with rosy cheeks, she's a top-heavy craft and even a moderate wave turns most of them bright green. But I had just one day left before setting off for a three week assignment in Canada. Rubbish conditions or not, I was going fishing.

There's a small estuary six or seven miles from our house. Around low water the sea-pool's shallow and weedy, it lends itself best to the fly. So an hour before first light I tied on a silver and white muddler minnow and started casting, letting the line swing around in the current. I like fly-fishing in the dark. I don't think I'm vain or overly self-conscious, but I'm not the most coordinated bloke you'll meet, and in daylight I've been told I look like a chimpanzee trying to swat mosquitoes with an overcooked noodle. But the line goes in something like the right direction and that's what counts. After quarter of an hour I felt a solid pull, then the reel buzzed and the pool echoed to the sound of splashes. My fish seemed to spend as much time in the air as in the drink, and it wasn't long before it was tired out. A seatrout of about a pound and a half. I always release my seatrout. Cornwall has a healthy population – we don't have any of those dreadful salmon cages down our way – and I imagine at some stage they'll need to transplant a bunch of our fish to replace the ones that have been slaughtered in the west of Scotland. I'm not sure how that would work. I read somewhere that a seatrout finds its native river using its sense of smell, and that it picks up the distinctive chemistry of its home water when it's way out in the ocean. Remarkable stuff. And you have to wonder how they tested the hypothesis. Maybe little blindfolds to make sure the fish weren't navigating on visual? And exactly how would you blindfold a smooth, wet creature that swims and leaps like a barracuda crossed with a wallaby?

But I'm wandering. Back to the sea-pool, and the tide was slackening, the water hardly moving at all. I tried stripping line at speed, and I was rewarded with a fat early season mackerel; and two or three casts later in came its twin. Great entertainment, a tasty supper, but where was my bass? Now the challenge with estuaries is also what makes them so attractive: they're full of a range of tasty treats: crabs, baby sandeels, fry, finger mullet, little shrimps, big fat prawns, tiny flatties. For an angler it's like being a waiter in a dim sum restaurant, every time you roll the trolley by, the customer fancies something different, spring rolls, dumplings, spare ribs, pork buns, squid.

So I tried a change of menu, a whiskery grub-shaped job on a curved size eight, something to suggest a tiny crustacean. And fair play to the canny chap who tied it – no applause please – it did the job. But not a bass, a mullet of about half a pound. The sun was red in the sky and the tide was starting to flood when I made one last switch, a big prawn pattern this time, a palmer-dressed number on a size one. And thump, a fat schoolie of a couple of pounds, mission accomplished. And enough fun to set me up for my Canadians.

Desperate Weather, Desperate Measures

'There's nothing in here moving'
Bob Dylan, *It Ain't Me Babe*

As a rule I go fishing because I love to go fishing. Also I often get up a few hours before dawn, and if New York's the city that never sleeps, Penzance is the town that rarely wakes up. There's not much to do at three in the morning, might as well go for a wander along the shore. But once in a while I head out because I really want to catch a bass. One June that was the story. I had peas and chard in the garden, oven chips in the deep-freeze, but the star of the supper plate was missing in action.

The weather was dire. Everyone was saying how delightful it is to see such clear blue skies at this time of year, maybe we're in for a proper summer, better stock up on sun cream. Gentle northerly breezes, Mount's Bay was as flat as a flounder, absolutely dire from an angler's point of view. One good omen, the tide was big, low at two o'clock. So I drove to a very exposed north coast beach, there might at least be some sort of wave there. It's white sand, crunchy and gravelly, and it's home to plenty of ragworms and sandeels. I nearly always have a packet or two of frozen eels for emergencies, so I grabbed one, a bag of baby mackerel as backup.

In the carpark I ran into two local chaps stowing their gear into a van. Not encouraging, they'd been at it all night for a small pollack, a flattie, and a weever. But looking at their tackle I wasn't surprised: tripods, six ounce breakaway leads, lugworms. When there's no surf to shift the bass treats around, I like my bait to be on the move instead, covering a bit of ground, searching out the bass lies. I tied on a one ounce bomb and a sandeel, stood well back from the water's edge, and lobbed twenty yards into the ripple. Bad choice, even one ounce was too heavy, sitting like a broody hen, like the pub regular who always bags the same stool and flies off the handle if it's taken.

'OK, I'll have to go weightless.' I often talk to myself when I'm alone and in darkness. 'I wonder what an eel weighs when it's mounted on a couple of three-zeros. Maybe half an ounce. It's not going to cast very well. But if I puddle through the shallows I'm sure to scare off the fish. Oh well, the tide's flooding, that'll make up for the lack of distance.' I stayed ten yards from the margin and flicked my bait as far as I could. Possibly fifteen yards, I could hear it splash so I know it landed in water. That was as much encouragement as I could expect, and better than the alternative – if it was on the beach I might have caught a shore crab or a seagull, a fish would be unlikely. I opened the bailer and backed further up the shore. Then I sat down and lit a ciggie. And a few minutes later I felt the welcome thump of a fat three pound bass, supper.

There were six sandeels in the packet: four bass and two flounders. When the dawn came up I watched my bait as I chucked it. It wobbled through the air like a dragonfly with banjaxed steering, touching down ten feet from the sand. That's where the fish were feeding, they must have been so full of eels that they needed to massage their tummies on the bottom.

There's Nothing to it

'You believe what you want to believe'
Tom Petty & The Heartbreakers, *Refugee*

When it comes to how you fish I'm with Robespierre: 'Liberté, egalité, fraternité'. The feminist in me would add 'sororité', but my point is that anglers are equals, we all should feel free to use the gear and methods we prefer. We don't need to guillotine the so-called purists – other handles include snobs or self-obsessed eejits – who make catty remarks about people with different tackle preferences, we should just ignore them. And if we can root out biases before they take hold, so much the better.

One September morning I drove to a north facing beach at about three thirty. The surf on my side of Land's End was puny, on the other coast it wasn't half bad, four feet and foamy. In the carpark was a chap with a whole optical warehouse of kit, a telescope, a camera with a massive telephoto lens, night vision binoculars, and other bits and pieces I couldn't begin to identify. A pleasant fellow too, he was hoping to take pictures of dolphins leaping in the moonlight. Maybe videos as well, his explanations were a bit technical for a bloke who struggles with anything more complicated than a Box Brownie. He asked me about bass, he was planning to start fishing with his pal Kevin. 'But he only uses lures. He reckons bait fishing's boring, nothing to it, you just chuck out a bunch of worms and wait. But lures are all about skill, watercraft, working out where to find the fish and how to tempt them.' 'Well,' I said, 'that's what any kind of fishing's about. Flies, lures, or bait, some people just wait, other people think and keep trying different approaches. Anyway, good luck with your dolphins.' I'd have chatted longer but the sea was calling me. Anglers always feel impatient to get that first line out, it's the flip-side of the way we linger for ever over the so-called last cast.

Twenty yards from the water I switched on my little torch to tie on a joey mackerel. But the sand at my feet was stippled with chunky sandeels. They weren't monsters but they were nine or ten inches long. I walked to the edge of the surf. By the glow of the moon I could see a few wriggling bodies in the froth, so I trapped one with my boot – good skills for a chap whose footballing career began and ended with handing out wedges of orange to the second eleven at half time. I mounted the eel and lobbed it out. Almost immediately a three pound bass grabbed hold, followed by two more. Then nothing for half an hour.

I tried a bunk along the strand to a spot where a ridge sticks out into the surf, drifting bits and pieces sometimes build up against it. Time for a fresh bait as well, but I couldn't find a single launce. Instead the shallows were thick with dead seven or eight inch squid, twenty or thirty of them. How so many wound up in that one spot I'll never know. Maybe some trick of the tide worked like a Dyson vacuum cleaner and swept them all together into a clump; maybe a passing crab boat had jettisoned its surplus bait; maybe I was looking at the aftermath of a calamari pop festival, and these were the music fans who'd overdone the cider and the MDMA. Either way I tied one on and the bass were appreciative, a nine pounder; then a lovely eating fish, four and a half and in prime condition.

Back at the car my photographer was full of questions, he'd been watching me through his night vision field glasses. How did I catch so many? How heavy was the big one? Why did I move? And weren't you supposed to put your rod onto a tripod? Had I run out of worms? So I gave him a quick guided tour of beach fishing for bass. Well, maybe not that quick, once I start talking about fish I bang on like an overworked cobbler.

'Wow,' said the victim of my lecture, 'that's nothing like the way my mate describes it. You're doing all the stuff he talks about, all this watercraft, thinking things through. I'm telling Kevin I want to have a go with bait first.' Then he showed me his photographs. He'd one of a dolphin, an absolute cracker, completely clear of the water with the pale half moon in the shot as well. He'd also snapped a seal that poked up its head and gave him a whiskery grin, and there were two pictures of me releasing bass. I had my back to him, that's my best camera angle.

Do as I Say, Don't do as I Do

'The rain came pouring down'
Van Morrison, *And It Stoned Me*

I'm a nocturnal bass fisher. Usually I stay till it's light, maybe I'm crepuscular as well, but the idea of a whole outing in the daytime, that's just not on. I'm convinced bass feed most actively by night, especially in the last few hours of darkness. But there's a social aspect as well. Make that antisocial, I love being on my own, the only living soul on a three mile beach or a rugged headland. And when there are people around they ask such annoying questions. 'Are you fishing?' That's a beauty. I'm holding a rod, my line's in the water, what d'you think I'm doing, waiting for a lightning storm so I can use eleven feet of carbon fibre to summon up thunderbolts and turn myself into a piece of crackling? 'Had any luck?' That's even worse. Luck has nothing to do with it. Sixty-odd years of experience, obsessive focus, local knowledge, a willingness to get out of bed in the middle of the night, a never-ending process of analysing conditions and responding as they change, that's what produced this handsome fish. Luck? That wins raffle prizes or fatuous talent shows on the television. But of course I don't say these things, I'm British for goodness' sake. I just grunt and change the subject. 'A bit damp, isn't it? But supposed to brighten up later, I hear.'

My last daylight session must have been over ten years ago. A client called and asked me to spend two weeks travelling between Bogota and Budapest. How those cities fell under one administrative umbrella's beyond me. Maybe someone chopped up the globe alphabetically. But it was an American multinational so I suspect they were random bits of the famous ROW, Rest Of World – which means everything beyond the US border. Either way I bought airline tickets and booked myself on that night's sleeper train to London. Which meant I had twelve hours in Cornwall before bombing off on a fourteen day trek around cities beginning with the letter B. So of course I went fishing.

It was late September, the end of the first big blow of the autumn, thirty knots onshore with steady light rain. That at least meant there shouldn't be many holidaymakers on the beaches. If they had any sense they'd be in amusement parks where families stay under cover and pretend to have fun while Mum and Dad knock seven bells out of their credit cards to pay for ugly souvenirs, ice creams, and rides that make the children throw up their ice creams. On the debit side of the ledger it was too rough to be on the rocks and I had no bait in the deep-freeze. In the end I decided to go to my local beach and sling a metal jig from the sand. Probably a waste of time, but at least I'd feel the spray in my face and breathe something pure ahead of a fortnight in air-conditioned aeroplanes and meeting rooms. I hate them. If someone suggested you eat food or drink water that had been recycled through another person's body you'd raise hell. So why do we put up with second-hand air?

But back to the beach, and it was deserted. I wandered up and down, raindrops dribbling up my sleeves and speckling my glasses. I was hurling forty grammes of shiny steel into the surf-table, pausing only to tweak scraps of weed from the line. Then after an hour or so my jig stopped dead. Maybe a big lump of wrack, I held the rod high and tightened harder. And I felt the unmistakable bouncy pull of a bass. In stirred up water I find fish generally don't pull much, but this one broke the pattern. She ran three times and it was ten minutes before I slid her in on a breaking wave. A five pounder.

At this point I realised I had an audience. A middle aged chap was standing at my side, staring wide eyed. 'Wow, that's a bass,' he announced. A blinding glimpse of the obvious, but better than 'Are you fishing?' He'd been trying to catch a bass for ages. He'd nipped into the local tackle shop looking for tips, the owner had told him the fellow who did best fished big baits in darkness. 'He described this bloke too. Skinny, beard, black woolly hat, patches on his waders, walks with a limp. Sounds a lot like you. So he was pulling my leg. I was planning to wait till it gets dark. But I should get started right away.'

When I try to help other anglers with a tip or two – try a shorter cast, switch to a squid, use a lighter weight – I often struggle to be taken seriously, they think I'm taking the mick. But convincing this man that the way he'd just seen me fishing, and beaching a fat bass, wasn't what I'd recommend, that stretched my powers of persuasion from Bogota to Budapest. I hope he saw the light in the end. The darkness at least.

Positive Thinking

'I've been working on the palm tree for eighty-seven years'
Neil Young, *Last Trip To Tulsa*

One of my employers sent the whole management team to a training session about visualising success. It was a spectacular waste of two days, low rent psychobabble and bloody silly exercises. But there was a highlight. As we came back into the meeting room after a coffee one of my colleagues was wrapping up a conversation about a sale we were working on. 'I don't care how you price it,' she said, 'they'll never buy it.' The instructor was all over her like a cheap suit. 'Naomi, please remember what we were talking about before the break, being positive.' 'OK,' said Naomi, 'I'm positive they'll never buy it.'

Anglers talk about confidence, how you have more bites if you have faith in your lure or your bait. I think that's right. Not because the fish pick up your brainwaves, I don't believe in ESP, unicorns, or fairies at the bottom of the garden either. But when you reckon you're going to catch something you make more effort. If you think the session's a lost cause, 'one last cast' translates into, well, one last cast. Unthinkable. If you feel you're in with a chance it reverts to its normal meaning: half a dozen chucks with the diving plug, then a few with the slider just in case, and ten minutes on the sandeel shad because you really never know.

When I started chasing bass in a serious way I fretted about conditions, I'd look at an online weather forecast almost hourly. If the BBC had said Cornwall was about to be invaded by reanimated dinosaurs I'd have thought, 'Westerlies, they'll lose a few landing craft in the surf. I'd better check the deep-freeze for squid.' Rough seas meant bait from the beach, calmer conditions were good for the fly or a lure outfit on the rocks.

Then one day my spinning reel died. Tackle buffs might care to know it was a Shimano Exage 3000. Also that its death wasn't a result of poor engineering or quality control, it died violently when I slipped on a rock, dropped the rod, and recovered my balance by stomping my foot down on the reel. I ordered a new one but I had to wait a week for delivery. It was a windless summer's week, and three mornings of fly-casting gave way to an evening of bursitis in my shoulder. So on the fourth day I took my beach rod to a stretch of sand not far from our house. I'd seen articles about freelining in a calm sea – what I'd never seen was anyone doing it.

The tide was slack low when I arrived, the water almost flat. I set up half a cricket pitch back from the edge and chucked out a mackerel. And it was weird. Normally I'd feel my bomb weight trundling through the surf, in wilder weather the waves would tug at my line while a wired lead kept the bait in the water. Today there was nothing going on, the joey was sitting on the bottom, the line was slightly slack, and the sky was inky. It was like being in a sensory deprivation chamber, nothing to feel and nothing to see. Then a chap I know came by, Sean, on his way to the rocks to go plugging. He asked what was on, I told him, and he said, 'You're up against it. If Nigel wanders by, tell him where I'm to. Quite honestly, you never know, but you're up against it.' Well thank you for that resounding endorsement of my chances, you really know how to give a bloke a shot in the arm.

Then his friend arrived and I took back everything. Because Nigel made Sean seem like a wild eyed optimist. Nigel's a man of few words, four to be precise. 'Pissing in the wind.' You're right, I said to myself, if only I had a lure I could search through some water, then I bet I'd find fish. But this was daft, I might as well have been dunking my mackerel in a cup of tea. With nothing else to do I decided to try a new bait. When I reeled in I realised the tide had started making, there was a current running across the beach and my joey had shifted twenty yards to my right, swinging around until it was almost on dry land. That was better, now my gear was covering water, it was almost like bouncing a shad along the bottom. Slowly perhaps, but at least it wasn't just sitting there. I cast again, then shuffled along the shore as the gear drifted. Twenty yards in ten minutes, but the tide was strengthening. After half an hour I was casting upstream then pacing steadily across the sand to keep up. And I was alert, convinced something was going to happen. I stopped for a minute and let my bait swing in an arc. It must have been twenty feet from the waterline when the line fell slack and I tightened into a four pounder.

Sean and Nigel stopped for a natter on their way back from the coves. They'd caught a few small bass and one half decent pollack. 'And you had that one out of the surf? Or out of the no bloody surf at all?' asked Nigel. 'How on earth d'you do that?' 'A nice mackerel wandering along the bottom,' I said, 'I reckon that has to be a way of finding a decent fish.' Not a word about positivity or visualising success.

With Thanks to James Joyce

'We've got to find a way'
Marvin Gaye, *What's Going On*

There's nothing like learning a new dodge, one you never would have come up with. It's even better when your tutor has a distinctive way with words.

The August sun was creeping into Mount's Bay and I was stumbling my way back to the carpark. There were sandeels in the coves and I'd had three bass on scrawny shallow divers, keeping a fat three pounder. But as so often in summer, first light turned into last orders, I hadn't seen fin nor scale of a fish for half an hour. Coming towards me was a tall man about my age, patches on his chesties and stains on his jacket. I warmed to him from the get-go. When I run into an angler with immaculate togs I'm sometimes self-conscious. Not that I'm a frustrated fashion model, just the feeling you have when you show up at a party in jeans only to find everyone else is in formal gear. Mr. Scruffpot peered at the bass hanging from my bag with a rueful grin. 'Shite and onions,' he said, 'I knew I'd have missed it.' Now I was beyond warm, positively toasty. I lived in Ireland for a while, never heard anyone say, 'Shite and onions'. Simon Dedalus uses the expression in Ulysses, but I thought James Joyce made it up. The stranger stuck out a hand. 'I'm Martin from Cork. And for the love of Mary don't tell me they were lepping onto the shore just now. I was going to set the old alarm clock, my wife told me not to bother. I was on holiday, she said, I should roll out of the stable when I woke up anyway. I shouldn't have listened. I set the clock so I'll be at work on time. And when it's something vital like a bucket of bass, I sleep like a donkey full of stout and miss the whole yoke.'

I reassured him, no buckets, just a few, and the one I kept was the biggest. He sighed. 'Sure there's a difference between a couple of fish and enough to fill Croke Park. But the big difference, that's between catching one and going back to the caravan for your rashers with nothing. I'll have one if I've to stay till the pope marries a Methodist.' He scanned the water. 'So they're after going down deep now, taking their siestas. Not to worry, watch this.' From a monster tackle bag he produced a popper finished in silver. But modified, the hooks had been removed. 'So now you're wondering,' said Martin, 'what do I do with a lump of plastic that's as much use as tits on a bull. And here's your answer.' He tied a foot of monofilament to the aft split-ring and attached a hook. Another rummage and he came up with a kitchen sieve. 'And now we're after making a cake. Or not.' He scooped the sieve two or three times through a rock-pool. A two inch blenny. Or maybe a goby, I can't tell the difference.

Martin nipped his hook through the tiddler's back and lobbed out into the chop. He pumped his rod and the plug shot along the surface in a welter of spray. 'See here's the notion. My friend the bass is dossing down near the bottom, snuggled up in the seaweed like a pig in straw. But a big old splash on the top, that's going to wake her up, make her wonder is there some excitement she's missing. Then she'll see my little livebait. And she'll think I really don't need another meal, my guts are as tight as a bank manager's grip on the old wallet, but that looks fierce tasty. Ah, might as well, it can't hurt to have just a nibble.' Another hoick, another explosion of froth around the lure. And in about ten minutes time Martin from Cork was fast to a frisky schoolie.

I haven't tried his trick yet, I try to avoid bright mornings. But he told me a little fish works fine, so does a prawn, but a strip of mackerel's a dead loss, you need something that flaps and makes vibrations in the water. Also a foot's the perfect length for the leader. Much longer and you wind up with tangles, much shorter and you don't have any bites. So a whole new way of fishing poor conditions. All I can possibly say is, 'Shite and onions'.

Bass

Clever Tricks from the Far East

'I don't think Hank done it this way'
Waylon Jennings, *Are You Sure Hank Done It This Way?*

Now and then someone shows you a fishing technique that seems intriguing. Then you muck about on a few websites and learn that it's standard operating procedure in another part of the UK. I suppose learning from upcountry anglers is payback for Cornish bass fans, making up for the frustration of the annual holiday invasion. Roads are like carparks, carparks are full of camper vans that take up three spaces apiece, and camper vans disgorge navies of surfers into the waves on our best fishing beaches. So we deserve something in return. Of course our economy depends on tourism, but nobody enjoys being overrun. In an American resort I once saw a tee shirt that summed up how we feel: 'Please don't visit our town, just send us your money.'

Anyway the chap who taught me this one was an off-season visitor, late in November. I was on a south coast beach fishing whole squid in a four foot surf, and it was slow. The tide was small but I'd have expected better. The only sign of life was the odd rattly nibble, after which my lovely bait would look as if it had been attacked by a very small hussar with a sharp sabre and an anger management problem. Whiting, aggressive little muckers, they make Bruce Lee look like a pacifist. The smallest hook in my pocket was a 2/0. I put it on, trimmed up a calamari nugget, and gave it a whirl. An eight inch whiting, so I switched to a 4/0 and lobbed that into the wave. To my delight it was grabbed by a three pound bass. The delight came partly from the fact that I'd worked for my fish, much faffing rewarded. And even more from the smug sense that I'd solved a knotty problem At least a whitingy problem.

Heading back to the car I saw a stout man with two stout beach-casters on a tripod. I stopped for a yarn, but mostly out of politeness, I didn't expect to learn anything. Maybe I'm a species snob but rested rods send me a message: this may be a wise and skilful angler, a bass fisher he's not. Our tackle stays in our hands, it's a regimental tradition like going commando under your kilt or marching behind a goat in uniform. But he was a pleasant chap, down from Dorset, and while we chatted he reeled in a schoolie. He unhooked it, put it back, then picked up a lugworm and went all Masterchef, chopping it into neat one inch segments. 'You didn't catch that bass on such a tiny nibble, did you?' I asked. No, not at all. His rig was a size six hook, a 4/0 dangling below it. The appetiser portion of lug went on the small hook. When he saw a rattle that showed a whiting had grabbed the worm he left everything in place until something larger picked up the livebait. It was a technique he liked on Chesil Beach, mostly for cod. You needed two rods, he reckoned, because sometimes you were waiting a while for your tiddler, best off having a couple of chances of hooking it. 'Thank you, that's amazing,' I said. 'You learn something new every day. Usually it's something boring and worthless, like how many bacon rolls the government says you can eat without popping your clogs, or what really happens to the stuff you sort into your recycling bins. But that's really nifty.' Then I went home and Googled Chesil Beach and livebait. And as he'd said, his two hook approach is used commonly all along the south coast.

I haven't had a go with it yet, I can't bring myself to buy the gear. Traditions have their place, and I'm a bass man. If I used a tripod it would be like dressing the regimental goat in a bikini and a baseball cap.

Unaccompanied Baggage

'That ain't no way to have fun'
Randy Newman, *Mama Told Me Not To Come*

One of the websites I look at has reports where parents take their youngsters out fishing. Often there'll be a snapshot of a very small child holding a fairly small fish, and the nipper's grinning like the cat that ate the canary, the parakeet, and then the whole aviary. These posts are popular, lots of thumbs-up messages about encouraging the next generation of anglers, showing kids there's more to life than mucking about with mobile telephones and making snotty remarks on social media. Quite right too, and if you take a child to the shore you should do everything you can to make the outing fun. Alas, some grown-ups don't see it that way. At least not without a nudge in the right direction.

I was on a Mount's Bay beach one July morning, a light two foot surf, when I came across a girl of about ten. She was sitting on the shingle, a spinning rod in her hand. Well, I say 'spinning rod', it was one of those everything-included outfits they flog in holiday resort shops along with plastic buckets, flip-flops, and lumps of styrofoam that pretend to be surfboards and fall to bits when they get wet. 'It's a bit flat this morning. Are you doing any good?' I asked. I hate it when people talk down to children. 'No, Dad said I could try spinning for mackerel, but the water's so shallow I keep getting stuck on the bottom. I don't think he expects me to catch anything, but Mum said he could only go fishing if he took me along. How about you?' I had a four pound bass in my bag and I'd put a smaller one back. 'Wow, that's a whopper. Dad's caught one, but not nearly as big as that. There he is, the man wading.' She pointed to a tall figure standing thigh deep in the wave. 'But I've only got wellies. And by the way, I'm Sophie.' I introduced myself in return. Then I had an idea. 'I think you're right about the mackerel spinning, but would you like to have a go for a bass?' Her eyes lit up. 'I'd love to, but Dad says you need to be able to cast out with a four ounce sinker, my rod's too light.' 'Possibly,' I told her, 'but we won't know for sure unless we try.' I nipped off her spinner and tied on a pair of 2/0 hooks, then mounted half a joey mackerel. 'What about a weight?' asked Sophie. 'No need, you can just let it drift around, keep the line tight, and when it washes up on the sand, chuck it back out and start again.' 'But I'll be fishing closer in than where Dad's standing.' 'So you will,' I said, 'but bass often feed where it's really shallow.'

She was a thoroughly decent caster. With a seven foot wand of cheap solid fibreglass she managed fifteen or twenty yards. And she was focused, holding the rod up, tightening as her bait rolled about in the wave. On her fourth or fifth chuck she stiffened and hissed, 'James, I felt a big bump'. The line went slack. 'Walk up the shore, Sophie, that should set the hook.' It did, and at this point I may have become a bit incoherent. 'Keep the rod high, is your drag loose? Let her go, don't try to stop her. The wave's pushing her in, crank as fast as you can. Let her go again, she's not ready. Rod high again, let her run. Wind like mad. OK, try to hold on, I'll grab her.' By the time I was slipping Sophie's bass up the beach Dad had come ashore to see what all the fuss was about. Three and a half pounds, that's what all the fuss was about. Dad, with an elegant rod, chest waders, and a peeler crab had managed a two pounder. His daughter, with a toy outfit and half full wellies – for which I'll take the blame – had one almost twice as big. To his credit her father was as bucked as a second-rate rodeo rider. 'Great job, Sophie,' he purred. 'you've got a talent for this. As soon as they open we're going to the tackle shop, you need a grown-up rod.'

Searching for Supper

'So that every mouth can be fed'
Desmond Dekker, *Israelites*

The supermarket frozen food counter amazes me. Who feels the need to buy carrots ready sliced into wheels, or Yorkshire puddings that can be plopped into the microwave? I understand that some people lead busy lives, but it really doesn't take that long to chop your own vegetables or whisk up an egg with some flour and milk. That said there's one convenience product I buy routinely, chips you cook in the oven. They taste great, and a fellow who used to be a fireman tells me they've done wonders for public safety. In the old days he'd be called out almost daily to deal with chip fires: a pan of oil bubbling on the stove can be a major hazard if you don't keep your eye on it. Forget a tray in the cooker and the worst possible outcome is shards of charcoal with your fillets.

One July morning I woke at about three o'clock with a fish supper on my mind. Maybe I'm shallow, other people can't sleep because they're worried about global warming or right wing nationalism, I get out of bed thinking of a juicy fillets and peas from the garden. It was warm and windless, the tide was small, and my last few bass outings had produced nothing but schoolies. So maybe a couple of fat mackerel were my best bet. I love mackerel anyway. A dusting of salt and pepper, a bit of minced garlic and chilli, then fry them for a couple of minutes without adding any oil, they release enough of their own.

An hour later I was on a local pier slinging a couple of 1/0 feathers and a thirty gramme metal lure into the gloom. And after another half hour I was wondering whether there was any mince in the deep-freeze. Not a nibble, maybe supper was going to be hamburgers. I tried letting my gear sink right to the bottom, perhaps the fish were down deep. Then a sharp rattle and in came a flounder as big as my hand. As I unhooked it a tiny wiggling wisp came out of its mouth, then another and another. It was like a film of someone slurping noodles, but running in reverse. Six or seven jelly-fry. Normally by mid-summer they've vanished, replaced by whitebait. Or maybe they've grown into whitebait. I'm not sure how you'd find out for certain, I suspect it would take a tagging programme, and it would be tricky to tag a one inch tiddler, like tying a beer crate to a sparrow. But when there are jelly-fry in the water they always seem to be the predators' meal of choice. Again I don't know why, maybe it's because they show up in such dense swarms that bass and mackerel can swim around with their mouths open, not so much hunting as filter-feeding. Or maybe they're fabulously tasty, like the evening meal I had in mind.

Either way I swapped my feather rig for a pair of size six sabikis and tried a cast parallel with the jetty. As the jig was sinking my rod thumped over and in came a three pound bass. Job done, home to pick peas.

Whenever you like

'What costume shall the poor girl wear?'
The Velvet Underground And Nico, *All Tomorrow's Parties*

People ask me when they should come to Cornwall for a bass fishing holiday. It seems rude to tell them the truth: 'I haven't a clue'. The tide table's reliable and springs are better than neaps. Beyond that you might as well chuck a stale squid at the calendar and pick the week that smells rankest. Because wave and weather are a mystery, like who's going to win next year's Grand National, where the stock market's going, or why people watch television shows about forgotten minor celebrities eating baboons' foreskins. Long range forecasts are as reliable as horoscopes, just less entertaining. Maybe the Met Office should juice them up, 'The month will be marked by deep Atlantic lows, even deeper discounts at your local supermarket. Don't be too proud to pick up some sausages.' Or they could tell the truth: 'Expect a combination of sunshine, rain, freezing fog, calm days, violent storms, blizzards, and perhaps a plague of frogs. Dress warmly but don't forget to pack a swimsuit.'

I'm not a year-round bass fisher. Not quite. January to March are slow, and cold water keeps the fish near the bottom. You can catch a few, but mostly on bait, and that means a risk of swallowed hooks. Lures and flies make for easy releases if you avoid trebles. But a bunch of worms or shellfish is easy to inhale, even for a little schoolie, and I'd hate to harm a bass that's undersized or breeding. But any time from April through December you can count me in, and sport can be great. Or rubbish.

The other question I hear from upcountry anglers is, 'What gear should I bring?' And that's another imponderable, up there with 'What is the sound of one hand clapping?' and 'Why do young people wear baseball caps back to front and sling their trousers low enough to show off their underpants?' Regardless of the time of year it can be still and sunny or a gale might come walloping in from the west, you may want to dibble a fly through the coves or sling a gigantic bait into a maelstrom of surf. There's only one thing you can bet on – that's bet, not necessarily win. In general bass change their feeding patterns from month to month.

Fashionable chefs chunter on about nose-to-tail eating and serving things in season. Big bass have been all over that trend for donkeys' years. They don't nibble at their prey, chewing up the choice bits and leaving the heads and guts for the crabs, they just open their mouths and swallow. And while you can always catch schoolies on worms and peelers, the best lure or bait for whoppers is something that mirrors what they're hunting in the wild. In spring they chase down a lot of weed maggots, along with the finger mullet that compete for these tiny treats. As things warm up they move on to jelly fry, sometimes prawns and sandeels. In mid-summer, when the tourists are scoffing ice creams, bass may be on the lookout for whitebait and mackerel. Then come the autumn squid. And in winter storms, razor clams, pilchards, and mussels slosh around in the stirred up surf. Exactly when the bass switch from one delicacy to another is yet another imponderable, it happens when it happens.

Take the late September morning when I was on my local beach a couple of hours before dawn. Dawn, I should say, was something I'd have to take on trust, the sky was black with rain clouds, there was no chance I'd see a sunrise. The breeze was onshore to thirty knots, the surf was churning, I had coffee and a banana in my tummy and hope in my heart. For a week I'd been doing well with whole joey mackerel, so on with a squeakily fresh one and await developments. Of which there were none. I tried poking a few holes in my mackerel so more blood and juice would leach into the water. Still not a chuffing wibble.

My backup bait was a small packet of squid. I thawed them in a pool in the sand, tied on the biggest, and lobbed it out. Within minutes my rod was hooped over and a nine pound bass was charging around in the breakers. As I released her she spat out my squid, followed by two more. And the next cast was an action replay, somewhere between six and seven pounds; followed by a smaller one, perfect eating size. At this point I realised just how much rain had dribbled up my sleeves while I was landing my fish. There was a puddle in my belly button and my Y-fronts had been rinsed thoroughly. Home for breakfast.

So when should you book your trip to the west? Up to you. Just come prepared for anything, never assume what worked last time's going to do it again, and bring plenty of spare socks and underwear.

A Snapper up of Unconsidered Trifles

'The poor man pawned his watch and pistol'
Professor Longhair, *Junco Partner*

There are lots of lure fans who lust after plugs. One website has a thread called 'Retail Porn', and it's aptly named. Reading the posts you can imagine people peering at their screens, cross-eyed with lascivious concentration as they wonder how to justify blowing twenty quid on a diver that accounted for three six pounders from a reef in Hampshire. And should they go with rainbow smelt or ghost sardine? What the hell, better have them both. Save the money that was going on those trousers, the old ones are fine, a few holes in the seat just mean better ventilation.

Now I'm sure we fish better when we're confident in our gear. If you clip on something you reckon's as attractive as an albatross gizzard you won't be ready for a take, your mind will wander, and you'll miss that unexpected pull. I suspect we catch more when we have full tackle bags as well. We stay longer. Yes, that was the last cast, but it was the last cast with a popper. Better have another dozen chucks with the slider. What I don't believe is that there's a magic lure out there, something so beautifully designed and assembled that it turns every session into a guaranteed triumph. And I certainly don't think there's a simple correlation between a plug's price and its performance as a fish magnet. Expensive jobs often are better made than cheapies, sometimes they're designed to cast further and more easily, but that doesn't mean they'll lead to more takes. A Chelsea tractor's built to a higher specification than my old banger, but I can drive down narrow Cornish lanes where the monster all terrain status-mobile leaves its wing mirrors in the brambles.

Horses for courses. The years I spent in Banjul, hauling in the school staff's meals on lumps of old broomstick, taught me that lesson. Work out what your quarry's eating, use something that suggests it – especially in size and profile – and you're almost home. And that's why there's never going to be a single world-beating lure. If there were it would have a built-in lifecycle like an insect, egg to larva to pupa to imago. In early summer it might look like a baby fry before growing to sandeel size, then putting on its whitebait costume until it was time to dress up as a joey mackerel. And it's not just time of year, where you fish makes a difference as well, different parts of the world throw up different bass fodder. I met a lad from somewhere in the east – OK, from my patch everywhere's east, but he hailed from Kent or Essex as I recall. It was early autumn and he said his local bass were chomping down small scad, turning up their fins at anything else. We have lots of scad in Cornwall – maybe scads of scad – from late summer through till the really cold weather. They can be a pain when I'm after mackerel or pilchards, hammering the feathers before anything else has a chance. But I've never found one in the stomach of a bass. Once I caught a schoolie on a scad bait, but it was one of those rare days when the wave seems to be solid with feeding fish. The scad was at the bottom of my otherwise empty bait bag, and it worked. But the bites were coming so thick and fast that morning that I reckon I'd have done as well with a scotch egg, but for the difficulty of tying it onto the hook.

Another time I ran into an Irish fellow on the rocks, and he was a superb angler. When we packed up he showed me some snapshots on his telephone, his favourite marks in County Waterford. And I couldn't help noticing the dozens of selfies mixed in, Michael with a double, Michael with a whopper on the fly. But just watching him fish I could see how good he was. He'd look at a little cove and unerringly cast straight to the best bass lie. I knew it was the best because I've been mullocking around in that water for almost twenty years, he just slitted his eyes, scratched his head, and dropped his lure into the perfect spot. So I was surprised he wasn't catching much. I had three bass, one decent one, he had a pocket sized schoolie and a wrasse.

After a while we sat down for a natter and he eyed up my plug. 'A bit small, wouldn't you be thinking?' 'No,' I said, 'mostly they're on sandeels right now, I think it's about right.' 'Sandeels you say?' Gobsmacked, I might as well have said wasps or doughnuts. On his home turf the day-to-day baitfish was pollack, they stuck around all season. 'Just sometimes you need a slip of a thing, sometimes a big fat yoke. But always a pollack. D'you see the underside of my lure, that pinky orange bit? Look at a pollack from underneath, that's the first thing you notice. But I'm guessing a sandeel doesn't have that blushing belly style. And I'm fishing something way too big as well.' As soon as he switched to a small skinny shad he started hauling in bass. Horses for courses again.

When I tell lure junkies there's no such thing as a plug for all spots and all seasons they agree. Then they add something like, 'But have you seen the Sasuke 140 Sand Bora?' In other words, 'Yes, you're right. But no, you're wrong. You just haven't found the holy grail yet. Here it is.' But the fact is that I've tried most of the upmarket lures. I haven't bought them, I wouldn't enjoy casting twenty quid into a spot where I'm unlikely to get it back. And if I worried about losing gear I'd steer clear of the weed and rocks where bass often feed. I've acquired my spiffy plugs under the law of salvage. Near our house are a couple of reefs popular with holiday anglers. On spring tides they're accessible in waders, and they're rich foraging grounds. I've snapped up several Feed Shallows, Patchinkos, Sammys, Skimmers, and who knows what else. Sometimes the model's printed on the body, but often I have to weigh my prizes in the kitchen, then Google something like 'bass plug 23 grammes 115 centimetres'. When I know what I've found I do a bit of maintenance, new hooks and split-rings, and they're ready to go. I'd be the first to admit most of them are jolly good. And as long as I use one that looks like the baitfish in the wave, it'll catch fish. But a brilliant horse on the wrong course, that's another story. It may look snazzy, it may fly through the air with the greatest of ease, but it won't interest many bass. It's just a retail porn star.

Vaulting Ambition

'I was waiting for the miracle, for the miracle to come'
Leonard Cohen, *Waiting For The Miracle*

A double figure bass, so many people tell me that's their life's ambition. Odd when you think about it, nine pounds fifteen ounces and they'd be cursing their luck, ten pounds and one ounce would have them dancing on the shore. Clumsily for sure, it's hard to do a Ginger Rogers on soft sand and in waders, but dancing for all that. Then again, why expect logic from anglers? We're people who spend all our pocket money on equipment we rarely use, steep our clothes in foul smelling midge-repellent or fouler smelling bait, and stand around in all weathers to catch something we could pick up from Tesco for a few quid.

Most years I land three or four proper trophies. I don't keep many; unless they're badly hooked I put them back. Bass over about five pounds are good breeding stock, and really big ones often have worms in their flesh. I'm sure they can be eaten without causing any harm, but most people don't fancy brown noodles wiggling through their creamy white fillets. I don't weigh my returns either, a marine biologist told me dangling them by their heads from a spring balance can do long term damage to their internal organs, and I couldn't be bothered with one of those sling efforts the carp fans use. So I just use a tape measure and the BASS length-to-weight conversion chart. At the risk of annoying anglers who've been trying for decades for that elusive ten pounder, once you've had a few, you really don't care about the next one's exact size.

What's more – and maybe even more infuriating to the people still dreaming of one – I reckon whoppers are fairly common. The reason we don't catch many is that schoolies feed much more actively than their great grandmothers. On calm early mornings I watch bass from the cliffs. Little ones zip around in groups in the surf, as quick as sugar-rushing toddlers raiding a buffet for extra chocolate pudding. Monsters lie inert and alone, like restaurant critics in comfy chairs, waiting for someone to bring them a heaping plate of goodies. Lures and baits are much more likely to be picked up by a busily searching tiddler than by a stationary lump. So the trick's to fish water that's full of food, but that keeps the schoolies away. In my experience that means the sort of wave that hits the shore like a heavyweight boxer in a strop, endless crashing swells. The only fish that can handle a stir-up that almost sucks off your waders are the great thugs, and when they're away from their tiddler relatives they can search out your bait in their own sweet time.

People describe big bass as lazy and greedy. I don't think that's fair, fish are too simple to have vices. It's not a character flaw, just instinct that tells them to burn off as little energy as possible and to eat everything they find. They're slow growing, they need maximum calories going in, minimum calories burned off in long distance swims. If you read an inane newspaper you might think people can change their shape with ease: 'Get a beach body in weeks on the kiwi fruit and coffee diet.' In real life it takes a while, and you need to eat less and take more exercise. Bass already have beach bodies, they need to bulk up, that's how they turn into egg laying champions. So a heaving surf's ideal, lots of squid and fish in the shallows, and everything's on the move. Our ten pounder can hold station and wait for the push of the wave to deliver a nourishing mouthful. And it needs to be nourishing, something from the body-builder's high protein buffet: none of your delicate canapés of worm, peeler, or sandeel, all my monsters have taken main course sized squid, large mackerel baits, a fat pilchard, or a juicy bundle of mussels or razors.

My last tip: fish close in. In a howler the water's most disturbed where it's shallowest. Out beyond the third breaker baby bass can frolic and feed in the relative calm, but nearer the shore's the adults-only zone. No explicit sex, but the surf's too violent for anything but a hefty giant.

One November the UK was lashed by a storm. These days their names are chosen in turn by the British and Irish weather services, and I can't recall whether this one had a common or garden handle or one of those Celtic ones that challenge English pronunciation – Aoibhe turns into Eva and Siobhan comes out as Shove-on. Either way there were several days of warm, wet forty knot winds. One morning I was on a somewhat sheltered beach an hour before first light. Emphasis on the 'somewhat': wind-blown sand was flying up the shore and stinging my face, in London I could have peddled my fishing trip as part of a skin conditioning régime, organic exfoliation and massage. I was in two minds about bait. Squid's a reliable standard, but a savage wave can be full of razor clams ripped from their burrows by the tow. As I shuffled down the strand I felt something crunching under my boots. Question answered, razors. I chucked my gear thirty yards into the mayhem and tightened up.

Then a chap appeared at my shoulder. His headlamp was turned off so I gave him credit for being a proper bass fisher – the clueless punters flash their beams all over the place. 'You're not casting far enough,' he told me, 'I've had four at distance, and one's a keeper, three pounds or so.' Before I could answer, my grip lead popped free and I scurried up the shore to tighten. According to the tape she was an eleven pounder. I'd go with eleven and a half, even her mother would have described her as big boned. Only after I beached and released another – seven pounds or so – and he'd had two more schoolies, did my new buddy decide it was worth trying my advice, a lob into the first wave. Fifteen minutes later he caught a well-muscled beauty. He'd a nylon weighing sling, brand new, still in its packaging. Ten pounds and three ounces, his first ever double after fifteen years of trying. He grinned so broadly I was afraid he'd never be able to close his mouth again. But once his beauty had posed for a snapshot and swum away he dug in his bag for a couple of bacon sandwiches, one each, and we both managed just fine.

Too Big, Too Small, Just Right

'Never let your big size fool you'
Carl Malcolm, *Hey Fatty Bum Bum*

Some bass fans seem to think there's a perfect size for any fly, lure, or bait. They're like the fashion designers who reckon a woman can be attractive only if she's a malnourished size zero, if she has that hollow eyed pout that says, 'I'm so slim and sexy'; or more likely, 'I could murder a bloody great meat pie with chips and gravy, then sticky toffee pudding'.

Fly-casters often have boxes full of Deceivers, Gummy Sandeels, Clouser Minnows; and just as often they're all between an inch and a half and two inches long, the size of a whitebait or a small launce. Lure enthusiasts are even keener shopaholics, their boxes are bigger, Patchinkos, Feed Shallows, Sammys, Skimmers, Gunfish, Komonos, Fiish Black Minnows, Senkos, and who know what else. And again often there's a specific size range, ninety millimetres to about a hundred and fifty, like a big sandeel or a small joey mackerel. Maybe they love neat rows, like the people whose boots are in military formation at the back door. And some beach fishers standardise on a particular hook size and tailor their baits to suit.

I'm more inclusive, and my boots are a random jumble. If the things I tie on the end of my line were catwalk models they'd range from short-arsed skinny waifs to heavyweight boxing champions. Bass can lock in on a single food source, and I like to offer what they're looking for, especially to give them something the right size. Not everyone thinks that's important, but I'm sure it is. One day I was after mackerel from a nearby pier. It should have been whitebait season, but I could see fry only as long as my fingertip, so I replaced my regular feathering rig with a pair of size six sabikis. There were two other people fishing and we all caught mackerel – they'll take anything from a bare hook to a stonking great popping plug as long as it's on the move – but I released three schoolies as well. One of the lads desperately wanted a bass, he was in a competition where you score points for every species you catch and photograph. It sounded a bit like autograph collecting to me, but I gave him a couple of the size sixes and his wish was granted on his third cast. Then he asked if I knew where he could go for a goldsinny wrasse. I went from hero to zero when I admitted that I wouldn't know a goldsinny wrasse if it bit me on the bottom; but I think my young species hunter would agree that an effective bass lure's about the same length as the prey species in the water. My smallest artificials are flies tied to size eights to suggest jelly-fry, baby shrimps, or weed maggots. My biggest's a glittery white, soft plastic a hundred and eighty millimetres long. I bought a few in the USA where they use them when striped bass are chasing monster sandeels. Stripers aren't related to our bass, but the same lures work for both species.

When it comes to bait, my hooks range from 2/0s to 6/0s. A pair of 2/0s is ideal for a runty little sandeel. On the rare occasions I use worms I'll load up a 3/0 or 4/0. And my standard big bass baits – mackerel, squid, pilchard, mussel, razor clam – load up a pair of 4/0s or 6/0s. Year ago I had a Kiwi friend. In a restaurant he'd beckon a waiter, then whisper, 'We'll see you right on the tip, and don't waste your time telling us how the chef wipes his nose or peels his parsnips. Just answer one question: which main course is the biggest?' That's the attitude of a healthy bass.

One early October morning I was fishing a five foot wave in Mount's Bay. The mackies were still around, though most of them were on the small side, nine or ten inches long. So I used a whole joey, snipping its nose off to put more blood and scent into the water, and mounting it on two 6/0s.

As I was releasing a six pound bass a young chap came along the sand. What, he wondered, was the secret of my success? He'd been into a local tackle shop where he found out that I was catching good bass at the moment, and that mackerel was the bait of choice. But he'd been at it all night for a couple of flounders. Then he showed me his terminal tackle. He'd a size two hook, a beautifully trimmed two inch strip of mackerel belly whipped on with fine elastic thread. I gave him one of my rigs. He stared at it quizzically, the way you might look at your dinner plate if the mashed potato were purple and the cauliflower were on fire. But fair game, he wandered off and gave it a go. Twenty minutes later he was back. 'Second cast, seven pounds and two ounces, that's amazing,' he yelped. 'I'd never have thought of using a bait like that.' I didn't say it, but I thought, 'Why on earth not? When bass eat mackerel they don't expect artfully cut pieces of sashimi, they expect mackerel.'

Fortune Favours the Fortunate

'I can't help it if I'm lucky'
Bob Dylan, *Idiot Wind*

I follow a couple of websites where anglers share reports. If you land a trophy you're congratulated on your skill and effort. 'Great fishing, you deserve it for putting in the hours.' Lose a whopper and your fellow rods tell you it was rotten luck, next time fortune will smile on you.

We're like the heads of the investment banks. When profits are rolling in they boast that this is because their traders are brilliant, the only people who understand the derivatives market, this proves they deserve salaries that let them buy a new Ferrari for every day of the month. And when everything goes paws-in-the-air, as in 2007, this was something nobody could have predicted, it was a once in a millennium event. Well, counting the dot-com crash, twice in a millennium. Add in 1987 and 1929, maybe an average of four times every hundred years. Anyway it would be unfair to expect the superstars of the financial markets to have seen it coming and could you please give us a few billion quid of taxpayers' money so our companies survive. Oh, and a few more billion so we can maintain ourselves in the obscene style to which we've become accustomed. Make your minds up, I say. If the brainboxes of Wall Street are paid for their all-knowing insight they deserve the sack when they turn out to be ignorant wankers. And if their success is down to greed and random chance, their earnings should be in line with those of people who look for winning tickets on the floor in bookies' shops. There's nothing wrong with being lucky, but at least own up to it for crying out loud, stop trying to cod us into believing it's anything else.

By the water I've seen fishers so jammy they must sleep in preserving pans. One who splashes to mind was an old boy handlining from a beach in the Gambia. As I walked past he hauled in briskly, it was a cassava fish of a couple of pounds. It came into the ankle deep shallows, followed about a foot behind by a four foot guitarfish (*Rhinobatos rhinobatos*). The venerable gent swung his catch to his feet. The sandshark lunged for the escaping snack, misjudged its landing, and wound up flopping on the sand ready for someone's supper.

Even odder was the summer visitor walking his dog along a local Cornish strand. In a knee-deep depression he saw a fish close to three feet long. He scooped it out with his hands. Then one of my tackle shop regulars showed up. The holidaymaker didn't know how to clean his catch so the canny local offered him a deal: gutting, filleting, and steaking in exchange for half the spoils. He brought the head and spine into the shop. We weren't entirely sure but we reckoned it was an albacore (*Thunnus alalunga*). And our boy said it was delicious.

Of course I've had some brushes with outrageous good fortune myself. One morning I headed off to a holiday campsite. They'd just replaced the pillows and duvets through the whole set-up, could our charity make use of the old ones? This was a thoroughbred gift horse, no chance I'd want to give it a dental check-up. Even if the bedding were in shite condition we work with another not-for-profit that bundles up rag and sells it to a recycler who makes stuffing for cushions. It's not a big money spinner but many a mickle makes a muckle, and better old rubbish be reused than dumped in landfills. Anyway there are two ways to the campsite, the main road and a back lane that crosses a little stream. Like most fishers I manage to persuade myself the route that takes you past water must be a shortcut, and I parked by the bridge for a quick glance. Under the span was a trout about twelve inches long. Not a man-eater but it's an acid stream, this wasn't a fish to be sneezed at or driven past in an unseemly rush to collect eiderdowns. My fly rod was in the car so I put on a home-tied tadpole effort with a gold bead head. The brook narrows at the bridge and I thought the weight of the bead would keep my fly from popping out of the water in the swift flow. I clambered onto the bank and dibbled my gear down current. A soft tug and my trout was away, zipping to and fro as the line cut the surface. Twelve and a half inches. And the duvets were properly tidy, half went to a local outfit that rehouses the homeless, the other half to a refugee camp in Greece.

Another morning I drove into town to open up the Oxfam shop for the rubbish collection service. I'm the only volunteer who gets up at foolish o'clock, they slot me in for a lot of early jobs. I was in good time so I stopped along the way to look at the sea. Flat as a dab, I'd try for mackerel next morning. At the water's edge I noticed a patch of dimples. I went for a closer look. Being an angler the closer look involved polishing my specs – I can drive with smeary lenses, but fish spotting's another story. I also grabbed my spinning rod. The pock marks in the surface were whitebait, half a dozen erupted into the air, one landing on the shingle between my boots. I nipped a 2/0 through my volunteer livebait and lobbed it a couple of yards. Within minutes I was releasing a four pound bass.

Seneca said 'Luck is what happens when preparation meets opportunity'. That's a kindly message, it lets even the jammiest so-and-so claim some of the credit. I'm a realist. Luck's what happens when you're lucky.

Bass-Nutty by Degrees

'This is serious business'
John Mellencamp, *Serious Business*

I think of myself as a bass nut. Then once in a while I run across someone who makes me think again. I'm just a mild eccentric but this bloke's a nut. One September night I was on a long beach fishing mackerel baits in a four foot wave. As I released a fish I glanced back along the shore. A hundred yards away was a small figure holding a rod. He passed the first test, no tripod, probably serious. What's more he was ten yards back from the water's edge, that put him on the cusp of nuttiness. A lot of anglers stand in the surf, maybe they're influenced by photos of people like Clive Gammon, he always posed knee-deep in the breakers. But proper job crazy bass fishers worry that a pair of boots in the froth might send their quarry off into the depths, they keep their distance.

Then came the confirming symptom of bass mania. Your man walked forty yards up the sand and tucked himself away behind a rock before switching on his headlamp. I turn my back to the sea to use my torch but I wouldn't go so far as to schlep up the strand and cower behind a lump of granite. Case closed, total nutter, I couldn't wait to meet him. It didn't take long. I had a two pounder which mangled my bait. It seemed disrespectful to follow my normal routine, tying on a fresh one on the open beach, so I scurried up to the outcrop, and there was my barmy bass man.

He was Alan from Sussex, his grandfather had taught him how to fish. 'Strict, he was. You did it right. He'd try not to move his feet, he thought the vibration would ruin your session. And to light his pipe he'd kneel down, turn his back, and put his hood up.' I watched as Alan whipped on a sandeel. Amazing, ten seconds and he had a neat little package. Now I've never been bothered about tidy-looking baits, I think a bass just wants something nutritious. As Einstein said, 'Leave elegance to the tailor'. I don't have a tailor, I leave elegance to other people. But mounting an eel always took me an age. 'That's because of your hooks,' said Alan. 'Offset points. Fine for squid or worm, fiddly if you're on razor or sandeel. Short shank Aberdeens, much easier.' As you'd expect of an obsessive bass man, he was right. I switched and there's no comparison. And I managed to do him a good deed in return. He'd brought eel and ragworm. He'd done OK, but all small fish. I gave him a couple of joeys, one produced a lovely fat five pounder.

Shopping for Skinflints

'If I only had a dollar'
Creedence Clearwater Revival, Lodi

One of the bass fishing websites I look at had a thread about rods and reels. Lots of people weighed in with their favourite models, a few shared horror stories of brand new fixed spools that fell to bits after a couple of outings, blanks that snapped for no good reason. Then someone announced, 'Look at the price tag, if it costs less than a hundred and fifty quid it's bound to be crap'. At which point I went to the garage and put all my gear in the rubbish.

Just joking. On average I spend about thirty pounds on a rod, sixty on a reel; then over its lifespan another sixty on WD40 and machine oil. I've never known a fish to snap my tip or jam the drag. My only serious tackle casualties are when I take a tumble on the rocks and break things; and if a clumsy eejit sits on it, it makes no difference how much you spent, your outfit's an ex-outfit, pining for the recycle bin. I don't have a problem with top-of-the-line gear. If you're careful, if you enjoy using something well designed and beautifully finished, and if you can afford to indulge your taste, I say you should go for it. Personally I'd rather spend my spare cash elsewhere, the fish can't see my modest reel or my battered rod until it's too late to say. 'I have my pride, I refuse to be landed on that old shite'. Anyway the kit that makes the difference between a blank and a bonanza often isn't the big ticket stuff, it's the little bits and pieces. Specifically the ones that give you more options as you try to tempt the fish into biting.

There's not much about bass where I'd claim certainty. Karl Popper said a theory's scientific only if it can be falsified by further evidence or experience, and that makes me a scientific angler. Often I think I know what to expect, always I'm prepared to be proved wrong when my silvery friends make a mockery of my ideas. But I have a strong belief that bass are fixated feeders. They lock in on a specific source of grub, and they'll ignore almost anything else as they fill their tummies with their chosen target. I can see where they're coming from. One of our local pubs does brilliant belly pork with leeks, parsnips, and red cabbage. I never even glance at the specials on their blackboard. They could be offering mussels or salt and pepper squid, two of my all-time favourites; they could be running a special where the cheeseburger's half price; but I don't care. No messing about, I ask for my pork, getting my order in quickly in case they run out.

I've never tried left-over belly pork as a bait – it's only Shelley's good influence that keeps me from licking the plate – but bass can be just as obsessive, especially when they're eating something small and plentiful. I notice this most in early summer with jelly-fry, silvery chaps under an inch long, and so slender you can hold one up to the light and see through it. Land a fish that's been scoffing them and it'll imitate something from a horror film, dozens of tiny wiggling creatures flopping from its gullet as you unhook it. And most regular lures are useless, there may be a swirl as a predator gives your plug a critical once-over, but that's how a bass tells you it thinks you're a halfwit. Switch to something the right size, that can be a different kettle of baitfish. I like a glittery fly on a size six hook, or a mini-sabiki, the type people use for pilchards and sandeels. And early in the season, when weed maggots can be all over the place, I use a grub-shaped effort like a pale Diawl Bach to suggest them. So I never go to the rocks without a few home tied patterns in a fly-box, total cost about a tenner.

One calm morning in early June a favourite cove was soupy, shoals of shiny noodles darting to and fro in the glassy moonlit shallows. I tied on a monofilament leader with a flashy fly on the dropper, a hefty weedless soft plastic on the point, and by the time the light came up I'd released a few bass and kept a three pounder for supper. Then a holiday visitor showed up and asked how I was faring. I told him, showed him the rig that was doing the job, and offered him a spare. No thanks, he'd stick to his Gunfish, it had never let him down. Ten minutes and he switched to a Skimmer, not enough wave for a Gunfish, the fish were chasing it but not taking. That's BSL, bass sign language again, it means 'Wrong lure, you absolute clown'. Then he went with a Patchinko. Still no hits. Finally he said, 'Maybe I'll take you up on your offer.' First cast, bingo.

There's another cheap lure that's saved a whole side of my bacon, the metal jig. We used to call them German sprats when I was a youngster, though mine came from somewhere near Birmingham as I recall. And they were available only in silver, nowadays they're finished in all sorts of colours, greens and blues that look almost sandeel-like, pinks and purples that would be more at home in a fruit salad than a fishing wave. But what matters most is that they're heavy and aerodynamic, easy to cast even into an onshore gale. Because wild weather keeps me off the rocks. Foolhardy people are washed away regularly, one of my friends flies a rescue helicopter and he's full of stories of prats who put themselves in harm's way and expect someone they've never met to dangle on a winch-line into a screaming storm just because Captain Catastrophe couldn't resist a few casts from an exposed headland. So for me a hoolie means sticking to the flat beaches where you can see how far the swells are going to reach. And when I'm twenty yards from the water's edge and the gusts are hitting thirty or forty knots I need a lure that's easy to cast – bass feed close in, but I've yet to catch one on dry land. So there's another cheap item for the kitbag: about two quid for a jig. Trebles can snag bottom in a shallow surf table, so add on ten pence for a single hook, a penny for a split-ring.

My beach fishing kit benefits from another low cost addition: a selection of weights. Some anglers standardise on four or six ounce breakaway leads. These let them sling out their gear, then prop their rods in tripods. I never rest my rod, it doesn't get tired. And as long as I keep it in my hand I can fish a sinker that's light enough to shift around in the wave and the current, trickling through the potholes and gullies in the sand where bass food piles up and bass pile in. In a savage surf I may need a wired gripper, but in anything less I stick with bombs, from four ouncers when it's lively, down to one ouncers in a wussy ripple. And if there's no wave at all I freeline my bait, usually a squid or a mackerel. I'm as near as damn-it certain moving baits lead to more bites than the same thing anchored to the sea floor, and beach bombs cost between fifty pence and a pound. Added to which you save money on snacks: if you hold your rod you can't eat sandwiches or drink tea on the shore, refreshments have to wait till you're back in the carpark.

My last blank-saver's bait. Obvious, you might say, you won't do much good if you leave it in the fridge – though there have been times when I've had to drive home and collect my little mackerel, along with my waders and my waterproof jacket. But what I mean's a selection of bait, I like to offer a balanced menu. Just like when I use lures, I find surf bass

– especially bigger ones – can be choosy, latching on to one particular offering and turning up their fins at anything else. A schoolie hardly ever refuses a bunch of worms or a peeler crab, but better fish are seasonal eaters. They target whatever's most abundant in the shallows, switching between squid, mackerel, pilchards, razor clams, and mussels. And when they're hunting razors even the juiciest calamari goes down as well as a cheeseburger at a vegan picnic. It's hard to be sure what'll tickle their fancies on any given outing, so I travel with one or two backups, usually frozen. Squid and shellfish are ideal reserve baits. Even if they thaw out a bit you can refreeze them for next time. If I were fastidious – unwilling to reek of stale marine creatures – I'd put my spare supplies in sealed plastic packets. But my jacket and my car are beyond saving, both smell like a supermarket fish counter in a heatwave; so I just stick an old shopping bag in my pocket.

One stormy November I had a week of terrific sport. A flat beach a mile from my front door was big bass central, every morning I had two or three over six pounds, one just short of eleven. And every morning I ran into a local chap who was doing more or less the same. The tide-line was dotted with dead squid, and that's what the fish we beached were spitting up as we released them. Then came a day when I showed up to find my partner-in-bass with the unmistakable air of someone who's been waiting a long while for a bite. It's a combination of boredom, grumpiness, and mystification, the look you see on the face of a railway traveller whose train's stuck in a siding while the public address announcer chirps cheerfully about the exotic coffees and Danish pastries available in the buffet car. 'Not a touch,' he said, 'I've been all along the shore, all ranges, dead as an Egyptian mummy. Someone must have run an inshore net and cleaned it out.' I took off my squid and replaced it with a razor clam big enough to load a pair of 4/0s. As I tightened into my gear the rod jumped in my hand and in came a nine pounder. I had only four clams left in my pocket, two each, and four more handsome fish between us.

A rod or reel that sets you back a small fortune certainly won't do you any harm, and it may give you hours of delight; but I think it's the cheaper odds and ends that make the most difference. And the money I save means more frequent visits to the pub, more plates of belly pork.

Pollacks to You

'You'll never know'
Jackson Browne, *For A Dancer*

July, warm and windless with a sea mist rolling in. The coves were full of sandeels, and walking across the sand I could see a few dead ones scattered like confetti after a big bass wedding. So no mystery about what they'd be eating, eels are greasy and fattening, the predator equivalent of a full English with fried bread and black pudding. I once sat on a fat launce, there's an oily stain on the seat of my waders to this day. Also a smear of dried blood, there were two 3/0s in my accidental cushion. It's quite a trick to remove a hook from your own bottom without leaving a messy scar. If I were a swimsuit model that sandeel might have ended my career.

Anyway I clipped on a shad with a long floppy tail. I like a big single hook in the summer, there tend to be a lot of tiddlers around, it makes them easy to release. I couldn't see the rocky reefs and outcrops in the fog, but I tried to remember where they were, dropping my lure between them and cranking it back with a stop-start retrieve. By the time the light began to change I'd had a two pound pollack and three schoolies. Maybe kindergartenies, they were tiny. Then a pollack about as big as my hand. Then another, and another.

Every cast was the same, as soon as the shad touched down it was grabbed. Finally I had a pollack baby that was badly hooked, bleeding profusely. No point putting it back, so I tied on a 4/0 hook and poked it through his back just aft of amidships.

Pollack

I lobbed out my just about livebait and lit a ciggie, the baler open, my fingertips pinching the braid. My fag was half smoked when the rod twitched, then thumped, and line started to vanish from the spool. The fish stopped for a few seconds and took off again. I tightened and all hell broke loose, a six pound bass flailing and thrashing on the surface. As I unhooked her she spat out three more small pollack. No sandeels in sight.

The New York State lottery used to have a slogan: 'Hey, you never know'. The same goes for bass.

Bass, Bait and Belts

'Like a worm on a hook'
Leonard Cohen, *Bird On The Wire*

One of the joys of angling is that you can help people so fast. If you want to improve your tennis, the coach may send you off to the gym to build up your strength and flexibility. Then you'll spend an age working on your forehand, backhand, smash, lob, serve, and positioning around the court. Physical skills develop slowly, some people say it takes thirty thousand hours of practice to master a new one. That's why charity shops are full of rackets, golf clubs, and cricket bats: 'Twenty-five thousand hours and I still can't hit the bloody ball, stuff it, my new sport's brewing beer.' But fishing's a mental activity in the main. Work out what you're trying to do and you're well on track to succeed. And little snippets of advice can make a big difference.

One September afternoon I was in my local tackle shop. I might have been picking up braid, hooks, or swivels, I buy as much as I can from physical stores. The internet can be cheaper, but you can't wander into a website for a natter. Anyway there was a teenager at the counter and the owner introduced him. 'This is John, he fishes your local beach and he wants to know how to catch bigger bass.' A pleasant lad, well mannered. He looked a bit daft, no belt so his jeans were slung around his thighs, a foot of polka dot underpants on display, but my generation had foibles of its own – kaftans, headbands, trouser bottoms like circus tents. 'So what are you trying at the minute, John?' He was using lug, plenty of schoolies, no whoppers. 'Makes sense. At this time of year the mackerel are still around, lots of them. A fair few wind up in the surf. I like a little joey fished whole or half of a bigger one, enough to load up a couple of 4/0s or 6/0s. And close in, on our beach that means under thirty metres.' Kids these days are mystified by yards. As for rods, poles, and perches, they'd think you were talking about coarse fishing kit.

I went away on a work trip but three weeks later I met John on the shore. 'James,' he said, 'thank you. Top man. Mackerel did the trick, some much better fish, one seven pounder. But here's the funny thing. This week I've had nothing, not a nibble.' I explained how the mackerel come and go in the autumn, squid the same, so you need to be ready to switch from one to the other. Then I gave him half of my squid. A few days later I was back on the same mark. As I walked across the sand John came sprinting in my direction. 'Just so you don't waste any time, James, it's mackerel again. They were on the squid until Friday, now they've switched back.' As I said, he's a very pleasant lad. And he wears chest waders on the beach so the silly underpants are hidden.

Carry-on Luggage

'You can get anything you want'
Arlo Guthrie, *Alice's Restaurant*

I travel light. Besides my rod I take a small knapsack to the rocks, a sand-spike and a medium sized backpack to the beach. There are lots of reasons: my knees are banjaxed, I hate carrying stuff, and I suppose I'm lazy. But looming largest is my belief that a bass fisher needs to be mobile. If I clobbered myself up with a giant box of bits and pieces I'd be inclined to go all Gumbie Cat: pick a spot, then sit and sit and sit and sit. And you catch fish mostly by casting where they're feeding and moving on from where they're not. Yes, you need to be flexible as well, to try a different lure or bait, but not as flexible as a contortionist.

Some lure enthusiasts disagree. I'm thinking of the ones whose kit boxes look like Madonna's underwear drawer, the ones who say, 'They don't fancy it in ayu, maybe I should try blue, or green, or rhubarb and custard, or ghost mullet.' Ask these walking tackle shops why they carry so much stuff and they'll say, 'Because you just never know.' That's fair, bass are predictably unpredictable. But never knowing isn't the same as never having a clue. There are patterns in nature, I'd eat my woolly hat –

squid-smeared as it is – if I needed to imitate a jelly-fry in November or a sandeel in March. So I take what I think makes sense, everything else stays at home.

But there are people who don't mind lugging around the whole inventory of a tackle emporium. I was on a Mount's Bay beach in November at the end of a three day westerly blow. A churning surf, that meant either squid or a big razor clam. I'd taken four of each from the deep-freeze, now which would it be? Fifty-fifty as far as I could tell, I started with razor, and in twenty minutes I had a plump four pounder. Then the weed came in so I hiked away along the shore. And that's when I ran into Simon and Darren, a father and son from Yorkshire. From fifty yards away I guessed they were related, identical profiles. They were well over six feet tall, broad shouldered and solid. Not fat, just solid: if they ran into each other on a football pitch the BBC would have been reporting a moderate earth tremor centred on Scarborough. They were sitting on crates like small steamer trunks, surrounded by a perimeter wall of bags and boxes, four big beach-casters propped on tripods.

I was disposed to like them from the get-go, Simon's first words were, 'Fancy a cup of tea? We just brewed up. Darren, where's the spare mug?' Darren rummaged in a duffel. It was so full that I'm sure if I'd asked for a flat white with almond milk he'd have come up with it. Actually if I asked for a flat white I'd be satisfied with anything warm and wet, I'm not sure what a flat white is, it's just something I've seen on the menu in overpriced coffee bars. I set down my fish bag and Simon stared. 'That's a cracker. We've had nowt, unless you count whiting so small my old mum's cat would eat them by the dozen. And we've tried everything: bluey and squid on my big rod, black lug and cuttle on Darren's, rag on the one scratching rig, mackerel on the other. And we're doing what the lad in the shop told us, keeping it close in, we're only casting eighty yards.'

I explained that for bass 'close in' meant twenty or thirty yards. A sideways look, but no argument. 'Aye, and what about bait?' asked Darren. I had three razors left, one each, it was going to be a short outing. But maybe we'd be OK with squid. Either way I wasn't going to bullshit my hosts, it was an excellent cup of tea. 'I had this one on razor clam. I've got a couple to spare if you want.' 'You're a gentleman,' said Simon, 'but we'll be right. Darren, where did we put the clams?' 'The small cooler, Dad, right hand side.' Simon opened a chest that would have made a kennel for an Irish wolfhound. 'Right, there's a dozen here, the others must be in the proper freezer in the caravan.'

They each had a bass to keep, and all three of us released a few. The fish were still taking well when I headed home, normally I wouldn't think of walking away from such good fun. But if I'd stayed to the end I'd have felt I ought to help them cart their stuff to the carpark. Not that I'm that lazy, I wasn't sure I'd be strong enough to pick up any of their boxes.

Don't Play with your Food

'I'm the innocent bystander'
Warren Zevon, *Lawyers Guns And Money*

I land things as quickly as I can. The more time they spend on the line the likelier they are to get rid of the hook. And if I'm going to release a fish I reckon it stands a better chance of thriving if it goes back fresh and frisky, not exhausted and stressed. Scientists can't say for sure how fish react to pain and exertion, but whatever suffering's involved a short period has to be better than a long one. And when I keep a fish with walkers or surfers watching, I operate like the most humane abattoir you can imagine, crank it in, a bash on the head, into the bag, no messing about. Whatever may or may not be going on in fishy brains, a body flopping around on the shore makes our sport look barbaric. If we want people to take our interests seriously we have to come across as responsible stewards of the environment. That's my take at least, others think differently. Some don't think at all.

One morning I finished my charity shop shift early. The town was crawling with summer visitors so I went the long way back to the car, following around the harbour. On the end of the pier was a figure with a rod. He'd attracted a crowd so I went for a closer look. He'd a heavy outfit and a long leash of feathers. The jetty was smeared with blood and carpeted with mackerel, some dead, some flapping and twitching. At a guess he had enough to fill a refuse bag; not one of the silly little efforts that rip as soon as you put in any rubbish, the big stout jobs they sell for building rubble.

The tip of the butcher's rod was bobbing, two mackies jigging around a few feet from the harbour wall. 'It's not worth reeling in for two,' he told his gallery, 'I'll leave it there till I have a few more.' I did my damnedest to be polite. I was careful to avoid words like disgrace, cretin, and dickhead. Just a modest suggestion that leaving a hooked fish in a harbour entrance was likely to attract a seal pup, and that seals tangled up in fishing line starve to death slowly and miserably. Our hero propped his rod against the wall defiantly. 'Bugger seals, they eat all the fish, nothing left for me to catch.' Before I could point out that even an elephant seal would struggle to put away the sixty-odd mackerel at our feet I saw a grey shape in the water. The rod bowed, the butt sprang up, the reel buzzed, and the whole lot flew into the air, the line pinging at the same time. Looking down I could see a bass of three or four pounds making off with its mackerel. Also a newish beach-casting outfit sinking slowly into four fathoms of water and a few more of tangled wrack. At eye level I saw an oaf on the verge of tears.

I'm not a man of faith but sometimes I wonder. Karma. There may be something to it.

Yesterday's News

'If California slides into the ocean'
Warren Zevon, *Desperadoes Under The Eaves*

There's a saying that generals spend peacetime preparing for the last war. A host of people are credited, I suspect nobody knows who came up with it first, but there's some truth in it. As a youngster I went on exercises with the Territorial Army and we shot at targets designed to look like Wehrmacht squaddies circa 1940. But maybe that's just because the MoD had printed millions of cardboard heads in coalscuttle helmets and there wasn't much opportunity to recycle them. And to be fair it's tricky to prepare for the next war, you don't know anything about it. Bass anglers often fish the last outing, and for the same reason. We know where the fish were feeding a

Bass

week or two ago – worst case we know where they weren't – but that doesn't mean we've any idea what's going on today. Of course there lots of variables – weather, wave, water temperature, light level, barometric pressure, what kind of sandwiches you have in your tackle bag – but to my mind two of the biggest things that change are: the availability of stuff for bass to eat and the underwater terrain where they find it.

Bass are pretty omnivorous. I'm much the same, apart from goat's cheese and factory farmed animal products I'll eat anything. With goat's cheese I dislike the taste, intensively reared chickens and pigs disgust me, anything else is fair game. So when people flatter me by telling me I'm related to a fish, maybe that's what they mean: 'Your man's coming for a cup of tea, he's first cousin to one of those bass that never stop stuffing their faces, hide the biscuits.' And like bass I follow a seasonal diet. I have a vegetable patch, I forage, so my ingredients change from month to month.

The difference is that I enjoy variety. Much as I love my home-grown produce I don't designate May as the month to live on broad beans. A balanced meal's healthier, tastier, and less likely to lead to outbursts of the wind. But bass don't bother with balance, I don't think they suffer from flatulence either, they binge eat whatever's most plentiful and easiest to find. When I clean my catches I look in their stomachs. Once in a while I find a mixture, more often they're packed with a single source of protein: maggots, little mullet, jelly-fry, mackerel, whitebait, pilchards, squid, or shellfish. For anglers this means being ready to change our lures or baits as the days and weeks go by. Just because a seven inch plug with a shiny black back did the job on Monday doesn't mean it won't be spurned on Friday, fish after fish swirling in its wake, their tails making rude gestures: 'Eejit, what makes you think I'd fancy that old tat?' The mullet may still be around, but if the bass have moved on to scoffing sandeels we need to change our tactics as well.

That's when those freakishly large lure boxes come in handy, all the days when the weather was shite so you amused yourself in an online tackle shop, doing violence to your credit card. With bait it's more of a challenge, but the principle's the same: try what worked last time, but have an alternative as well. If you're hell bent on avoiding a bass blank, a few lively ragworms or peelers are a great fall-back. I rarely use them these days because they attract so many tiddlers, but they'll get you the odd bite almost regardless of what the bass are feeding on.

The other big shift comes from the force of the sea, and I suspect we run into it more in west Cornwall than you might in points east. Atlantic waves and tides are powerful, like fleets of JCB diggers. And they're random, they bunk rocks and sand around as if those JCBs had drivers with bags on their heads and flagons of cider in their cabs. What used to be a gully fills up overnight, a spit vanishes, boulders as big as family cars trundle along the shore. Areas where baitfish were pushed about in the current or squid piled up in potholes turn into flat, smooth, fish deserts. The places where predators and scavengers find their self-service canteens show up somewhere else. To find our bass we need to stay on the move. So try the old spot for sure, but not for too long. If it doesn't deliver, take a hike.

On most of my regular marks I expect to be alone. I look for out-of-the-way coves, strands where you have to walk a fair distance. Anyway most nocturnal anglers work the evening slot, heading home about the time I'm rolling out of bed. But there's a high tide beach I share with a chap who lives in the closest village. Luckily he's the ideal fishing companion for an antisocial git. If I start before he does I can expect half a dozen words when he shows up, and vice versa: 'Any good? Squid again? Or mackerel?' Perfect, at half past daft, that's as much conversation as I fancy. I don't want to know about football or which forgotten third rate pop star choked on her lizard tails on the television last night, just let me get my gear into the drink. Anyway one autumn we saw the promised land.

Thirty yards from the high water line was a depression in the sea floor. It was half the size of a rugby pitch, maybe two feet deeper than the surrounding sand. As the tide flooded it would fill up with flotsam, some weed, lots of bass fodder. Through early October we had two dozen fish over six pounds from our scour-out, a couple of doubles. Then came the day when the well ran dry. No, more dramatic than that, the well turned into a badly maintained public lavatory, lousy fishing and there was a nasty whiff blowing in across the bay. We tried mackerel, squid, razor clam, and mussels. Two schoolies – play-schoolies, perhaps, they'd have fit in my woolly hat. 'Some bastard must have run an inshore net again,' said my chum. 'I'm going to work, why don't you have a geek at low, see if there's any sign of commercial gear?'

So I did. No trace of monofilament mesh, but our hollow in the sand had marched quarter of a mile along the shore and moved ten yards further out to sea. Our old reliable area was covered in dredging spoil, flat and slimy with a bouquet of dead lugworms and seagull shit. And the nearest dredger was dumping its mud three miles away, I'll never know how it wound up filling in our magic crater. The tide's like William Cowper's god, it moves in a mysterious way, it plants more than footsteps in the sea. But next morning I saw my man's headlamp as I clambered out of the car. 'Follow me,' I told him, 'and cast a bit longer, half a cricket pitch.' He had a five pounder and an eight, I had two sixes. And a month later there was another new war to prepare for, a howling storm rebuilt the whole beach all over again.

Nothing Marks the Spot

'He just grinned and shook my hand, 'no' was all he said'
The Band, *The Weight*

Once the word gets out that you catch good bass everyone wants to know where you fish. Anglers who blank a lot believe that somewhere lies a magical land of *Dicentrarchus labrax*, a mark where every cast produces a bite and every bite's from a monster. Of course they're wrong, bass move around, they follow the richest clumps of food which rarely stay in one place for long. So yesterday's hotspot can be today's central blank, mobbed with people as dismal as any economist.

I almost never let on where I've been. The best you'll hear's something like, 'a south-facing beach' or 'a cove in the bay'. One baby step ahead of 'in the water' or 'where the land meets the sea', but not exactly giving the game away. Mostly this is because my angling brethren and sistren love to talk about their sport, and loose lips sink populations of inshore fish. Once an area develops a reputation in the tackle shops and on the websites, commercial skippers take note and move in. And although I have no problem with professional netters – everyone has to earn a living, and even dredging's more honourable than working for a people smuggling ring, a tabloid newspaper, or a hedge fund – the ones who target angling marks often set their gear illegally, use undersized mesh, and flog their catches direct to cheap and insanitary restaurants run by fly-by-night scumbags who think regulations are for suckers and cleanliness is next to bankruptcy. (There's an establishment like that near our house, the owner's asked me to bring him a few fish. He's been prosecuted twice for housing his employees in unsafe accommodation, twice for food safety violations, and he just bought a Porsche. I see no need to take him on as a charity case.)

Anyway as long as I refuse to dish out ordnance survey map references, what am I prepared to say about places to fish? Quite a lot, to be fair, though other anglers often refuse to believe me, some even accuse me of taking the piss. Perhaps because my first advice is to avoid the most popular areas. You know what I mean, the beaches that are written up in catch reports all the time, the headlands where local tackle dealers send visitors. Personally I hate fishing in a crowd, I like to know it's just me and the Atlantic Ocean, no cheery groups out for a dangle and a bit of banter – which seems to involve cackles of laughter broken up by belches, farts, and shouts of 'I'm in' or 'Jammy bastard'. OK, that's just me, not everyone's an antisocial grumpus. But well frequented marks have other drawbacks. On a deserted stretch of the shore you can keep moving. If bites are slow, if weed comes in, up sticks and take a wander. When you're shoulder to shoulder you have to stay put. Even worse, busy areas look like villages at Christmas time, gleaming with headlamps in red, green, and blazing white. Especially when it's calm, lights on the shore drive the bass away. I don't know where they go, maybe Blackpool – 'These clowns are useless, let's go and see some proper illuminations' – but they certainly don't stick around.

The next thing I look for is shallow surf, another bit of advice that earns me sideways glances: 'Right, let me slip out of my waders so you can pull my leg'. Anglers love deep water, we grew up on Jacques Yves Cousteau and Jaws, we can't believe big fish hang about in spots you can reach in wellies. But it's true. A feeding bass doesn't have to work as hard for its grub when the wave's only a couple of feet deep. Out in the ocean she'd hunt high and low, in thin water they're one and the same place.

Snags and obstructions are good too. Lure fishers stare at me with horror when I tell them to look for rocky lumps and bumps. I'm sure they're thinking, 'Great, lots of places for my twenty quid plugs to get hung up, any bass I pull out of that tackle graveyard's going to wind up costing as much per ounce as platinum, saffron strands, or authenticated slices from Elvis Presley's last fried peanut butter sandwich'. But again I'm not kidding. Obstructions break up the push of the swell and tide, they create eddies that bash baitfish around; and a sandeel or a whitebait swirling out of control through a stir-up makes an easy meal for a predator. By the same token, junk on a surf beach – weed, bits of netting, waste plastic – shows you're in an area where all manner of flotsam and jetsam wind up in the shallows; including dead worms, crabs, squid, and fish. And where their food goes, so go the bigger bass.

Last of all it makes sense to seek out marks where the wind's onshore. To me this is as obvious as the need to use sharp hooks, as plain as the lies in an election manifesto or an advertisement for alternative medical potions, of course you want the weather to be pushing bass treats in. But again some people just aren't having it. 'I like the wind behind me, it makes long casting easier.' 'If I can find some shelter I can put up my bivvie and get out of the rain.' True enough, but if I wanted my gear to go the Isles of Scilly I'd put in on the ferry; and I can stay warm and dry by sitting in the carpark with the windows closed and the heater cranked up. I want bass, and standing in the teeth of a damp gale's a small price to pay.

One October conditions were far from typical. In autumn we expect a string of lows to come in off the Atlantic; instead we had a week of south-easterly breezes, my west-facing marks were calm and all they were producing was schoolies and the odd flattie. So unusually I needed to find somewhere new. I picked a flat two mile long beach, there was a half decent wave at the far west end, and there were tangles of wrack and rubbish on the sand, everything seemed to be drifting in that direction. Better yet, it was a fair hike from the nearest road, that tends to keep a place pretty deserted.

For all their talk about fresh air and healthy exercise, not many anglers appreciate a long trudge in soft sand and waders. Between four and five in the morning I had two double-figure catches. Unfortunately one was a clump of weed, the other was a length of nylon rope tied to a balk of timber. But as soon as I found a clear patch things looked up. Two three pounders on joey mackerel, then I switched to a fat nine inch squid for what I designated as my last cast. Of course that meant about as much as it usually does; I missed a bite so I needed a last-last cast. Then I beached an encouraging six pounder, so there was just time for a last-and-no-bloody-kidding cast. That resulted in a thump, six feet of slack line, and a beauty which the tape measure put at eleven and a bit.

Finding a good fishing spot really doesn't have to be a game of picking other people's brains, and it isn't that complicated either.

The Insomniac's Reward

'He's been up all night'
Warren Zevon, *Mohammed's Radio*

August can be a trying time for Cornish residents. The roads are jammed and vehicles have the herky-jerky manner that tells you the driver's trying to make sense of a barrage of orders from the little person who lives in the satnav. 'At the roundabout take the third exit. Go around the roundabout again and take the fifth exit. At the next ramp pull into the carpark and let someone else take the wheel. Someone who listens, you cloth eared moron.' Our beaches are crowded too, as soon as the light comes up the holiday surfers parade on the sand before chucking themselves into the wave right where you're fishing. So generally I tried to book lots of business trips in high summer, top up the bank balance before the autumn gales and the coming of the big bass.

One year I tried a bit too hard, four back-to-back weeks in airports, anonymous hotels, and tacky corporate boardrooms. At the end of the month I headed home. The train to Penzance runs along a mile of Mount's Bay and I peered at the ocean in the evening sun. A smallish wave, but a welcome wave. Early to bed, I was too whacked to think of setting an alarm clock. Also a pre-dawn start would send an unfortunate message: 'I missed you, it's good to be home, so I'll spend a couple of hours in the marital bed before crashing around the house and waking you up in the middle of the night.' But at two thirty I was staring wide eyed at the ceiling, it was mid-morning in Melbourne, Calgary, Singapore, or the circadian balls-up of my brain. So a packet of tinker mackerel into my fishing bag and away to our local beach. It was moonless and the surf sounded lively.

On with a four ounce bomb weight and I lobbed out before changing my mind. The four ouncer was sitting on the bottom as still as weekend traffic on the A30. I like my bait to bounce around, seeking out the scours where dead crabs and fish pile up. I switched to a three ounce sinker. Perfect, I could feel it trickling along in the cross-flow. And on my second cast it stopped trickling and headed for the Isles of Scilly. A seven pound bass, with two more to follow before sunrise. When the eager beaver surfers showed up and began hurling their bodies at my gear I was too cheerful to be annoyed. 'Have fun,' I yelled. And I was home before the traffic.

Reuse, Recycle, Remarkable

'Sure know how to use it'
Hoyt Axton, *Never Been To Spain*

You won't see it on the front page of the *Financial Times* or the *Wall Street Journal* but the developed world has a market glut of used soft toys in good condition. The charities I work with collect donations for reuse and sale and we drown in furry playthings. I suspect lots of relations buy them for babies. After all it's hard to know what a pre-verbal seven or eight pound tiddler really wants, something cute and squishy looks like a safe bet. So the new arrival winds up with a whole safari park of fluffy animals and an overflowing cot. A lot of charity shops don't even try to sell soft toys, they take up floor space and the only people who buy them want to pay fifty pence for something the dog can shred on the lawn. But when Shelley and I started working with displaced Yezidis in Iraq we found they were crying out for anything their little ones could play with. The toddlers were born since the 2014 genocide, they've been in tented camps all their lives, and toys have been a low priority for the agencies that help them out. Anyway we started collecting and shipping boxes of furry creatures. Then Shelley found a charity called the Teddy Trust. In 2018 it sent 35,000 cuddly toys to children who've been traumatised by wars and famines, and now our Iraqi nippers are on its list. If your house is packed with a zoo of bears, Google it, it's satisfying when something that's gathered dust since your children were small has another life.

I hate waste in general. These days, that makes me worthy and in tune with the times. I might even be 'woke', who knows? But it's nothing new, I think of myself as a common or garden tightwad, the sort of chap who uses old butter wrappers to grease pans and digs mackerel guts into the vegetable garden. Even chucking surplus bait into the sea causes me physical pain. I don't care if it's free or cheap, I want it to catch fish not feed seagulls. But one summer morning I thought I'd be emptying my worm box into the briny before too long. I'd bought a tenner's worth of rag to cover two outings. The wave was moderate, the water clear, ideal conditions for a bunch of wriggling worms in the shallows. But my first session was cancelled when the Oxfam shop called at the last minute to ask me to cover for someone. On the second trip I could see my rag weren't going to make it to a third day, a few were dead, the rest were candidates for extreme unction. Fair enough I'd released a few schoolies but I hadn't had ten quids' worth of fun yet. And now the light was coming up, one more cast and it'd be time to head home.

On with a 6/0 hook and I stuffed it, nipping each worm through the head. I must have wound up with thirty or forty. When I dunked them in the shallows they looked like something from a low budget 1960s science fiction film, *The Alien Octopus Ball Strikes Back*. As my weight settled in the breakers I felt slack line. Then a fish took off for the Atlantic. Eight and a half pounds, a very good bass for July. And would it have taken a smaller bait, two or three worms on a 3/0? No idea, but that would have left me chucking the rest away. And I don't think that would be woke.

Forage of Discovery

'That path is for your steps alone'
The Grateful Dead, *Ripple*

Free food's a delight. I love to eat things I grow in the garden, even more things I pick from hedgerows and footpaths. In a blind tasting I might not tell the difference between blackberries from a supermarket and ones I've picked, but I really fancy a bowl of berries only when my fingertips are stained blue and my wrists have been scratched by brambles. A favourite wild crop's sea spinach. More properly it's sea beet (*Beta vulgaris maritima*) but it was spinach to the locals when I was growing up. It's bad luck to change the name of a boat. It's a seaside plant, I reckon it's covered by the same nautical mumbo-jumbo, sea spinach it remains. It grows best in sandy soil, always in spots where it's sprinkled by salt spray. The plants are dormant in winter, going to seed in summer, so the seasons for gathering it are spring and autumn when it has new glossy leaves. The flavour's like regular spinach but a firmer texture, no trace of sliminess.

Anyway I was out on the coastal footpath with my bag, one still and sunny October morning. The regular picking spot looked iffy, tractor prints through the middle where the farmer had overshot at the end of the field. I don't like vegetables sprayed with pesticides or slurry so I walked on. After half a mile I was overlooking a shallow weedy bay. There were two young fellows fishing, I sat down on a tussock to watch. They were obvious lure enthusiasts: chest waders, sunglasses, peaked caps, and bum-freezer jackets. And they seemed clean – bait fishers often look as if they've been rolling around in seaweed and mackerel scales. The lads had waded to the mouth of the bay and were slinging their plugs miles out into the open water. I rolled a ciggie and settled into my grassy seat to enjoy the show. In half an hour they had a pocket-sized school bass, a wrasse, and three big garfish that jumped like Desert Orchid on a springboard. As I stood up to carry on with my vegetable hunt I took a look at the water between the shore and my lure fishers. It was frisky with mullet. Then I saw fins cutting the water, decent-sized bass. I thought about trying a yell, 'Turn around and fish towards the shore, you've waded past all the good ones.' But who's going to pay heed to some stranger with a bag of leaves screaming advice across a hundred yards of water? On to the next clump of spinach.

Next morning I retraced my steps just before first light. The water was shallow so I clipped on a black and silver weedless soft plastic bait. Standing ten feet from the edge I wandered around lobbing my lure twenty yards into the ripple. By the time the sun came up I'd kept a fat four pounder and released two more.

Then the chaps from the day before arrived. This time it was OK to engage them in a chat, I had credibility. I was in waders, I had a rod in my hand and a bass hanging from my bag. When I told them where the fish were feeding they looked at me as if I'd asked to borrow a twenty pound note for a magic trick involving kerosene and a box of matches. Then I pointed out fins poking through the shallows, a shoal of mullet. 'But I can't fish there,' said one, 'My plug dives to a metre.' Their lure boxes were like interior designers' shade charts, full of the same swimmer in every colour imaginable. I think it was a Feed Shallow, which would explain their hesitance: twenty-five quid last time I looked.

I gave them a couple of soft plastics. They wanted to pay me, were dumbfounded when I told them they cost about a quid. We fished together for half an hour. They both lost fish – I think they were used to tightening too quickly – but they beached a couple as well. And that bay's become one of my regular stamping grounds, all because I eat my greens and I'll walk an extra half mile rather than pay for them.

Very Local Knowledge

'They march you to the table, you see the same old thing'
Leadbelly, *The Midnight Special*

Bass often feed in small and very specific areas. This isn't a strange idea for people my age. When we were little, people fed in very specific areas. You ate at the table. Now and again, in suitable weather, we were allowed tea and a snack in the garden, but that was a treat. Maybe that's why there was less childhood obesity back then. In the 1950s parents could keep track of their nippers' diet, we weren't demanding crisps and sweets at the supermarket checkout or vile burgers every time we drove past a junk food outlet. Of course we also used knives and forks, chewed with our mouths shut, and asked permission to leave the table. But that's another story, a curmudgeonly one.

With bass it isn't manners that confine them to their spots, it's the need for plenty of net energy: the calories they shovel down their throats adjusted for the ones they burn off by hunting their snacks. If you run ten miles to pick and eat a small punnet of blackberries you'll lose weight, the exercise will slim you down more than the berries bulk you up. But if you sprawl on your sofa, click through an online fried chicken place with free delivery, and scoff a value bucket of greasy drumsticks and chips, your next lounge suite's going to need extra large seats to accommodate your ever expanding arse. Bass, especially big bass, go for the sedentary option. They're inefficient converters of protein, that's why they grow slowly. Their systems can't afford a long energy-guzzling hike for a tiny nibble, they need big lumps of grub deposited in front of their noses. Right in front.

One summer morning I was pottering back from a lure outing at low water. In a stretch of flat, featureless terrain marked only by small round boulders – bum-crunchers, the sort that make it easy to tumble onto your bottom – I noticed two lumps of granite. They were the size of cows. Not monsters, small-to-medium cows, Jerseys or Belted Galloways. They lay at ninety degrees to one another, there were two or three feet between their heads, their tails were eight or nine feet apart. I made a mental note of the spot, this was a natural funnel.

A few days later I went back in the middle of the ebb. In the moonlight I spotted my cattle. Not Florence and her chum themselves, they were underwater, but there were swirls and eddies on the down-current side, where the flow was squeezed between them. In my imagination I could see baitfish being swished along in the tide race, flipping helpless as the narrowing channel pushed them around. I plopped a shallow diver into the stirred-up area and a bass grabbed hold before I'd started to retrieve. I had five, all from within a yard of the cows' noses. From the rest of the bay, not a chuffing wibble. No snacking on the fin, my bass were sitting at the table, their parents would have approved.

Another day, this time in October, I'd been chucking squid into a small surf in Mount's Bay when I saw a familiar figure on the sand. He's an elderly gent, easy to identify because he always turns out in a high visibility jacket, wellies, and shorts. Delivery drivers like short trousers because they're often caught in rain storms. You can dry wet legs with a wipe of a towel once you're back at the wheel. Soggy trousers, on the other hand, stay soggy, not to mention clammy and cold. But this old boy's retired and he used to work on cargo ships, I don't know what his excuse is. Maybe nostalgia for his days in the boy scouts. Maybe someone once told him he had good-looking legs. Or maybe he's just odd.

Anyway I noticed he was casting much shorter than usual, less than a cricket pitch, so I asked him what was on. 'The grandson's got all this diving gear, flippers and goggles and so forth. He went out right here and there's a hole in the sea bottom fifteen yards from the drain pipe. He reckons there was so much rain running off in the last storm that it kind of dredged it out. It's a fathom deeper than the surrounding area. Small, my robin, only about as big as a hay barn. But worth a try. The boy said it was full of dead crabs and stuff.' I chucked my gear out twenty yards, then inched it in until I could feel the weight start to trickle downhill and towards me. I don't think it even found bottom, a nine pounder snaffled it en route. Mister Short Trousers had one as well, but his was a schoolie. He always fishes sandeel, another grandson works for a company that flash freezes them, he gives grandfather the odds and ends. I shared my squid and we had two more good fish apiece, between five and seven pounds. But if you cast too far and missed the hole, not a twitch. Another sign that bass don't leave the table till they're excused.

Low Pressure, High Hopes

'I hear hurricanes a-blowing'
Creedence Clearwater Revival, *Bad Moon Rising*

I defy any self-respecting bass fisher to sleep through a hooting autumn gale. When leaves slap damply at the bedroom windows and the front door rattles in its frame I'm driven to roll out of the duvet, slurp a coffee, and head off in search of a whopper. One October the pull of the rising wave was so strong I couldn't fall asleep in the first place. Fair enough, my body clock was somewhere between west Cornwall and western Canada, but I could always take a nap after the sun was up and the bass were snoozing. And so to the shore.

I'd been away a while and the only bait in the deep freeze was razor clam and squid. Razor serves me best when the sea's been stirred up for a while, this was the start of the hoolie, so I thawed my squid in a bucket while the kettle boiled. In case Shelley should read this, let me be clear, the bucket was outside the back door, I didn't break my promise to keep bait out of the kitchen. Parking by the beach I was buttonholed by two policemen. The first young chap refused to believe I was going fishing. 'It's lashing rain, you're crazy.' His colleague was an angler, more understanding, 'A lovely surf building, tight lines my handsome, stay safe.'

I tackled up in the carpark. Normally I tie on my weight right at the water's edge where I can see the strength of the sea but even from afar this clearly was a day for a wired lead. Also for a securely-lashed bait, lots of elastic thread to keep the hooks in place in the boiling surf. Mindful of the second copper's advice I stood back from the margin to cast then turned my back on my gear and put up my hood.

After ten minutes I was beginning to wonder about checking my rig. In a proper howler a squid can do the eightsome reel, winding itself around the mainline or the spikes on the sinker. I tightened hard ready to pull my gear clear. Something tightened back, a hefty thump, then slack line. Two long runs and a nerve-wracking trip through the breakers and I had an nine and a half pound bass at my feet, a silly grin on my face. I tried to release her but she kept washing back onto the strand, and the undertow was too powerful for me to stand in the shallows and revive her. Anyway a friend had asked me for a whopper to serve at a Christmas lunch; so a biff on the head and into the bag. I didn't want to risk having to kill another, time to head home.

The policemen were still in the carpark as I loaded my fish into the boot. I don't think they're too busy just before dawn on a soaking wet October morning, maybe Cornwall only has fair weather criminals. 'Nice one my beauty,' said the angler of the pair, 'I told you he wasn't insane.' 'And you were wrong,' snorted his partner, 'he looks like a drowned rat, he's got a lump of seaweed hanging from his hat, and he's smiling. If that isn't insane, what is?' Sleeping through a big blow, that's insane. But I kept my mouth shut, just a conspirator's wink for his partner.

It's Crazy but it Just Might Work

'Fill my mind with tales of mystery'
Van Morrison, *Fair Play*

One of the great things about anglers is our diversity. I don't mean just that we come in all shapes, sizes, genders, ages, ethnicities, sexual orientations, religious persuasions, socio-economic classes, and so forth. We do, and that's terrific, the more the merrier. But chatting with a teenager, a Tunisian, or a Taoist may or may not give either of us any new ideas about how to have more bites. What produces fresh insights is when we pick the brains of people who cut their sporting teeth on different types of fish in different waters.

Some tricks are so odd that I've never been tempted to try them. In Southern Africa tilapia are supposed to go well to a piece of an alka seltzer tablet. You stick it to your hook with candle wax and let it fizz away in the water. The fish, they say, follow the trail of bubbles and chomp away at its source. Or maybe Zimbabwean tilapia suffer from hangovers and indigestion. Either way I can't imagine buying my bait from the pharmacy. A Spanish chap told me chicken skin's brilliant for sea bream. He didn't offer any advice about preparation, maybe garlic, thyme, and paprika, but again I don't think I'll take his tip. Besides, the skin's the tastiest bit of a chicken, I'd rather eat it myself.

Then there's an Iraqi friend whose cousin goes for carp and catfish. He flings hand grenades into his lakes, and he's a tackle tart. The grenades left behind by the British and American armies are best, he claims. Russian ordnance is unreliable, prone to explode in the boat. Another approach I don't fancy for Cornish waters.

More mainstream, and less likely to blow themselves up, are anglers from coarse fishing backgrounds. And the dodge they rave about is groundbait. Match fishers, carp hunters, bream fans, they chuck vast amounts of the stuff into their swims, and some have proprietary recipes they guard like military intelligence. Aniseed, garlic, ground-up dog biscuits, menthol oil, the so-called nutritionists and alternative medicine peddlers could decant a decent carp mixture into small bottles and flog it at a tenner a time to cure acne, halitosis, and bowel cancer. But please keep it under your hat or the feckless money-grubbing bastards will do just that.

I hardly see anyone using groundbait in the sea, the only routine exceptions being the people who target mullet and sharks. I wonder whether bass fishers might be missing out, but the evidence so far is skimpy. I met a chap on a surf beach using a swim feeder tied to his weight. It was a cage-like gadget about the size of the canisters we once used for camera film. His was stuffed with a mixture of bran and smashed up herring and he reckoned it leached out enough oil to attract bass to his hooks. I'm not so sure, I had twice as many bites as he did. We were using whole squid, a big one dribbles plenty of appetising juice into the wave by itself, especially if you change your bait every twenty minutes. And his gear was out of the water a good deal while he mucked about with herring mince and a teaspoon. Another lad was on a rock mark, he had an old pillow case full of mackerel frames. His theory was that the scent would attract baitfish, then bass would pile in. Again I'm not sold, he had a pollack, I managed three schoolies. But on the credit side he hauled up his chum bag to find a large edible crab clinging on like grim death. I hope it later had a less than grim death. I'm told you put must them in a pan of cold water and bring it to the boil slowly, that way they feel no pain.

Only once have I come close to seeing a real result from groundbait. It was early autumn, breezy, and the mackerel were still around. For a week I fished the same mark every morning. My car was having one of its moody spells, the starter motor was misbehaving, so I stuck to a beach where the carpark's on a slope. That way if the engine wouldn't fire on the key I could roll downhill and do a jump-start. I picked a spot on the sand, marked by a big conifer, and stuck with it. At the end of every session I took my unused joeys and the remains of the ones that had been chewed up, then buried them nine inches deep at the water's edge. Next time the tide flooded, I reckoned, a pop-up bass café would open; and with any luck I'd be casting into a queue of whoppers waiting for tables. The results of my study: I had a good week; my catches improved as the days went by; and on the three days when other anglers showed up, my pine tree area produced more fish than their random spots. Hardly proof that my buried treasure was doing the job, but definitely interesting. If I were an academic I'd conclude 'Further research is indicated' which means 'I need more grant money'. As a bass fisher I'd say it's worth trying again. Certainly a better bet than alka seltzer, chicken skin, or hand grenades.

The Ragworms of Human Kindness

'I can't do it all by myself'
Buddy Guy & Junior Wells, *Help Me*

To catch bass you have to be willing to change your mind. You may think you picked the ideal lure for the conditions, but if it doesn't do the job, try another. The water can look perfect, if there's nothing happening, take up your rod and walk to a different spot. The only time I like to stick with Plan A is the very start of an outing. Too often I've woken up, looked at the weather, decided to fish a beach in Mount's Bay, then had second thoughts. The breeze isn't fresh enough, it'll be too flat, better off driving to the north coast instead. Whenever I go through this palaver I end up peeved. Because on the way home I stop for a quick look at my south-facing beach and the wave's perfect. Even if I had a good session up north I'm cross: I wasted forty minutes in the car when I could have been fishing.

It's the same mind-changer's remorse – expect an academic paper in a psychology journal any day – that kicks in when the specials board in the pub has too many things you fancy. You plump for the squid, but as the waiter starts writing you switch to the crab cakes. Then your order arrives. The crab cakes are tasty, but they're tiny, and the only other thing on your plate's a salad garnish Peter Rabbit would eat in one bite. Meanwhile your dining companion's served a Matterhorn of calamari dribbling with garlic and chillies, a fistful of tomatoes, and a whopping chunk of crusty bread to mop up the juice. So at the table or on the fishing mark I try to stick with my first decision. It may turn out to be wrong, but at least I won't torture myself with what might have been if only I hadn't dithered so.

One July morning I was on a long Mount's Bay beach to fish the bottom of the tide. The mackerel were running so I'd thawed a packet of babies overnight and grabbed a few squid as my just-in-case substitute. There was a headlamp on the strand, that persuaded me to hoof it to the end. Then I looked into my bag for a juicy joey. The wretched thing was full of dead batteries. I keep them in the car until I'm going to the tip anyway so I can put them in the special bin. And they, like my mackies, were in an orange supermarket bag. The rewards of trying to take care of the environment, now I was looking at a two mile long schlep to fetch the right bag. It was hardly going to be worth fishing at all. Half way to the carpark I stopped for a yarn with the chap with the headlamp. He also seemed to have a hover-pack, the man was walking on air. He was on holiday, trying for as many types of flatfish as he could. And he'd had a brilliant night, a plaice, a flounder, a dab, and a sole. 'And now,' he grinned, 'back to the caravan for a short course in death. D'you want my spare bait? I've got a fresh order coming in tomorrow. Today, I mean.'

Plaice

I knew I'd be more confident with a juicy mackerel on the end of my line, mackerel was what I'd set out to fish, and first thoughts so often are best thoughts. On the other hand I wouldn't catch much if I spent the whole session marching up and down the beach and muttering darkly about why bloody fool supermarkets make their bags from opaque plastic for crying out loud. So I thanked him, tied on a 4/0, and nipped half a dozen ragworms through their heads. I dunked them in the shallows to toughen them up, they looked like a brittle starfish in a disco. Out they went into the froth. My flattie-man had barely left when my rod lurched towards the wave. A five pound bass, followed by a three pounder for supper. And the mackerel didn't go to waste, the cat had them for breakfast.

A Healthy Diet

'Eat your pork and beans'
Howlin' Wolf, *Back Door Man*

A lot of tasty foods are bad for us. Bacon, clotted cream, cheeseburgers, Yorkshire pudding cooked in beef dripping (and if you don't use dripping you might as well not bother at all). So it's a delight to find something delicious and learn that the medical profession says we should eat it as often as possible. And by the way, when I say 'medical profession' I mean doctors and academics who rely on verifiable data and run replicable trials. When so-called nutritionists provide dietary advice in irresponsibly rubbishy newspapers, most of it involving wild claims about the benefits of inert supplements, I take them just a little less seriously than the joker who writes the horoscope page. You can't cure skin cancer with guava juice and the droppings of Indonesian fruit bats, telling people you can keeps them from seeing their GPs, the people who actually might be able to help. And don't get me started on the iniquitous bollix the tabloids spewed out about the MMR jab.

What I loathe about people who flog bogus therapies is their cynicism. To make a dishonest living they, and the tabloid hacks who promote them, are happy to peddle useless shite to the vulnerable, the desperate, and the dying. A good friend spent a fortune on homeopathic and alternative supplements as he struggled with a painful and incurable illness. He'd have been better off with aspirin and whisky, but the bastard who supplied him with little bottles of tap water and spices from the supermarket laughed all the way to the bank.

But back to healthy treats, and one of my favourites is the humble pilchard, peddled these days as the much more self-assured Cornish sardine. They have to be properly fresh, I always cook them the day I catch them. But as long as they are, all they need is scaling, gutting, a wipe with some oil and garlic, a sprinkle of salt, and a few chopped chillies if you're that way inclined. Then two or three minutes cooking on each side, on a blazing barbeque or under a dangerously hot grill, and you're in for a treat.

On my patch they show up in late autumn, so a calm November morning found me on a local pier an hour before first light. I fished a string of mini-sabikis with a jig to carry them out into the depths, and it didn't take long to find the little beauties, five into the bag. They weren't very big, I needed one more, three apiece would make a satisfying meal. Maybe that makes us gannets, who cares, oily fish are good for your heart, brain, and bones; and they're delicious, they do wonders for your mood as well. Another cast, but this produced three, one on each lure. So two in the fridge just in case a beach fishing wave should pick up. It did. By evening the wind was walloping in off the Atlantic, rain slapping at the kitchen window as we sat down to our fish supper. And at four-thirty next morning I lobbed one of the leftovers into a boiling surf.

Then a regular showed up, a pleasant chap and a good bass fisher to boot. He was on razor and a blank. 'Maybe that bit too soon,' I guessed. 'I like razor when it's been howling for a couple of days, it seems to take a while for the wave to wash them out of the sand.' 'What are you using?' 'Pilchard.' He's local, I'd no more talk to him about a Cornish sardine than offer him a lamb and mint pasty or suggest putting the cream on your split before the jam. 'Interesting,' he said, 'I've tried them, never any good.' At which point my lead broke free and I backed away up the beach to tighten. A lovely fat bass between six and seven pounds. She'd chewed up my bait, but she spat up another one in pristine nick. I grabbed it, gave my chum the one from my pocket, and we each had a five pounder. Bass are healthy eaters too. And even if they're not, how would you make a full English breakfast or a Yorkshire pudding stay on the hook?

Unfair Weather

'Pressure going to drop on you'
Toots & The Maytals, *Pressure Drop*

My brother Mick and I used to work with a water-keeper in the north of Scotland. If we had a few sunny days the old boy would shove his hands in his pockets and grunt, 'Terrible weather for folk'. Pause while he lit a ciggie. 'Nice for the tourists, mind.' Although I'm clear our holiday visitors are human beings with all the rights and obligations associated with the species, I know exactly what he meant. His was a spate river, the salmon ran only when it rained. I'm a bass fisher, we like an onshore blow to stir things up.

You can't always get what you want – sing along if you must – and once in a blue moon the far south-west of the UK lives up to the billing given to it by the Victorian spin doctors of Great Western Railways: the English Riviera. In general our palm trees look as if they're wondering what moron planted us here as they bow apologetically before westerly gales, their bark shredded by hailstones. But most summers we have a few weeks when they seem to belong in Cornwall, light airs wafting through their fronds under balmy sunshine. Of course if you're planning a bucket and spade getaway you never know which weeks those will be. And the same's true in reverse if you come to the far west for some bass.

There's a reason anglers like a good blow, it's not just that we take perverse delight in watching canvas windbreaks cartwheeling across beaches or sunbathers cowering in swimsuits, woolly jumpers, fleeces, and cagoules. Waves bring bass close to the shore. They batter baitfish against the rocks, making them easy prey; and they drag worms, crabs, squid, shellfish, mackerel, and pilchards into the shallows on our beaches. When the sea's calm it's harder to know when, where, and how to find our silvery friends. I meet people who think it's impossible. It isn't, not as long as you make some adjustments.

First let's look at when – and in still conditions you have to channel your inner vampire. Well, you don't need to spend the daylight hours in a coffin, but I wouldn't waste them on the rocks. Bait fishers are nocturnal anyway as a rule, but lure and fly enthusiasts often work the day-shift. When the sea's like a mirror I reckon they're up against it. Ruffled water makes bass feel well hidden and secure in the shallows but when the surface is glassy they venture inshore mostly under cover of darkness.

Next, if there's no surf, I look for something else to concentrate bass treats. One option is current. Long beaches and open coves can be swept by cross-flows, especially in the middle of the tide. Estuaries, narrow bays, and harbour mouths sometimes swirl appetisingly on the ebb. And wherever the water's on the move there are spots where bits and bobs accumulate. Some bits are tedious – weed and rubbish – but some bobs are bass magnets. Rivers carry fry and prawns downstream to the sea, and fishing ports have all sorts of edible leftovers sluiced from boat decks. I'm not impressed when commercial crews drop bits of netting and plastic rope into the briny, but heads and guts are fine by me.

Another possible buffet area for predators and scavengers is something that sticks out into the current and prevents tiddlers from escaping. If you want to meet people at a function, the best place to loiter is beside the bar.

A wall or an obstruction works the same way for bass. I've watched them herding shoals of fry along a pier in summer, clobbering them when they could escape only by swimming through granite and concrete. In spring I've seen them bashing mullet up against a steep shingle beach. And I've caught more than a few good fish on strands where a spit pokes out into the sea and traps stuff as it drifts along the shoreline.

Lastly, I try to compensate for the stillness of the water by being a bit stealthy, and by injecting extra motion into my lure or bait. I'm never a wader, but if it's calm I stay back from the water's edge, ten yards or so. And when I'm on the rocks with my fly rod or my spinning gear I scurry about like one of those nitwits who barrel along with their eyes glued to their telephones – then seem surprised you're not delighted when they run into you. Five or six casts, that's all before I bunk down the shore and try somewhere else. On beaches I use a lead small enough to have my gear trundle around in whatever current I can find. My standard surf kit includes bomb weights in all sizes from one to four ounces; and if even the lightest sinker doesn't budge, I nip it off and freeline my bait.

One August we had two weeks of what the Met Office was calling barbeque weather, and I was itching for a change. I love a charcoal-cooked burger, mackerel, or chicken thigh, but that wasn't enough to make up for the slow fishing. One morning I took my spinning rod to a nearby pier. In an hour I had enough mackerel for hot smoking, so I took off my feathers and tried with little sabikis. Three giant launce, more like snakes than sandeels, the biggest was sixteen inches long. It may show how sad I am that I measured it. I made up a couple of rigs, short shank 4/0 Aberdeens separated by a foot of mono.

At three thirty next morning I was on a long beach for the middle of the ebb. A mile from the carpark there's a finger of boulders running out from the sand. It's a spot that's done me well over the years, and I always have it to myself, nobody else fancies shuffling that far in waders. I stayed back from the water, put on one of my eels, and freelined it in the ripple. The tide was pulling, in a few minutes my line was at thirty degrees to the shore and my gear wasn't far from running aground. As I started to reel in, the rod hooped over and an eight pound bass took off for the depths. She'd swallowed the hooks so she had to go in the bag. I had another between three and four, safely released. Then my last eel was chewed up by a weever. As I arrived at my car a chap with a four-wheel-drive BMW full of tackle gave me a nose-in-the-air look and a few words of advice: 'Wasting your time in these crap conditions. You'd never do any good with a rubbish outfit like that anyway. And where's your flaming weight, for heaven's sake? Don't you have any idea at all about fishing?' I didn't bother trying to change his mind, some people are beyond enlightenment, not to mention bloody rude. I just nodded and set an eight pound bass in the boot, with an unnecessary flourish I have to admit. 'How on earth did you catch that?' spluttered Mr. BMW. 'Crap conditions, rubbish outfit, no weight, some sort of idea about fishing. You should give it a try,' I said as I drove off. I was ready for breakfast.

Speaking of food, I mentioned smoked mackerel. I'm not sure how to do them on a gas barbeque, I'm an old-school pyromaniac, strictly charcoal, but I'm sure you could work it out. You need to fillet your fish, but don't bother with the pin-bones, they're easier to remove after cooking. Make a brine with two parts sugar to one part salt, as much as you can dissolve in a pint of boiling water. Chuck in garlic and herbs to taste. Then add enough ice cubes to cool the brew. Soak your fillets in the brine for an hour and a half. Make a small fire, six handfuls of charcoal, and push it to one side of the grill. Cover the grid with foil, otherwise you lose the odd portion between the railings and local children learn new vocabulary. Pat the fish dry, then spread them out on the opposite side from the fire. Lob in some smoke chips, put the lid on the barbeque, and cook for an hour, adding more chips once or twice. If you want to go all Masterchef, mix chopped chillies with maple syrup and lime juice and drizzle this stuff over your fish ten minutes before they're done. Once the fillets are cool you can tweak out the pin-bones if you like, and dinner is served.

A Sign

'Better think of your future'
The Specials, *A Message To You, Rudy*

I'm a devout atheist. Working with refugees I find myself shoulder to shoulder with good people of all faiths and I'm delighted I do. Worship whatever you like. If it inspires you to peel potatoes, rattle a moneybox, or collect sleeping bags, that's wonderful; and next time you say your prayers please tell your god I send my thanks to him or her for all your effort. The only time I'm bemused is when someone refuses to accept that I behave the way I do without believing in a higher power. That strikes me as bleak:

you don't have to long for heaven or fear hell to want to live without being a scoundrel. And not going to church, mosque, or temple gives me more time for my charity stuff. And for fishing of course.

One summer's morning I was on the closest beach to our house. It sits at the foot of the village, if it's still you hear the clock bell of the church where my grandfather was vicar in the 1920s. I hadn't planned my outing, I just woke early and decided to go for a wander with a rod in my hand and a packet of frozen sandeels in my pocket. Eels aren't a favourite bait, there's a fair amount of faffing involved in mounting them, and then often all my hard work is undone by baby schoolies. And looking at the wave I thought they'd be a bit small. It was a five foot surf, plenty of suspended sand, I'd have been happier with something fat and juicy, a big aromatic lump sending its scent far and wide in the stirred up water. But needs must when there's not much in the freezer.

As I walked down the strand I saw a baulk of timber. When I was a child people collected their firewood from the shore. If you found a bit that was too heavy you put a pebble on top and came back with a friend. Once your plank was marked nobody would think of picking it up. Nowadays our fuel's delivered by a tree surgeon, it's his patients that didn't make it. So it was just curiosity that had me grab the end of the beam. The underside was alive with crabs, three to four inch shells. I stuffed a couple in my bag, then a few more. Bait's addictive, I remember digging worms as a child and finding it so exciting that I hardly cared to stop and go to the river. But I resisted the temptation to fritter away my morning grubbing through weed and wood. Down to the water. I tied on a 4/0 and mounted my bait the way we used to do it for blackfish in New York: poke the hook point into a leg socket, out of another one, job done. When the shell's hard you don't need elastic thread, especially if you're not going to cast too far.

In ninety minutes I had seven bass between three and five pounds. For summertime that was an amazing result. I kept one and dropped it off at a friend's house. She asked how I caught it. I don't think she was interested, I'd say she was thanking me for her supper by giving me the chance to burble on while she at least pretended to listen. But when I told her about the crabs there was an intake of breath. 'Wow,' she said, 'that was a sign.' She's a spiritual woman, I reckon she was thinking of divine intervention. But I agree, it was a sign: a sign that the surf was crawling with crabs, and bass eat anything that's plentiful and nourishing.

The Colour Purple

'Purple haze, all in my brain'
Jimi Hendrix, *Purple Haze*

Much in life can't be predicted. Almost as much, after it's happened, seems as if it can be explained. And often the explanation's bollix. Investment gurus for example. On Monday they tell their clients to buy bonds. On Tuesday they tell the same clients bonds fell because, without warning, employment rose in the thermal sock sector and the head of the central bank wore a tartan tie. Yogi Berra, the American baseball coach, said, 'It's tough to make predictions, especially about the future.' Niels Bohr, the Danish physicist, said the same. And these financial fortune tellers would have to agree, all they can predict is the past. But real mysteries are opaque beforehand, just as unfathomable looking back. Like bass. What'll they do? No idea. Why did they behave like that? No idea. And that's why they're such a challenge and so much fun.

One calm July morning I was wandering along a rocky stretch of the shore with a rod in my hand and no notion what to try next. I'd gone through my boxes, lures and flies to suggest sandeels, whitebait, jelly-fry, prawns, small mackerel, everything short of a bramble crumble. Not a sniff. And it was two months to blackberry season anyway. I ran into a local chap I know, he had the same sad tale to tell.

As we were chatting philosophically about how you can't win them all and at least it wasn't lashing down rain, a boy scrambled onto the nearest outcrop. And two minutes later his rod was bouncing in bass mode. Not a whopper, but he landed a two pounder. Two or three casts later he repeated the dose, so we went for a closer look. He was about thirteen, he'd never fished in the sea before, but he thought it would be a bit like going for pike at home. The tackle shop had sold him a few plugs from the bargain bucket. The one he was using was a skinny shallow diver in a colour scheme best described as grape jelly and gorgonzola, lurid purple with white and blue-green flecks. It looked like nothing you'd imagine in the natural world unless you were a colour blind acid head with a migraine.

The youngster asked how we were doing. Shamefacedly we owned up: blanking. 'Maybe your lures are wrong. You can use one of mine if you like. The geezer in the shop said they had great action in the water, just that nobody liked the finish. They'll be good for zander anyway.' He dug out a box: two more of the purple jobs, three in saffron and dog turd livery. 'Just that if you lose them you've got to give me £1.99 so I can replace them.' Safety first, we both opted for synthetic grape and blue cheese. And the three of us caught bass after bass. We tried the yellow and brown version, it was useless. We went back to our more conventional lures, they were the same. But a small purple stick wiggling through the ripple was dynamite. I'd never have expected it, and I'll never know why.

Evidence-based Bass

'How can he really expect to be happy?'
Withered Hand, *Religious Songs*

They say that if you open your mind too much your brain falls out. I'm inclined to agree, especially when I take one of my rare looks at Facebook or Twitter, where gullible oafs repeat as gospel truth rumours that were started by primary school pranksters, crazed conspiracy theorists, or – least credible of all – tabloid journalists who claim to write about health and medicine. But I'm just as leery of people whose minds are closed. They stick to their opinions come hell or high levels of improbability, even in the face of clear evidence. They might as well say, 'I know what I'm going to do, so don't confuse me with the facts'. It's an attitude you see in a lot of senior business types. 'Leadership means taking decisions,' they announce proudly. True, but decent leadership means taking decisions after taking the time and trouble to find out what's going on.

Anglers often overcommit to their views, and a lot of them do it unconsciously. Or maybe they fall in love. Either way they pick an approach and stick to it, even when the data show they're barking up the wrong tree in the wrong forest on the wrong bloody continent. Take the holidaymaker I ran into in a shallow bay early one August morning. There was a light chop on the water and I could see little disturbances here and there. They looked like whitebait: I'm not sure quite what they do, it may be a flick of the tail, but they make a splash that's all their own. To bolster my judgment there were a few dead whitebait tangled in the weed on the high tide line. Now I don't suppose it makes a world of difference what lure you fish when the bass are scoffing two inch tiddlers, but the two inch bit's important.

Bass

Use something the right size and I have takes galore, go with something huge or tiny and it's not a chuffing wibble. I like a small Toby. It's easy to cast, it's cheap enough that I'm happy to fish it through snags, and as long as I replace the treble hook with a big single it makes for easy releases. So I was lobbing away with my spoon, two or three bass to my name, when the visitor came and asked what was the secret. I tend to be longwinded about fish – ask my wife – but not this time: 'The water's full of whitebait about 50 millimetres long. This is what I'm using, but I reckon a little shad or plug would be fine too.' 'Interesting,' he peered suspiciously at my Toby, 'but I'm going to stick to what I know works. Patchinko 125, the best lure I've ever run into.'

After an hour and three more bass I was ready to head home. On the way back to the car I ran into 125-man again, he was on a blank. I tried to be tactful. Nothing like, 'Of course you're blanking, you're fishing something two and a half times as big as what they're eating, it's like serving up a thirty inch pasty or an eight egg omelette.' I offered him a Toby but he was having none of it. 'I'm going to order some new lures,' he said. 'I love the Patch with the yellow back, but I reckon the semi-transparent one might be what I need down here.' I wanted to say, 'Go for fully transparent, then they won't see how bloody enormous it is', but I managed, 'Is there a small version, a Patchinko-mini or something? I suppose that might be worth a go.'

Then there was an October outing, proper autumn weather, mists, mellow fruitfulness, and a thirty knot onshore breeze with the odd horizontal shower. I'd been mackerel fishing in a calm sea the day before and I'd taken home a dozen joeys as well as a few better ones. I don't know why for sure, but when the little mackies show up, the big bass often follow them right up to the shoreline and tuck in like fat seagulls behind a trawler. Maybe the babies slip through the ring-netters' mesh, a fair few of them damaged and dying. Or maybe whole shoals come inshore but only the bigger, stronger fish can deal with the waves, the smaller ones washing into the shallows. Either way fresh joeys produced two bass in three casts. Then I saw a pair of headlamps coming my way. They were a few yards away when my third fish took, somewhere between eight pounds and nine. 'Beauty,' said one of the lads, 'are you on peeler?' 'No, mackerel close in. I've got some to spare if you want to give one a try?' 'But there's nothing to beat peeler,' said his pal, 'bass go crazy for peeler, totally bloody crazy. We brought thirty quids' worth down from Sussex.' An hour later I'd had two more chunky fish, the better an eleven pounder according to my tape measure. The young chaps had managed a schoolie between them. 'Listen,' I said, 'I'm going home now, you really might as well have my leftover bait, it's no use to me.' No thanks, it wasn't nearly as good as crab, crab was like crack cocaine for bass. So I filleted the surplus joeys and the cat had a treat while I ate two eggs on fried bread.

Can you be too open-minded? For sure. Too committed? For sure, most obviously when you see concrete data that tell you what's working, and you squeeze your eyes shut.

Please Give Your Reasons

'I don't understand this bit at all'
The Sex Pistols, *Holidays In The Sun*

As a species we love explanations and we show absurd levels of respect to people who provide them. Our forefathers sucked up to jokers who claimed to understand that spring or the Nile flood came only because the community built massive useless structures and gave all the best food and clothing to high priests, chieftains, and other kleptocrats. These days we pay whopping salaries to self-styled experts who tell us what's going to happen; and when their forecasts turn out to be bollix offer plausible excuses for being wrong. Television sports pundits for example, before the game they'll assure you Barcelona are bound to win, afterwards they'll offer a litany of reasons they lost: the pitch was sticky, the half time drinks were too sweet, and the goalkeeper was unsighted by a flock of pigeons released by their opponent's supporters. Investment analysts are cut from similar cloth, just flashier togs, longer words, and worse grammar.

Anglers aren't immune either. And like the overpaid wafflers on *Match of the Day* or *Bloomberg News* we're more thorough about failure than success. A great outing's easily explained: I fished like a champ, and that new plug's brilliant. A blank takes more creativity: there was too much rainwater run-off in the surf, my fishing companion kept distracting me by singing Leonard Cohen songs in the wrong key, and it's always tough when there's a rising moon in Leo and a pompous prat in Ten Downing Street. In fact it's really hard to explain triumph or disaster. Experience is the best guide we have, but it's unreliable. Years by the water tell us a seven inch shallow diver with a silvery blue finish does a good job when the joey mackerel are about, but those years can't say why that plug produced three good bass on Monday, one emaciated pollack baby on Tuesday. And sometimes we're completely clueless.

One May morning I fished my way along a run of weedy coves and bays. A week previously I'd seen shoal after shoal of finger mullet, so I started with a black-backed shallow diver. Not a touch. Maybe they were in the really shallow stuff, a dozen casts with a weedless soft plastic in the same livery. Also useless. I'd been on the pier recently, some fat early mackerel on size six sabikis that suggest baby jelly-fry. So I tried a small streamer fly on a dropper. Not a chuffing wibble. By now the dawn was breaking and I could see bass swirling all over the shop. They were small, but they were bass. I sat on a boulder and watched them charging through the ripple. Then another angler showed up, his name was Mark and I think he was from Sussex. But it might have been Surrey or Suffolk, down in the far west we see anything east of Helston as an undifferentiated jumble. Anyway Mark was on a blank too. He was a proper job bass junkie, two enormous boxes of plugs, shads, and softies. He'd tried almost everything he owned, the schoolies weren't even following or taking short, just ignoring his lures the way sensible people ignore headlines about the life-threatening properties of brown ale and Cumberland sausages. But we kept at it, not so much fishing the water as trying to flog it into submission.

Finally I clipped on a twenty gramme Toby, silver and white. It's my favourite when the whitebait are in so it was a long shot. A real long shot, about as likely as the Derby being won by an armadillo ridden by a meerkat, I don't expect to see whitebait until June at the earliest. But I slung it out and started cranking. Twenty feet from my boots it vanished into a slurping boil and I was playing a small bass. 'What did it hit?' shouted Mark. I told him and he rummaged in his bag. 'I've got a Toby here, a copper one.' But still no interest. I beached another schoolie then I shuffled over and gave him my spare silver and white job. We must have caught ten between us. I was tempted to keep one just so I could gut it and inspect its stomach contents, but they weren't big enough to be worth eating. So what on earth was going on? They'd only hit the whitebait coloured spoon, I can't think they were just snapping at something because it was moving fast near the top, Mark's coppery one did that, and they ignored it. Why? If I earned a seven figure salary for talking tosh about the Champions League or the bond market I'm sure I could come up with an explanation. But I don't, and I've no idea.

Muddling Through

'They took all the trees'
Joni Mitchell, *Big Yellow Taxi*

I love my fly fishing. Some people take their dogs for walks in sites of natural beauty, I take a light rod. No rucksack, just a couple of fly boxes and some monofilament in my pocket, off I go. And while the folk with pooches come back with plastic bags of poo – as long as they're not part of that scummy subpopulation that leaves neatly wrapped turds hanging from the hedges like foul Christmas ornaments – I come home with supper. I once focused my fly fishing on members of the trout family: brownies, rainbows, seatrout, the odd try for salmon. One September morning I headed to a local reservoir just before the dawn. If the breeze picked up there ought to be daddy longlegs (maybe daddies longlegs) all over the water, if it stayed still the trout had been bashing rudd fry of late. So it was with a glad heart that I wandered down to the water.

Five minutes later I was back in the carpark, my line still dry, muttering darkly about the bailiff. Over the winter he'd hacked down a fair few trees along the bank. I'd reasoned with him, warned this would destroy our fly life and let fertiliser and slurry run straight into the water, but he was as unyielding as a VAT inspector after an assertiveness training session. And now the inevitable had come to pass, a spell of warm weather, a few heavy showers, and the lake was full of shite from the fields around. The whole reservoir looked like a giant bowl of split pea soup and smelled like the wheelie bin outside a vegetarian restaurant with terrible hygiene. I drove off, I didn't even care to wait around for the bailiff to show up. There can be a certain satisfaction in saying 'I told you so' but not when you've lost a favourite fishing spot.

Nobody should arrive home in a filthy mood and a cloud of filthier language so on the way back I stopped for a look at a shallow sea pool. Mullet mavens sometimes set up camp beside it, ladling their browse into the water like the witches in a Cornish Macbeth: 'Eye of scad and pilchard scale, loaf of bread and garfish tail.' Thick-lips go well to the fly and they pull like stink, a buzzing reel might help me over the disappointment of losing my trouting.

The tide was half and ebbing so I had to cross two streamlets to reach the main channel. They were twenty feet wide, twelve inches deep in their gullies, but I waded as slowly as a nervous heron in case of soft patches in the sand. And then I saw a solid grey shape in the water. It was flicking its tail like a trout holding station in a riffle. But this wasn't a trout, not jerky enough. And it wasn't a mullet, too static. It was a half decent bass. I nipped off the shrimpy nymph on my leader and rummaged in my pocket for a fly box. Something to suggest a fry or a tiny sandeel, pale and flashy. I tied on a size six muddler minnow, white head and wing, silver body. I cast downstream dropping the fly a few feet in front of the bass. Next cast, I thought, I'll put it a bit closer. There was no next cast. I twitched my line and saw a swirl and a puff of sand where the bass had been, then came a thumping take. The fish ran, the reel sang, and if I could carry a tune I'd have joined it. After five minutes or so I beached a three pounder. I had two smaller bass from the little hollows in the sand, then the ebbing tide emptied them completely. The main channel was as dead as slow cooked mutton, nothing but drifting weed and supermarket carrier bags for my trouble. So home to fillet my bass.

Next morning the tide was forty minutes later, I fished two hours of the drop. I had three schoolies followed by a properly solid fish. On her second run she took off across the stream, misjudged her turn like a racing driver on a surface of greased eels, and grounded on the opposite bank. She went six and a quarter pounds, easily my best ever bass to the fly. Stuff the green slime at the lake, this was fun. But I still wish we could have our trees back.

Fluff and Stuff

I'd never describe myself as a saltwater fly fisherman, more of an occasional bodger. I use a trout outfit that casts a number seven weight forward line. The rod's seen better days and that's the way I like it. Some of my favourite coves call for rock scrambling and I'm a clumsy buffer with creaking knees. It hacks me off when I take a tumble and bruise my bottom, I'd be hopping bloody mad if I smashed up a brand new carbon fibre blank as well.

Mostly I use the fly for bass when it's so rough I can fish only in the shelter of a sea pool, when it's so flat that even a tiny soft plastic lure looks crude and obvious, or when I feel like a change of pace. But I'm glad I have the option. One of my finance professors started every class by having us chant 'Adding a degree of freedom can never diminish total utility'. Translated from Pompous-Bollix, the official language of economists, he was saying it's great to have a trick up your sleeve even if you play it only now and again.

One early June was windless and clear. The coves were speckled with jelly fry about an inch long, I'd been catching bass on a little shiny fly on a dropper in front of a spoon. So why not leave the spinning rod at home, shove a fly box in my pocket, and go for a wander? I'd turned two or three fish loose when I noticed a figure along the shore. He was belly button deep out from the beach, I paused to watch.

Some people realise they're not athletic so they don't try to cast long, just enough to get by. I count myself among them. Some use their size and strength to bully their fly into the next parish. Watch them in action and you hope their partners are massage therapists and they have cupboards full of painkillers. And some seem to be standing still, working as hard as a tree sloth at nap time while a whole fly line snakes across the water. This fellow was one of them, steady stance, tight loop, effortless grace. But no fish. After a while he came ashore. Anglers always eye up one another's gear, it's like dogs with their bottom sniffing. His rod was beefy, a nine or ten weight, his line looked like a fast sinker. I could see him registering my trout outfit, the blank coated with scales, the line smeared with goop. But he was too polite to comment, he just asked if I was doing any good. 'A few back there in the shallow stuff, they're hitting the tiny fry.' He'd looked at that water the evening before, he'd thought it not deep enough. 'See I had a guided boat outing last year, mostly you wanted the fly five or six feet down. And those coves are eighteen inches deep. But maybe I should switch to a floater and give it a go. I'll tie some flies and come back tomorrow.'

I offered him one of mine, it's a pattern I call the whatever-comes-to-hand-and-silver-muddler and it does what it says on the tin. But bass can be particular about size and shape, much less so about colour. I could see my new pal frowning as he swapped spools, then tied it on; but again he was too well mannered to ask whether this ragbag of deer hair and tinsel really delivered. It did, we each had three or four fish before the ebbing tide emptied the cove and we wandered up to the carpark.

Next morning I had a mooch in a different bay. At the end of my session I noticed an envelope on my windscreen. Two beautifully tied fry patterns with a note that read, 'I know yours do the job but I'm one of those sad gits who washes his line after every session and rearranges his fly box twice a week. Thanks for your help and tight lines.' One of his flies caught me a three pounder. You run into the best people when you're fishing.

Right First Time but not Every Time

'You won't have to think at all'
Van Morrison, *Cry For Home*

When it comes to bass I'm obsessive about being willing to change your mind. If there's nothing doing, try a different lure or bait, cast longer or shorter, go for a stank along the shore and find another spot. One of my favourite quotes is from Albert Einstein: 'The definition of insanity is doing the same thing over and over and expecting different results.' But in everyday language we celebrate people who stick to their guns, they show grit, determination, stamina, decisiveness, and the courage of their convictions. They're more worthy than the flip-floppers and U-turners who can't make their minds up. We seem to admire the bloody fool who never owns up to being wrong, to despise the thinker who looks at the evidence and follows where it leads. That might have something to do with the abject shower of shite we elect as political leaders.

And anglers wade into the same trap. Look at a catch report where someone's landed a trophy, half the comments are about how much you deserve it for putting in the hours. Stuff and nonsense. Blanking for yonks because you had the wrong bait in the wrong spot at the wrong time of day doesn't mean the sea owes you a whopper. Bass have never heard of karmic debt, they just eat; and you deserve your fish when you work out what they're eating and where. That can call for trial and error. So you might wonder if I ever go to the shore with a plan A and have a good session without diving deeper into the alphabet. And yes I do, thank you for asking. Now and again I hit the nail on the head without first bending it flat and bashing my thumb with the hammer.

For instance one July we had a couple of weeks of bucket-and-spade weather, warm with a light onshore breeze. High summer's not the best time for big bass. I don't know where they go, I just know where they aren't. I find the holiday season trying myself, the roads are jammed with caravans, drivers are prone to sudden turns across the traffic when someone in the back seat spots a sign that says 'Cornish Ice Cream, all you can eat', and there are queues at the pasty shops. Maybe it's the same at sea, the whoppers are fed up with being stuck in traffic as styrofoam surfboards bump into air mattresses and boy-racers on jet-skis make the whole ocean sound like a demolition derby in an earthquake.

Anyway there were plenty of mackerel about so I spent an hour on the pier, six for smoking, two bags to freeze, a few in the fridge, and four for supper. Two each may make us piglets, but we like mackerel, especially with new potatoes and kale from the garden. As I was walking back to the car I met half a dozen youngsters with spinning rods. Enterprising nippers, they were going to fillet their fish and flog pan-ready meals to holidaymakers. At which the cogwheels in my mind whirred. Slowly perhaps, oily fish is good for the brain and we hadn't eaten ours yet. But still they whirred. Through the day and into the evening these boys and girls were going to chuck dozens and dozens of frames off the jetty, this was a groundbaiting operation on a massive scale. The tide was still ebbing and I tried to work out where on the nearby beach a mackerel head would wash in. I spotted a clump of weed and watched it drifting along. Extending its course gave me my landing zone.

At three o'clock next morning I was scuttling across the sand, looking for the big white rock that marked the spot. There was no surf, just a ripple, so I tied half of a decent sized mackerel to a pair of 4/0s and lobbed it out with no weight. Then I started twitching it in a foot at a time, letting it sit a couple of minutes before repeating the prescription. When my bait was twenty feet from the water's edge the line went slack. I tightened and a four pound bass thumped emphatically. My second fish was a five pounder, my third was just under eleven according to the BASS length converter. My last was a perfect size to make a meal for two, about three pounds. Hey, I've already admitted we're piglets when it comes to fish.

Cover of Darkness

'Three a.m., I'm awakened'
Jim White & Aimee Mann, *Static On The Radio*

I believe bass feed most actively in the hours just before sunrise. Fishing on a bright summer's day fills me with as much confidence as the number eleven in the village cricket team would feel heading out into the middle to face Wes Hall or Joel Garner. Although a late evening outing can work the oracle I reckon the fish eat through the night in the leisurely style of nibblers in a tapas bar, or party guests who didn't expect there to be canapés and stopped off at the chipper on the way. But when the first hint of dawn's about to creep into the eastern sky, that's when instinct tells them the kitchen's going to shut soon, dig in now, a value meal portion of worms or squid before the buffet closes for another day.

Like a lot of anglers I'm an obsessive student of the weather forecast as well. Some people are online stalkers of celebrities, tracking their every word and poring over their photos. I stalk the Met Office, grunting at the prediction of north-easterly breezes, smirking at the prospect of a hefty blow out of the south or west. And of course I peer with special fascination at the section of the chart covering the early morning.

The winter of 2015 started calm and warm. In November there were still blackberries on the brambles, most years they're blown off by hooting gales by the end of October. The fishing was pleasant enough, small and medium sized bass to lures, and I enjoyed being able to wander through my little coves in a tee shirt and a rain jacket. (I'm in Cornwall after all, I'd as soon go without my trousers as leave my waterproof at home.) But in spite of reliable fun with the schoolies I lusted after a decent blow and the chance of a big wave whopper. Finally the colours on the Met Office website began to change, the pressure was dropping, a howler was in the offing. The exact strength and timing kept changing. Ever since 1987, when Michael Fish announced there'd be nothing like a hurricane in the UK just before a hurricane flattened half the country, the weather gurus have erred on the side of caution. They're like the drug companies that advertise on American television channels: 'Side effects may include slight abdominal discomfort, skin irritation, and dry mouth; oh, and also terminal liver damage, fatal heart attacks, and episodes of homicidal rage.' But in the end the boffins settled on a breeze that would pick up through Friday night, forty-odd miles per hour by Saturday lunchtime.

Promising stuff, I love the very start of a good storm. The bass seem to come in even before the wildest of the winds – I suspect they're more weather-wise than Michael Fish, their instinct tells them what's in store – and the beginning of a hoolie often lets me fish before the lumps of weed and tangles of plastic junk turn the water into a black hole for terminal tackle. So I shoved my beach rod and backpack in the car and thawed a bag of nine or ten inch squid. The mackerel had vanished after their summer visit, I only do well with razor clam when we've had a few days of stirred up seas already, squid was a no brainer. It's a bait I like a lot, the only drawback being that the smell of stale squid endures in the car like the perfume of jasmine on a summer breeze – except that it hums like a seagull sewage farm during an outbreak of gastroenteritis.

Our house is sheltered from south and east winds, it seemed only moderately breezy as I slurped my four o'clock coffee next morning. But shuffling down to the water on an exposed beach told a different story, the weather was screaming, gusts up to forty-five miles per hour and occasional showers of horizontal rain slapping against my spectacles. I tied on a squid and a four ounce wired lead.

My first cast was a thirty yard effort, and effort it was, just standing up in the gale was hard work. I made sure the weight was holding then decided to sit down on my backpack. It converts into a stool, handy for a creaky kneed old so-and-so like myself, and I thought a lower profile on the shore might expose me to less of the blast. But as I plopped my bottom seat-wards a gust carried the pack stool away up the strand and my arse hit the deck with a thump, leaving me sprawled like a beetle on its back. I held the rod up to keep the reel out of the sand, clambered to my feet, recovered my stool, and tightened the line. Except it wouldn't tighten. A yard, five yards, still slack. Then came a mighty thump and the start of a forty yard run into the depths. It was an eleven pounder. Some friends had asked me for a big bass to freeze for their Christmas Eve supper so I bent down, biffed her on the head, and started to unhook her. And in a trice my vision blurred, I couldn't see the hook. My spectacles had blown off my nose and cartwheeled away up the shore. With my pocket torch between my teeth I must have spent twenty minutes on my hands and knees quartering the beach, my face eighteen inches off the ground, before I found them buried in a tangle of monofilament gill net.

And that's one more reason I like to fish before sunrise: there's nobody around to see me making a fool of myself.

The Beach for Me

'A little bit of heaven here on earth'
Bruce Springsteen, *Cadillac Ranch*

In my parents' wills they asked that their ashes be scattered in fishing spots by all of their sons together. Father outlived Mother by a few months, and my brother Mick was in the Pacific when he died. We waited for Father's little ceremony until the three of us were in the same place anyway. This turned out to be when Shelley and I were married in Connecticut, so for a few years the old boy's mortal remains lay in a plastic bottle in my booze cupboard. Father enjoyed his dram, it seemed an ideal place to park him, between the Gordon's and the Talisker. Mother, on the other hand, went straight from the church service to the water's edge, and we sprinkled her into a light surf on a strand where she'd gone swimming a lot. She was a hardy soul – or a nutter – and she bathed almost daily. One cold and stormy December morning a rescue helicopter tried to pull her out of the briny. The crew refused to believe anyone would be daft enough to flop around in such wild and frigid water, but she was having the time of her life until the winchman got in the way.

Mother's beach is only about six hundred yards long, shallow and gently sloping. If I were allowed to fish just one place for the rest of my days – even after failed appeals to the high court, the general synod, and the judges on *Strictly Come Dancing* – it's the spot I'd pick. And not just for sentimental reasons, it has a lot going for it.

It's rarely crowded, at least in the hours of darkness. I think this is because local anglers reckon it's a place with weed problems and a magnet for schoolies. And it's both, but only if you fish like an old school bass hunter. Cast beyond the third breaker and you're almost bound to wind up landing a double figure bag of kelp. Use worm or peeler crabs at range and you'll spend most of your outing releasing undersized tiddlers and wondering when you're going to run out of bait. But different tactics lead to different results.

The sand's uneven, long ridges and channels running parallel with the water's edge. When the tide's all the way out it looks like one of those concrete playgrounds where loud teenagers on skateboards fly from ramp to ramp and passing orthopaedic surgeons sigh at the inevitable increase in their workloads. As a pensioner I find noisy kids exhausting. I've always thought trains, buses, and restaurants should be segregated, bouncy youngsters kept apart from grumpy old gits who want to read the newspaper in peace. Bass agree. On my beach a fling into the second channel out – thirty or forty yards as a rule – has your gear among the frisky juveniles. A lob into the closest channel – often less than a cricket pitch – gives you a chance of the sort of grown-up fish that'll do anything to get away from a shoal of hyperactive nippers.

One July morning I headed down at about three thirty. The wave was puny, that was a drawback. Two headlamps, that was another dark cloud. The silver lining: hardly any weed and a big tide sweeping across the beach. With a whole joey mackerel and a three ounce bomb weight my tackle jigged along like a cod Irishwoman in Riverdance, smack in the middle of the nearest depression in the sand. In forty minutes I had three bass, no giants, but I kept a four pounder and released a couple of smaller ones.

Then I wandered over to see how the other fellows were faring. Two chaps from east London, a father and son, and they'd been trying all night, three nights in a row, for a dozen basslets and a few flounders. They peered at my fish like lions eyeing up a butcher's shop window. 'What are we doing wrong?' asked the lad. 'Everything' would have been an honest answer. But perhaps tactless. So I sorted them out with light sinkers to replace their six ounce breakaways, gave them my last two little mackerel instead of their peelers, and told them to shorten their casts to fifteen yards or so. 'Fifteen yards, that's a rum,' said the boy. 'A what?' 'A rum, a rum and coke, a joke, innit?' 'No,' I told him, 'fourteen and three-quarters would be a joke, fifteen's dead serious.' Twenty minutes later they had a keeper apiece, three pounds and three and a bit. 'Our camper van's in the carpark,' announced dad with glee, 'and we're going to cook these for breakfast. Three nights running my missus has been laughing at us, buying a cockle's worth of crab, staying out till all hours, and coming home with diddly squat. This morning she's going to eat her words. Along with the freshest bass she's ever put in her north.' At which his son added, 'North, north and south, mouth.' Simultaneous translation, English into English. And that's another reason I love my beach.

Conspicuous Consumption

'Huh, I'd like to meet his tailor'
Warren Zevon, *Werewolves Of London*

A calm July morning with the sky starting to pale. I was shuffling along a run of shallow coves chucking a Toby into the wavelets. The shallows were skipping with whitebait, earlier I'd seen half a dozen foxes eating them on the beach where they'd been stranded. The bass were slow but steady when I saw a trim figure approaching, a man twenty years my junior. We introduced ourselves, he was Mark, on holiday from Kent. 'I thought I recognised you,' he said. 'I've seen some of your magazine articles. My friend's reading your book right now, he said I might run into you around these parts. And that you'd take one look at me and bust a gut laughing.' 'Why would I do that?' He wafted his hands over his neatly fitting waders, then pointed to his rod, his reel, a landing net dangling from his belt, a massive kit bag, and a jacket festooned with clip-on tools. 'Because,' he said, 'I own every expensive bass fishing gadget know to humanity. And if I don't, it's on back order. And my friend says you find tackle tarts hilarious.'

That's not true. I find it depressing that some people don't take up bass fishing because the peddlers of expensive kit have done their damnedest to persuade us you'll never do any good without spending the gross domestic product of Lesotho on your outfit and the annual budget of a medium-sized municipality on your lure box. It makes my blood boil when wealthy anglers sneer at others who have to make do with more modest kit. And I know from experience that you can catch plenty of fish on fifty quid rods and reels and with terminal tackle an average teenager would fund by washing the family car once a week.

But I have no issue with bass nuts who like to spend their spare cash on spiffy equipment. Some people collect vintage wine or antique silver, some have to own the latest mobile telephone as soon as it comes out, I buy more books than I'll ever find time to read, we all have the right to fritter away our money in the way that gives us pleasure. I explained all this to Mark. 'Makes sense,' he said. 'And you're right, I know my reel's not going to make any difference in how much I land, I know I don't need a knotless landing net with a carbon fibre frame, I know you can cut braid with a penknife instead of a titanium steel bladed clipper. And anyone who gets snotty about someone else using cheaper tackle, that's just an arsehole with no manners. But I can't resist well made fishing gear.

And one thing about being a tackle addict, my wife can always find me a good birthday present. She just types 'new bass gadget' into Google, makes sure it's not a guitarists' website, job done. But tell me, James, are you really that frugal? Isn't there anything in all my bits and pieces that you'd be prepared to spend money on?' My eyes locked in on a hook file, it was on a cord so you could clip it to your coat. 'That,' I told him, 'is a really clever idea. I'd buy one of them, I use a stone and I'm always scrabbling to find it.' He unsnapped it and passed it to me. 'I get one free every time I spend fifty quid. I've got two in the car, more in the shed. And I hope you'll take this as a compliment, but you are one cheap so-and-so.' I did and I do.

A Dark and Stormy Night

'Don't want to land in no Buzzards Bay'
Jimmy Buffet, *Volcano*

Living in Cornwall you develop a respect for the power of the sea. Three times I've pulled out people who were heading for a watery grave. All three, in the technical jargon of search and rescue, were complete shitheads. An old lady walked her dog past a sign warning of beach subsidence, ignored warning shouts from three anglers, and wound up in an eight foot swell. We made a human chain, a beefy bloke as anchor, a midsized one in the middle, and a long skinny one – myself – on the end wielding the gaff. Another prat took his little boy onto a rock that was being washed by giant waves. The third showed off to his lady friend by haring up and down a flat beach in a gale, racing the breakers until he was flattened and concussed by a big one. What's more I know people who used to be on the Sea-King helicopters out of RNAS Culdrose, their stories would scare a jellyfish stiff.

So when a fellow came up to me in a waterside carpark and asked if I thought he'd be OK on the headland I was direct. 'No bloody way.' We were in the middle of an August gale, eight to ten foot waves bashing in. 'So where are you going to fish?' he asked. 'From the beach. It's flat, you can see how far back you need to stand.' 'But you've got a lure rod.' Which was true, I'd just come back from a work trip and there was no bait in the deep-freeze. 'I sometimes do OK in the surf table,' I told him. So we wandered down together. His name was Paul and he was on holiday, staying in the local village. He lived in the Midlands, mostly he was a pike man, but he'd had a few outings after bass. 'Never caught one though, my girlfriend says she's beginning to wonder if they still exist. She reckons they might be extinct, like dinosaurs and ferret fanciers.'

We watched the sea for as long as it took me to smoke a fag, to be properly sure we know how far the swells were rolling up the strand. Then Paul opened his kit box. 'What d'you think I should try?' Some bass nuts carry enough lures to start an online retail business, this chap could have set up as a wholesaler. Either pike are very choosy customers or Paul's the captain of the Warwickshire tackle shopping team. The box had cantilevered trays, four I think, with a dinner service worth of spoons, an aquarium of realistic soft plastic fish, and a slew of plugs, shads and grubs with curly tails. 'The problem's going to be casting into this headwind,' he said. 'I reckon all my baits have too much drag, they're just going to blow right back in my face.' I dug out two thirty-five gramme metal jigs, one each, single hooks instead of the original trebles. 'Sling it as far as you like,' I said, 'then scoot it in along the bottom, stop and start style. And keep fishing it till you're sure it's on dry land, sometimes they take right at the edge of the water.'

By first light he'd beached two bass, I'd had three. Nothing of size, the best was a two pounder, but Paul was as happy as Larry, not to mention Curly and Moe. He kept a fish to show his girlfriend: ferret lovers may be an endangered species but bass still exist.

By the way, if you have a smallish bass – two pounds is ideal – you can make delicious ceviche. Fillet and skin the fish and cut the flesh into strips about an eighth of an inch thick. Squeeze four limes and one orange, add a couple of finely chopped chillies, a minced clove of garlic, a good pinch each of salt and sugar, and a small handful of chopped coriander, stalks and all. Pour the brew over the fish and leave it for half an hour. Then drain and eat with crusty bread. Some people are funny about raw stuff, but ceviche really isn't raw. When you grill or fry, the heat denatures the protein in your meat or fish. Acid – vinegar or lime juice – does the same thing at room temperature.

Too Soon or Too Late

'If it wasn't for bad luck I wouldn't have no luck at all'
Albert King, *Born Under A Bad Sign*

My brother Mick works overseas but he has a house in Cornwall ready for his retirement. When he's on leave we always find time for a few bass trips. Shelley's bemused by our conversations, especially on the phone. 'That was quick, what did you talk about?' she'll ask. 'I'm picking him up at three, he'll bring ragworm, I've got mackerel.' 'And that's all?' Of course that's all, what else needs to be said? If his plane had crashed he wouldn't have called, if the family were smitten by some dread disease he'd baulk at getting up in the middle of the night. And I don't need to remind him to bring waders and waterproofs for heaven's sake, he's my brother, breeding will out.

Mick only has a few weeks off each year and that's made me feel for professional bass guides. How often must their clients show up, full of bacon, eggs, and optimism, only to find the sea's as flat as a freshly ironed pancake and the coves are weedy enough to pass for Neptune's noodle soup? And when you know someone booked the trip a year ago and has been dreaming of it ever since, it seems inadequate to say, 'Last week was great, this week looks crappy, but that's fishing. Sorry, lap of the gods.' More than inadequate, an invitation to smack you with a lump of kelp, chuck your gear into the depths, and scream that the pictures on your website are photo-shopped fakes from the seafood counter at Sainsburys. But lap of the gods it is. The weather gods at least.

2017 was typical. It must have been September when Mick and I had our first outing together. Now September can bring fishy Atlantic gales. Not this time, we spent a good few pre-dawn hours in search of a decent wave. Even a fizzy ripple would have cheered our hearts like a pasty and a fair few pints. We caught some fish on lures and on worms fished with very light sinkers, twitching them through the millpond. But Mick had a wife and two grown children at home, a modest keeper apiece wasn't going to lead to feasting in his kitchen.

The day before he was due to head off to Heathrow the breeze began to pick up. The surf was still puny but it was at least building. We walked the beach to find the best-looking wave, on with chunky half mackerel baits. I had a couple of schoolies, Mick not a wibble. As the eastern sky grew

Bass

pale my imagination drifted towards a hot coffee, a bacon roll, a big yolk running into the butter. Then to my left I saw my brother edging gingerly down the sand in the half light, a healthy bend in his rod. He beached his fish then biffed it on the head with a smooth stone and a broad grin. It was a five pounder, his best to date.

The wind stiffened through the day, by next morning there was a proper stir up. I was on the shore at four, home by five with an eleven pounder and a six pounder to my name. At the risk of being a pain in the backside, some advice: if you really want more big fish, step one is to retire.

A Very Present Help in Trouble

'We can run with our arms open wide before the tide'
Bruce Springsteen, *Sherry Darling*

As I grow older I'm more and more convinced that people in general are decent and well meaning. A few exceptions: politicians, investment bankers, peddlers of bogus medical therapies, tabloid journalists. But Norman and Norma Normal are good eggs.

When we're raising funds for our Yezidi children I'll see someone with a face, as they say in Lancashire, like a bulldog licking pee off a nettle. Here we go, I think, I'll get a thousand words about how we shouldn't be helping bloody foreigners, why not support a local school, charity begins at home, rhubarb, rhubarb, rutabaga. And I'm ready with my prepared speech, show me a Cornish town where the men and old people were murdered, the women sold as sex slaves, and you'd have a point. Otherwise why don't you bugger off and have a good day. Then the crosspatch scowls, hands me a tenner, and says, 'Effing sorry it's not more. It's an effing disgrace our government's doing eff-all to help, effing good show that you lot are trying to make an effing difference. Keep it up.' A grumpy egg, but a good egg regardless.

One autumn morning I had a similar meeting on the shore. I'd headed out with some joey mackerel and a few ragworm from my local tackle dealer. They were on their last parapodia – the little flappy bits that look like legs – so he gave them to me. I'd checked a surfie website overnight, it predicted one metre waves in a light breeze. Rubbish, their forecaster must have bonked his head on the board one time too many. The wind was fresh, the breakers were between five and six feet, and I had the wrong bait. In stirred up water I like something juicy and aromatic, a big fat calamari would be ideal.

OK, I thought, maybe I should drive home. I'd waste half an hour on the road, but it might be worth it. As I pondered I heard a yell across the carpark: 'Hey you, bloody fisherman, look at this.' A stout man in a lycra outfit strode up to me waving a small bag. 'Spud picked it up. We were heading onto the sand for our exercise session. Right beside a rubbish bin, easy enough to put it where it belongs. And if he ate it he'd get sick.' Spud was a Heinz 57 outbred to a Heinz 57, a portly golden retriever superstructure on a corgi undercarriage with spaniel ears and a whippet tail. 'Never mind the bloody plastic, that could wind up strangling his intestines. Nobody should be leaving their crap around the bloody place.' He waved the offending item in my face. Half a dozen big squid in a vacuum pack. 'Quite right,' I told him, 'but it isn't mine. Here's my bait bag, worms and mackerel.' At which Spud's master said, 'Oh, sorry about that. Must have been someone else then. Never mind, I'll chuck it.' 'No, please don't. I can use the squid, then I'll take the plastic home with any other rubbish I pick up on the beach, OK?'

Half an hour later Spud and Spud-master came galloping back from their workout. I gave them a fat four-pound bass. Both seemed delighted and the biped of the party was amazed. 'Fair play,' I told him, 'if you hadn't given me the squid, I bet I wouldn't have caught her. And maybe a bit for Spud, he found them?'

A Twenty Pounder

'What do we have for entertainment?'
The Clash, *The Magnificent Seven*

Late December, a warm damp gale walloping in from the south and a sucking surf. In other words it was a perfect morning for a bass fisher who hoped he'd put on the right rain jacket, the one with no holes. The water was bubbly and coloured so I tied two big razor clams onto a pair of 4/0 hooks and lobbed into the margin. There was a fair amount of weed in the wave but I could keep my gear in the water for five or ten minutes before I had to reel in and clear the junk from my line. Any longer than that had me playing a giant tangle of the vegetarian catch of the day. On my fourth or fifth cast I felt a slack line take. In stirred up water I find bass don't pull that hard and it didn't take long to beach an eight or nine pounder. A friend had asked me for a decent-sized fish for a supper party so she went in the bag. It's easy to wind up with a swallowed bait in rough water so I decided not to risk another chuck, I'd head for home.

In the carpark I ran into a youngster. He was on holiday, staying in a cottage right by the beach. 'I was hoping to fish but it's too rough to be any good,' he told me sadly. I'm not sure whether it was my silver tongue, my silver beard, or my silver bass but he soon changed his mind and went back to grab his rod. He'd only picked up ragworm for his outing so I sorted him out with a pair of bigger hooks and a bunch of juicy clams. Then I sat down to see how he'd fare.

But I felt awkward peering at the lad, some things are best done without onlookers. Sex comes to mind, along with shaving, making spaghetti sauce, and talking to the cat about politics. But fishing's up there too, I enjoy my outings most when it's just me, the water, and the bass. So I went for a wander along the strand. Soft sand, trouser waders, a hooting wind to blow you off course, not a bad workout. Forget about rowing machines or elliptical trainers, someone should come up with a piece of gym equipment that simulates slogging along a beach in a storm. Maybe a bit of virtual reality to enhance the experience, set your goggles for a Caribbean shore with palm fronds and coconuts flying through the air, freezing rain in the Baltic, or the full Cornish with soggy fronds of wrack and raindrops like golf balls slapping your chops.

Twenty minutes of stomping through the weather and I was ready for a mug of coffee. On the way to the car I stopped to see how the lad was doing. Very well indeed, he was fast to a whopper, something capable of running against the resistance of a stiff drag on a hefty beach outfit. 'It's been on for ten minutes, no idea what it is,' he told me. I watched the thumping of the rod tip, steady and emphatic. 'I'd say it's a bass and a good one.' What else would it be in shallow roily water, shaking its head like a school teacher dismissing a cretinous answer? 'If you can bring her into the shallows I'll gill her ashore.'

Ten more minutes and I was convinced this was a monster, maybe even a record, line screaming from the reel as his fish bored away in the undertow. The first weak gleam of the dawn was in the sky by the time my young chum had the upper hand. Watching the wave I scooted out up to my knees and peered into the froth. The weight was wrapped in a huge skein of black plastic bags and there was a fish on each of the two hooks of his pennel rig. I flopped the bags over my arm and strode up the beach with a two pound bass and a ten pound huss. I was crushed, I was a philosopher's stone in reverse gear, the man who could turn gold into dross; a trophy into rubbish, a schoolie, and a none too attractive wrecker of rigs. But the youngster was grinning from ear to dripping ear. 'Breakfast,' he pointed to his bass, 'and a personal best,' the dogfish. 'And what a fight.' I suppose that was his nod to the bin bags.

Too Much Weather

'It's a wonder tall trees ain't laying down'
Neil Young, *Comes A Time*

Once in a while a stranger recognises me from something I've written. It's not like being a rock star, nobody asks to take a selfie with me. And nobody says, 'You changed my life'. I'm glad, if a few ideas about bass fishing and the odd quirky observation transformed your outlook on the world I'd have to wonder which rock you were living under. But the people who buttonhole me are anglers, so of course we wind up having a natter about fish. And it's lovely when some of my advice is helpful.

One October I was in the Oxfam shop when a thirty-ish fellow showed up. He'd bought a copy of my book from our local bookstore, and the owner had told him where to find me if he wanted it signed. He did, and more importantly he wanted a shoulder to cry on. His name was Stu, he'd read some of my magazine pieces and planned a Cornish fishing holiday. 'And just look at it,' he pointed at the window. A light drizzle was falling. No, that's not true, it wasn't falling, it was flying horizontally up the road at forty-odd miles per hour, perhaps touching down in Devon. Or maybe Middlesex, Maastricht, or Moscow. 'I had a day booked fly fishing in an inshore boat. Cancelled, too rough to launch. I looked at a couple of rock marks to try some lures. I'm no wimp, but they had ten foot waves crashing in, they're not safe. So I've driven three hundred miles and I'm not even going to get my rod out of its bag.' 'Have you thought about bait?' I asked him. That can be a delicate subject, some people react as if 'bait' were a euphemism for crack cocaine, indiscriminate violence, or bestiality. But no, he just said, 'I didn't bring any beach fishing gear.'

Now one of the things I never do is to tell people where to fish. I've learned my lesson: let one angler know about a mark and the grapevine sprouts like genetically modified Japanese knotweed. In a week the carpark's jammed, the shore's ablaze with headlamps. And in another week the illegal netters zoom in for an almighty slaughter. But in this case I made an exception. The poor chap had taken time off work and he wasn't going to see fin nor scale of a bass. I sent him down the road to a local tackle shop to buy a cheap surf-casting outfit and a bag of squid, I told him which beach to try, and to be there between three in the morning and first light. 'Will it be any good even in this storm?' he asked. 'For sure, just don't cast too far, thirty yards maximum.' 'Really?' 'Yes, really.'

Next morning I had a bit of a lie-in, it was four o'clock before I arrived at the water's edge. In the moonlight I could see a figure a couple of hundred yards away, bound to be Stu. But before checking in with him, just one chuck. And as my lead bedded in it promptly bedded out, yards of slack. I tightened, and in ten minutes there was a seven pound bass in the shallow foam. At which point I realised Stu was beside me. 'D'you want me to gill her in?' 'No, we'll let her go, just see if you can wiggle the hook free. And how've you been doing?' 'Brilliant, two good ones. And like you said, really close in.' Well, yes.

The Sizes of Things

'I been in the right place but it must have been the wrong time'
Doctor John, *Right Place Wrong Time*

A lot of common expressions are due for an update. I propose, 'Look after the pennies and while you're messing about with them an online fraudster can swipe the pounds from your bank account.' 'See a pin and pick it up, then wash your hands, dogs shit on the ground.' 'Jack would be as good as his master if he had a private education, friends in high places, and a trust fund.' And one of my favourite bits of idiotic folklore: 'It's the little things that make a difference.' Of course little things can be important, but so can big things and medium-sized things. When my car has one of its tantrums I want the mechanic to wipe the grease from the steering wheel after he's fixed it. I also want the right spare part fitted, and make sure you tighten up the bolts while you're at it.

I run into anglers who overlook important details. They're religious about washing the salt from their reels, lubricating the bearings, cleaning scales from their rods with soapy water and a toothbrush. But the last few yards of their line are so worn that they seem to be developing dandruff, and their hooks might have been adapted for use in a nursery school where only teacher's allowed things that are sharp. As frugal as I am in general I can be a spendthrift when it's going to make the difference between landing a trophy or wiping bitter tears from my cheeks with an unused fish towel. I cut off the end of my line if it looks remotely dodgy. I replace any lure hook that won't hold a surgical point, and my bait rigs go into the compost at the end of every outing – a 4/0 rusts away to nothing in about six months, and iron in the soil seems to help my sweetcorn crop.

But for all the attention I pay to the nitty-gritty, what matters most's on a grander scale: finding feeding fish. One September morning I drove up north – as in Land's End, not Manchester or Inverness – in search of a decent wave. I found one too, three or four feet and bubbly. There were mackerel on all my marks, but nothing fancied my joeys. I bunked up and down the beach, tried casting longer, then shorter, never a touch. Then I saw three familiar figures, a large man and two enormous dogs. They're mastiffs and they always make me smile. They'll gallop straight at me, then put the brakes on ten feet away, skidding along on their bottoms in a blast of flying sand. But mostly I grin because I know their back-story. My man took his wife to see them when they were about a month old. In a well planned conspiracy, his pal, who'd bred them, tucked their mother away out of sight and assured her they'd grow up to be the size of golden retrievers. A year on and the poor woman's sharing an old fisherman's cottage with a pair of animals that could pull a plough.

My bait was past its prime so I slipped it off and grabbed a fresh one. Malcolm, the two-legged member of my gallery, looked at it. 'That's what we had for supper last night. We were walking by the breakwater and one of the boatmen gave me half a dozen. They were lovely, just pop them under the grill with some garlic. And the bones are so fine you don't notice if you eat a few. So why don't you ever see the baby ones at the fishmonger?' 'There's no market for them,' I said. 'If you look at the prices from Newlyn they sell what they call larges for, say, a quid a kilo. Then mediums would make maybe sixty pence. Smalls twenty pence. It's not worth gutting them and driving them all that way for coppers.' 'Right, that explains it,' said Malcolm. 'The chap in the boat gave me six, a few more to Agnes, the woman with the standard poodle, and he dumped the rest over the side. There must have been over a hundred.' 'Wow, that's great. Thank you. Excuse me, Malcolm.'

I grabbed my gear and took off along the sand, the desperate scurry of a man with a train to catch. Or a bass to catch, even more urgent. Lots of delicious debris at the very end of the beach, of course that's where the fish would be scavenging. Twenty yards short of the harbour I stopped and cast into the sheltered water in its lee. Five minutes later I beached a four pounder, quickly followed by her twin sister. By this time Malcolm and his mates had caught up with me. They went home with another fish supper.

So yes, the little things make a difference, I'm glad my hook points were like needles, my line wasn't scuffed. It's a good job I hadn't left my elastic thread in the other jacket or worn the waders with the banjaxed belt that pops when I move too quickly. But big things matter too.

I Don't Know Much

'One thing for certain'
Bob Seger & The Silver Bullet Band, *Fire Down Below*

I like George Orwell's non-fiction. OK, some of his ideas about gender and race seem primitive these days, but he died in 1950, attitudes were different back then. One of my favourite essays is about Dickens. It ends by describing him as 'a free intelligence, a type hated with equal hatred by all the smelly little orthodoxies which are now contending for our souls'. Dead right then, dead right now, one of the most depressing things about the twenty-first century is the number of people who tell us how to live our lives on the basis of political or religious dogma. Argument gets you nowhere, they just quote something from Hayek, Marx, or the book of Genesis. Case closed, they say, I'm not a bigot, I'm just right, the sacred text proves it. Drivel, the text shows that some long dead geezer had an opinion, but this still-living geezer has a different point of view.

Bass fishing can give us too much faith in our ideas. Or maybe that's overly general. You may be open to persuasion, I sometimes have too much faith in my ideas. The warning sign's when I say, 'I don't know much but ..'. What always follows is a categorical statement: but trophy fish feed hardest in rough weather, but jelly-fry show up in early summer, but big baits are best. All of which are true. Except when they're not. There's always the chance of a surprise, with bass there's a good chance. So what I ought to say is, 'I don't know much,' and leave it there.

One summer's morning I was on the way back to the car when I saw a young chap scrambling out onto a headland. I'd caught a couple on sandeel shads, but once the light came up the bays were dead. The lad seemed to be using a small popper, a jet-propelled popper. He was a brilliant caster, even into a freshening onshore breeze his lure was going fifty or sixty yards. Now years of mucking about on the rocks have taught me that inshore bass feed in the snaggy shallows where their prey's easy to grab. I'd never waste my time flinging a plug half way to Saint Michael's Mount, in fact I generally cast at forty-five degrees to the water's edge. That way the whole retrieve's through the thin, stirred up water I like. But after a few minutes the youngster had a solid pull. What's more it was almost as his lure hit the water, way out in the bay. A fat two pounder. 'Oh well,' I thought, 'every dog has its day.' Then the dog had another day, a slightly better bass. And then it had a doggy long weekend, a third half decent fish.

I'm not sure I can fling a plug fifty yards into the wind, so I clipped on a Toby. And on my first heave, as the spoon sank, I felt a heartening double thump. Four bass in under a dozen casts, and then they stopped dead. I reckon there must have been a shoal of whitebait out there, maybe herded into a ball, but that's a guess. Here's what I know for sure: bass often feed close in. But the idea that they always feed close in, that's a smelly little orthodoxy and I'd be a better fisher if I denied it the chance to contend for my soul.

Why am I Here?

'Even the losers keep a little bit of pride'
Tom Petty & The Heartbreakers, *Even The Losers*

We all have outings when common sense says we should have stayed in bed; at least that we might as well cut our losses and head home for a cup of coffee. But the fishing brain really doesn't run on common sense, does it?

It was July and I woke to the sort of weather the Cornish Tourist Board would have us believe they see only in Devon, steady rain falling vertically through a windless sky. But the forecast reckoned it was becoming lighter, clearing about breakfast time. OK, I thought, at least it's warm rain. And there were sandeels on all my marks, you don't notice a spot of drizzle when there's a bend in your rod. In the carpark I debated whether to wear my waterproof cap. It has a long peak, it keeps my specs clear of annoying drips. But it also has permanent ear flaps and in calm conditions I like to listen for the slurps and swirls of feeding fish. I stuck with the old woolly hat. The way down to the cove crosses a sheet of sloping granite. I patted myself on the back for my foresight: it would be like sheet glass coated with olive oil so I slithered safely down on my bottom. Standing up at the end of my bobsled ride – or bumsled ride – I felt moisture in the seat of my bags. An outfit malfunction. To say I had a hole in my trouser waders would have been like saying the Hindenburg suffered slight smoke damage: two square feet of shredded vinyl were flapping around my bottom like a grubby Hawaiian grass skirt. I keep a length of cord in my knapsack, I tied it around my hips so I wouldn't trip on my new tails.

But at least I was by the water. Flat as a dab, maybe a weightless plastic lure, skinny and in sandeel livery. And the box of softies was nowhere to be found, I'd rigged a few new ones, must have left the whole kit and caboodle on my desk. So Plan B, a shallow diving plug, that would be almost as good. I clipped it on, only to realise the line wasn't running through the end ring. Make that the gizmo formerly known as an end ring – the wretched thing had fallen to pieces, the ceramic insert was flopping about on the braid. So out with my penknife and rig up again.

It's possible to cast without an end ring. Not something I recommend, but possible. Make your normal insouciant flick and the line wraps itself around the eight inch piece of carbon fibre at the very tip of the rod. But a gentle lob was OK, followed by a careful squizz to make sure there were none of those fankles that would lead to smashed tackle if a decent fish took hold. And that didn't seem likely anyway, forty minutes scuffing along the shore, not a chuffing wibble. Then the weather came in, the steady rain replaced by the sort of downpour that had Noah saying, 'What did I tell you idiots? Thirty-nine days and twenty-three hours to go, and no, I don't have any last minute cancellations, the ark's fully booked.' Bloody Met Office, I thought, they should flog off their new computer system and pick up a few pine cones.

As the sky began to pale damply in the east I tried to scan the water for signs of life. Nothing visible, but hard to be sure, my glasses were running with rivulets, should have put on the cap with the long peak. I tried a mackerel-sized diver, then a Toby in case of whitebait. No interest. OK, I thought, when you've no idea what to imitate, maybe it's time for a lure that looks like nothing in nature, a black flying condom. Now I like flying condoms, they're terrific for seatrout, but I'd be hard put to tell you what they suggest. Maybe a toy paddle steamer designed by a lateral-thinking incompetent.

But long ago The Jock taught me that an opportunistic predator sometimes goes for a small morsel that might be edible, especially it it's whipped along the top of the water. And sure enough my third cast resulted in a savage yank. The fish missed the hook and I almost burst into tears. Stiff upper lip, I let the lure sink, then raised the rod briskly. Another thump and a three and a half pound bass started jogging around the cove. Triumph. I shoved her in the bag for supper. But skin that's been drenched for a couple of hours loses its toughness, I stabbed my thumb on a fin. Only a scratch, but it must have hit a baby artery because in seconds my hand looked like a prop for a slasher film. I reached for my kit bag, a towel to mop up the mess. And as I leaned forward there was a sound like a flatulent carthorse on the high fibre diet plan. The ripped waders had turned into three separate items of weather wear: a right wellie, a left wellie, and a deconstructed vinyl kilt in Clan McHalfwit tartan, pale olive green with black squid ink stains and a blood red overcheck.

In the carpark was an elderly lady with a retriever. She looked me up and down – the lady I mean, the dog just sniffed my fish – and sighed. 'Good morning. You've been in the wars. Was it any good?' 'Good morning,' I said. 'Not just good, it was absolutely brilliant.' Because it was.

You're Never Alone with a Bass and a Hat

'I don't want to be your boss'
Bob Dylan, It Takes A Lot To Laugh, It Takes A Train To Cry

When I worked for big companies they went through management models the way teenagers go through snacks. We had the flat organisation, empowerment, behavioural competencies, matrices, centres of excellence, and a scad more I've forgotten – thank goodness, some memories are painful. None of these fads lasted long. The firms that peddled them had to come up with a new idea every couple of years, even if this meant admitting the last one was a load of rubbish. Otherwise they'd have nothing to sell.

The only one I found intriguing never got off the ground. It came from a retired general, and his theory was that some people are like dogs, some are like cats. Dogs are pack animals, wolves with manners. They live comfortably in a hierarchy. You know who's your boss, your peer, your underling. The top dog's treated with respect and obedience, the runt does what it's told, the ones in the middle vie for power and authority. In a domestic setting most dogs put their human keeper in the role of pack leader: this is my person, the one who takes care of me and calls the shots. Cats are solitary. Structure means nothing to them. All they want is to be left alone to do what they fancy. Give a house cat free rein to live by its own code and you have a pet that'll sit in your lap when the mood strikes, hide under the bed when it doesn't. And if you try to impose rules, your furry friend's going to show an opinion by using the carpet as a litter box. According to the general's advice there are a lot more dogs than cats in business. Employers should test their workers' preferences and manage them in very different ways. I lobbied in vain to have the company give his approach a try. Because I'm a cat. Except that I can be counted on not to wee on the rug.

I'm the same way when there's a rod in my hand, maybe that makes me a cat-fisher. I don't want to go to the shore in a gang, I have no interest in competing with other anglers, I follow my own timetable, and I'd hate to be in charge of anyone else's sport. I suppose that's why guiding drove me so far up the pole. But give me water, absolute freedom as to which bit of that water I fish, and I'll purr with delight.

Of course my love of solitude doesn't mean I hate people, I just don't want them chattering at me while I'm trying to think about bass. And when I run into other anglers, especially the ones fishing by themselves – other cat-fishers – I always stop for a yarn. And here's the best thing: the ones in groups, the dogs, natter about all sorts of boring bollix. They'll tell me about last night's football, a coded message that says, 'I'm an Arsenal supporter, my pack's bloody brilliant.' Or they'll ask me whether I've ever caught a double, a prelude to saying, 'I've had two, does that make me the Alpha dog around here?' But the solitary bass hunter doesn't waste time establishing status, it's straight down to business, what's going on in the water, how can we get more bites?

One September morning I shuffled onto my nearest beach a couple of hours before the dawn. It was the time of year when the mackerel come and go, the squid the same, so I had half a dozen of each. I always imagine little blackboards in the surf. One day they read 'New season calamari, fill your boots'. Next day it's 'Mackie season ending soon, eat up now while stocks last'. I could see a short figure by the water so I made a quick detour. A woman in her fifties, I'd say, though I might be doing her an injustice: we all look older than our years when we're wind battered, dripping with rain, and anointed with smears of seaweed and bait. 'Any joy?' I asked. 'No, a cracking bite first cast but I dropped her in the last wave. That was on a joey.' Typical cat, no mucking about, straight to the stuff that matters. 'That joey was the only one I had, the boys have been in my bait freezer. And worm's done me no good at all.'

She marked my card, I returned the favour, half of my little mackerel into her bait box. I wound up with three bass, she had two and a very respectable pollack. At a guess all our fish were between four and five pounds, but we didn't compare sizes or work out who'd done best. That would be a dog trick, cats don't care.

Going the Extra Half Mile

'And you need a helping hand'
James Taylor, *You've Got A Friend*

Most of us have good intentions. Often they don't lead anywhere, we're distracted by the day-to-day bullshit of life and we never get around to dropping off the baked beans to the food bank or making sure our elderly neighbour's OK. It's easy to let noble plans go by the wayside. A Brummie I met in Calais put it neatly. We were chopping onions to make hot meals for the migrant population, he'd been at it for a month or more. He seemed devout, every time his mobile telephone played the call to prayer he'd excuse himself for a few minutes. Someone asked him about his faith, maybe curious as to whether he was a Sunni or a Shiite. He said, 'I believe in the god of the backside, the one who says, 'I'm jolly glad you worship me, thank you. Now get off your arse and do something useful.' And I too admire the people who find the time to follow through on what they think they ought to do.

One wild autumn night I drove a mile or so to a slightly sheltered bay. Through three days of a storm it had been a magical spot, a few good bass every morning, all on razor clam. Right in front of the carpark was a chap with a beach rod so I stopped off for a catch report. Nothing but small whiting. I asked what bait he was on. Ragworm, he'd been told it was the best. 'It's good,' I told him, 'but in stirred up water I like something bigger and juicier. Razor's been working lately.' 'Thanks,' he said, 'I've got a packet, I was going to try them if I ran out of worm. But I'll give them a go now.'

I scuttled four hundred yards along the sand for my first cast, and it wasn't long before I beached a good one. By the time the eastern sky was lightening I was out of clams, but had four fish between three and six pounds. 'Can't complain,' I thought, 'though it would be great to have one more chuck.' Then along came the other fellow, flushed and out of breath. 'I wanted to say thank you for the advice, four bass, one of them was my personal best. I've got to go now, I'm in charge of breakfast for the kids. But I've got one razor left, you might as well have it.' Then he turned and beetled off to his car. The magic of the last cast, a real beauty, eleven pounds on the BASS tape measure. And all because your man was prepared to walk eight hundred yards in soft sand to do what he thought was the decent thing in the circumstances.

Correlation, Causation and the Need to Fish More

'I want to know'
Creedence Clearwater Revival, *Have You Ever Seen The Rain*

To be satisfying a statistical conclusion must be supported by the data and there has to a causal explanation as well. In other words we can see a relationship and we can say why it holds. It's easy to do one without the other. When I was a student we were given an assignment to find a single variable to predict gross national product. We did it in pairs and my colleague's father worked at the Harwell atomic research centre. That meant he had access to a computer. In those days even big companies didn't buy the things, they rented time on other people's. Anyway my pal's dad wrote a programme and came up with some figures for us. We presented our findings to the professor, almost perfect correlation, we'd found a metric that showed the trajectory of the national economy. 'Very good,' said the prof. 'What's the independent variable? I'm guessing stock market performance with a lag time.' 'No,' we told him, 'it's the number of goals scored in the year by Accrington Stanley.' I've never trusted finance types who pretend to be mathematicians.

As anglers we come up with all sorts of data. Our sample sizes are small – that's a hint to our families and employers, we need more outings – but often we're fairly sure we know what's going on. What we rarely know is why. One early summer morning I was sauntering along a rocky patch in rather too calm conditions. 'Sauntering' sounds posh, as if my waders had spats. More prosaically I was moving slowly, my knees were knackered. The ripple and the pools held sandeels and jelly-fry, plenty of both, some darting about and some little corpses. Now my experience tells me bass will eat tiny fry whenever they're to be had, even if there are other food sources on offer. Correlation but no causality. I had a little pale muddler minnow on a dropper, a soft plastic on the point to give casting weight, and a couple of schoolies to my name.

Then I ran into a lad of about fifteen. People my age can be pissy about teenagers: they're rude, ill disciplined, and so on. Not the ones I see fishing. They can be exhaustingly energetic, but I find them delightful.

Maybe the younger generation's bad behaviour comes from spending too much time in lonely communion with telephones and tablets, maybe it's cured by dashing around on the water. That's a causal explanation with very inadequate correlation data. Anyway the boy was called Bruce, he hailed from Glasgow, and he was planning to take biology for his Highers. 'I'd like to be a marine scientist. I mean, can you imagine studying sea life and getting paid for it?' I told him a little about my brother, he's a fisheries advisor, mostly working in the Pacific islands. 'Sweet,' said Bruce. That's youngster-speak for excellent; groovy, as my generation might have said.

Bruce was using a shad. 'I can see sandeels, but they're not having it.' I told him my experience with jelly-fry. A small data set, no plausible causality. But would he like to have a bash with a dropper rig? Indeed, and it didn't take long to pay off, a schoolie and a good eating fish. 'Wicked,' he said, another synonym for groovy. 'Now my mum won't be able to say I'm wasting my time. But I wonder why the bass prefer tiny wee dots like the fry when they could be putting away eels that are so much more nourishing.' He scratched his head. 'Maybe they're easy to catch, something to do with conserving energy. The babies look like they're swimming in circles. Maybe bass lie still in one spot, wait for a shoal to happen by, grab a meal, then go back to lying still. You know how to find out?'

Now he was animated, waving his rod like an operatic conductor as the fat lady enters stage right. 'You need someone with diving kit. Just to sit on the bottom and watch. And wouldn't that be a grand way to spend a few days.' If you say so. And certainly I'd love to know why bass seem to lock in on jelly-fry. It'll be a few years before Bruce finishes school, then his bachelor's degree, but I'm waiting for his doctoral research project.

Are we Surprised?

'You can seek the rhyme and reason, but in the realm of the unknown'
Jim White, *Alabama Chrome*

I'm always banging on about how bass are unpredictable, you must expect the unexpected. So fair enough that people ask me if I'm ever truly gobsmacked by their behaviour. If a quantum physicist explains a research paper and the only words you understand are the auxiliary verbs and the articles, are you taken aback? No. If you see it coming you can't be non-plussed when it arrives. Thus speaks the voice of reason. The voice of experience isn't so sure.

One March we had a spell of warm, damp weather. The wind was southerly and the wave in Mount's Bay was between wild and bloody furious. Perfect conditions for a big bait and a big bass, so I took myself down to a flat strand a mile from the house. Perfect for vegetarian anglers as well, great lumps of weed everywhere. I reckon some of it might have been dulse. They say it's delicious stuff, good for you to boot, but not what I had in mind when I rolled out of bed at half past daft. There's another beach even closer to home, I decided to give it a few chucks, see if I could find some clearer surf. And as I arrived at the water's edge I saw a boy with a rod shaped like Cornish palm tree, bent and bouncing in the weather. 'If you can hold her in the last wave, I'll bring her in,' I told him. A lovely five pounder. 'Well done, young man, that's a beauty. What bait are you on?' A little sandeel. At this point I went a bit Lady Bracknell. In the hooting wind it might have sounded as if I said, 'A handbag?' But no, it was, 'A sandeel? In March? In a gale? A sandeel?' Yes, a small sandeel, the fellow in the tackle shop had given him half a packet for fifty pence, and he'd been running out of pocket money. And his prize had taken his very last bait. 'He's a nice man, very generous, I think they're two pounds fifty as a rule, when the bag's full.' Indeed, I thought, and that's a fair price when there are sandeels in the water. But in March? Might as well have given the little chap a chipolata or a custard cream. And that was when his bass flopped on the sand and spat out four tiny eels.

'I tell you what,' I said, 'I'm going to leave my rod and bag right here. The tide's ebbing, you won't need to move it. I'll be back in ten minutes, I live on the hill, and there's a big bag of baby launce in my freezer, plenty for both of us.' It was indeed a generous packet, and a good job too. We ran through a dozen of the wee chaps. My best fish was about eight pounds, my young companion had one of nine pounds and two ounces, beating his previous record by more than four pounds. But sandeels in March, holy *Hyperoplus lanceolatus*. Yes, I was gobsmacked.

Where Have all the Anglers Gone?

'There's a lone red rider'
Neil Young, *Misfits*

Bass are unpredictable. As for the people who chase them, our behaviour's more programmed. We respond to the pull of the moon and a drop in barometric pressure the way Pavlov's dogs reacted to his bell. Most of us don't slobber but we feel an overwhelming hunger to be on the shore. So when a westerly autumnal blow arrived in the middle of a set of big tides I scratched my head a while. I wasn't wondering whether to go fishing, that was a given. I'd as likely stay home as replace my early morning coffee with an infusion of camomile and black pudding. My dilemma was where to go. In general I don't like to see other people, I'm the Greta Garbo of the bass community, I want to be let alone. And in wild weather there's a practical matter to bear in mind as well. Rough seas bring weed, you sometimes need to shuffle up and down to find a clear patch of water. When your mark looks like an energy-saving version of The Strip in Las Vegas – no topless dives or roulette wheels, but tip-lights and brightly coloured headlamps all over the shop – moving can be a challenge. In the end I picked a long beach, even if a few other bass fishers showed up, I'd be able to keep my distance. And I decided to start at four o'clock, the time the overnight brigade heads home.

At three forty-five – I always wake too early when conditions are promising – I pulled into the carpark. Deserted, save only for a vixen which jumped out of the rubbish bin with what looked like a takeaway curry or chicken fried rice – our foxes have a varied diet these days. But not a car in sight, what on earth was going on? OK, it was raining horizontally, but if Cornish anglers were put off by getting wet they'd be few and far between: the odd lazy lump who props a rod and sits in the car to watch it, one or two carp hunters who live in waterside tents, and a couple of chancers crossing the Tamar to rustle cod from Plymouth aquarium. Maybe I'd missed something on the news, a forecast of asteroids landing in Mount's Bay, a threatened invasion by shock troops from the Proper Pasty Liberation Front. Anyway I'd take my chances.

Casting was hard work. Even for a thirty yard chuck I had to wait for the very end of a gust, then try to have my wired lead settled into the bottom before the next one. Standing up was tricky, if I unzipped my jacket I'd have turned into a hang-glider. But within ten minutes I felt a thump, slack line, then the comforting head shakes of a decent bass. It was a four pounder and I put it in the bag. I fancied a fish supper anyway, and when I come home looking like a rat that's been drowned by a water cannon my wife tells me I'm crazy. 'Yes,' I'd be able to say, 'crazy like a man with top quality seafood.' There were four squid left in the bag. I tied on the biggest, a ten-incher. It would create a lot of wind drag, but it looked so good I was tempted to have a nibble myself. And it produced a fish I measured at eleven and a half pounds before turning it loose. Time for a ciggie break, but lighting it was a bit of a trick. The wind's always slower close to the ground, friction, so I lay on my tummy, pulled my hood way forward, and flicked my Bic repeatedly. Finally I managed a small flame and a relaxing puff, so I got to my knees.

At this point a fellow with a spaniel showed up. 'Any good?' he asked. 'Terrific. A big one and a beauty for supper. I just can't imagine why there aren't more people fishing.' He peered at me: kneeling with sand and weed all over my front, woolly hat dribbling down my neck, glasses speckled with rain drops. 'Well,' he said, 'I'm no expert but I think I can.'

Craftsperson Needed, Bodgers Need Not Apply

'Looked like something death brought with him in his suitcase'
Warren Zevon, *The French Inhaler*

T.C. Wickham was a Winchester doctor in the late nineteenth century and his name will live forever. As far as I can tell his professional career was unremarkable. He doesn't seem to have treated members of the royal family or discovered a ground-breaking therapy for housemaid's knee; probably because he bunked off from the surgery as often as possible to muck about by the water. And he gave his name to the Wickham's Fancy. William Greenwell was a Church of England cleric. We don't remember him for theology or sermons. In fact I reckon he may have chosen his career so he could put in a long shift on Sunday then spend the rest of the week fishing – and inventing the Greenwell's Glory. I'd love to give my name to a fly, to know that a hundred years from now anglers would rummage through their boxes, tie on something pretty, catch a bass, and wonder 'Who was this Leakyboots? He did a good job anyway.' And I have the concept, it's just the execution that's holding me back.

Most people who fish flies for bass use sinking lines and streamers. I love to see a take on the top and I fish the shallow stuff, so my line's a high floater. Through the summer there are jelly-fry and whitebait on my marks. Both make tiny splashes. They don't jump clear of the water, you just see spits, maybe as their tails flip over. I decided the Leakyboots Lure would work like a skinny popping plug, a slight disturbance when you tweak it along. Easy so far, but there's a wrinkle. Bass never seem to eat small fry right at the surface. They swirl at sandeels, but jellies and whitebait meet their maker a bit deeper down. So my fly needs to come up to do its sprinkler trick, then sink into the feeding zone. Just a smidge heavier than neutral buoyancy, that's the goal. Still so far so good. There's a substance called plastazote, like dense wetsuit material, it's used for orthotic insoles. Also for floating flies like gurglers. So the plan was a cone of this plastazote, flat end at the front to stir up the ripple; some fine lead wire around the shank to help the fly sink between pops, a silvery coating on the cone, and a tinsel tag and wing. The tinsel admits of variations, a bit of red for a Bloody Boots, yellow for a Lemon Leaky, and so on.

Design phase complete, I moved on to manufacture. I tried carving my cone with a razor blade, then making a slit so I could fit it over the shank. Two hour later I had nicks in my fingers and foam shavings everywhere. In Banjul I whittled my broomstick plugs with ease. It's a lot harder when you're hacking at something the size of skinny wasp, and when your material bends itself out of the way of the blade. It's only a footnote in art history but Michelangelo went on the record as saying, 'A synthetic foam David? Stuff that, I'm a genius but I'm not a bloody magician.'

And by the way, a tip you won't find on the fly-tying websites: buy plastazote the same colour as the stair carpet. The little offcuts stick to your trousers, then fall off as you wander about, and if they're yellow it's obvious who's to blame for the mess. I abandoned the sculpting method and cut thin strips with a view to winding them around the hook, more turns as I reached the eye. That was promising until I added the fine lead wire underbody. With that enhancement I lost my conical profile, the whole thing looked like a miniature salami in a banana skin with multiple hernias. I never got as far as the nail varnish, there's an unopened bottle in my desk drawer to this day. I'll hang onto it, I might be invited to a glam-rock fancy dress ball. Or I might even run into someone with the patience and fine motor skills I so clearly lack. Until that happens my lure remains on the drawing board, my name unknown in the fly fishing community.

Of course it's disappointing, I'd like to be a household name, even if that house is small and occupied only by nutty fluff chuckers. But I don't feel inadequate. A hundred and fifty years ago doctors and vicars had help. Maybe Wickham interviewed his nursing assistant by asking her to spell 'headache' and to whip up a Coachman. Maybe Greenwell's organist could bash out *Onward Christian Soldiers* with one hand while the other crafted a Connemara Black. I don't have a resident tyer on staff, just a cat. So if I'm to join the immortals I'll have to come up with a new wheeze.

Up Against It

'You're all just pissing in the wind'
Neil Young, *Ambulance Blues*

Sometimes we go fishing because there's a chance of catching something. Sometimes we go because we're convinced there's a trophy bass out there with our name on it – in a good blow on a big tide. And sometimes we go fishing because we're anglers and that's what anglers do.

One April morning I headed for a nearby beach. The tide was coming up to high, once the water reaches the shingle it's a fairly steep drop-off. There was no sort of wave but I was betting baitfish might be herded against this barrier. And anything's possible when you've a rod in your hand and delusional optimism in your heart.

I came across a chap I know, he fishes there from time to time. Not today, just an early walk for his dog before he went to work. 'A tough one, my handsome. Chance of some mackerel, I suppose, I've heard they're starting to find them from the boats.' And that wasn't a bad idea. I walked the length of the bay flinging a guesswork jig at the horizon. That's the trouble with mackerel, no clue where to find them. They seem to belt around at random, like the clowns who stare at their smart phones as they stride through town, nonchalantly flattening toddlers, grannies, and shopping trolleys. But unlike 5-G eejits, mackerel have a redeeming virtue, they're tasty. And bloody mindedness was rewarded, a mile into my route march I found a couple of big fat ones.

Bass

Mission accomplished, not bad for such a hopeless-looking morning. I set off back to the car, wondering whether to fry them with garlic and chillies or a light dusting of curry powder. And that was when I saw a swirl a yard out from the shingle. I pulled up and collapsed into a creaky kneed squat, a human shape outlined against the moon can scare away the fish. Peering along the water's edge there were tiny fins in the surface film, then another whirlpool like the last trace of a sinking boat. Fair enough, it would have been a small boat, maybe crewed by a dormouse, but adrenaline enhances my vision. I rummaged in my knapsack for a plug with a black back and a shiny white belly. A toss parallel with the water's edge, two turns of the reel, and a four pound bass tore off into the gloom. And that's why we go fishing even when conditions are dire.

Just Desserts

'It's always cold and windy down here'
Mental As Anything, *Fringe Benefits*

The technological advances of the last twenty years have left me colder than charity. I remember a financial type telling me to buy shares related to devices with some number of Gs as a prefix. I said no, what bloody fool would want to watch videos on a telephone for heaven's sake. I acquired my first ever mobile in 2020. I didn't want it, Shelley insisted I have it for when I'm on the road. She struggled to find one that meets my criteria: it makes calls. It also receives calls, but only rarely, most of the time I can't remember which button to press. And that's the lot. No texting or social media thank you very much, I don't need that guff in my life. And only once can I recall being glad of one of these clever dick gizmos.

It was on a north coast beach in the middle of a late summer storm. It had a name, so it wasn't many years ago, rough weather was anonymous until 2014. In the carpark were two big station wagons, rod tubes on the roofs, tackle boxes in the luggage spaces, and four large men sprawled on the reclining front seats. Evidently waiting for the wind to drop below forty knots, maybe for the raindrops to be smaller than sparrows' eggs. I tackled up on the tarmac, the sand was flying. As my bait went on I saw a small figure approaching, rod in hand. Political correctness might have me refer to her as a young woman. Stuff that, she was a tiddler, thirteen or fourteen years old I'd guess. Not exactly dressed for the weather either, a rain jacket, jeans, and wellies.

Her name was Erica, her family had a caravan close by. 'And I'm going to catch their breakfast,' she announced, 'I've read that bass bite well when it's wild.' Her terminal tackle wasn't quite up to the conditions so I sorted her out with a wired lead, a pair of 4/0s, and half a mackerel. Then I delivered a stern warning about staying well back from the water's edge. I'm good at that, all those years teaching.

I also set up a good deal closer than normal, only twenty yards between us on the sand, so I could see when Erica's rod hooped over. 'I'll come and help you bring her in,' I yelled. But as I pulled my gear clear of the bottom my rod thumped as well. We each had a fish of about four pounds. 'There's breakfast,' she chirped. Twenty minutes later we had another tandem take, twins again, this time seventy centimetres. Erica took snaps on her telephone, then we released them into a pool. The tide was making, it would be underwater in half an hour or so. 'You did a brilliant job,' I said. Then I looked her over. She was grinning like a quokka doing stand-up but her trousers were soaked and she was shivering. 'Erica, I say we call it a day. You should get back to your van and put on dry togs. Besides, we've each had one to eat and a good one to go back.'

In the carpark a fellow from the station wagons was up and doing, nursing a coffee as he peered through the rain. He looked at Erica's breakfast bass. 'Well done, little girl,' he said, 'a decent fish for the conditions. But you never get big ones when it's this rough. That's why we didn't bother.' My daughter Bailey has a look that says, 'You are such a cretinous waste of skin.' It's a combination of incredulity, resignation, and disgust. Erica gave him that look as she dug out her phone and showed him her photos. 'We didn't do so badly.' 'Well,' announced the bloke, 'you really are a lucky girl.' And this time the look came from me, I can't stand it when people talk to children as if they were idiots.

'She's not at all a lucky girl. She fished ideal big bass conditions, she fished them really well, she stuck it out in filthy weather, and she earned her bass. Keen, yes. A nut, perhaps. Lucky, not a bloody bit.'

A Proper Job Expert

'Oh John the wine he saw the sign'
The Incredible String Band, *A Very Cellular Song*

As a bass fisher you have to realise there's a great deal you don't know. The more experience you develop the more you understand that the fish always have a few more tricks up their scales than you could imagine. For some anglers that's a dispiriting idea: I'll always be lost. For me it's a source of delight: I'm less lost than once I was, but there are enough mysterious highways and byways to keep me learning for the rest of my life. And sometimes I meet a person who can show me a section of the map I've never seen.

One calm summer's morning I was on a pier in search of mackerel, big ones for supper and babies for the bait area of the deep-freeze. Some anglers have dedicated bait freezers. I just try to keep my joeys and razors away from the peas and oven chips, I'd hate to shove a packet of squid in the microwave by mistake, or arrive on the beach with wheels of frozen courgette from the garden. As the sun crept over the bay an elderly gentleman pottered onto the jetty with his dog. Now when I describe someone as elderly I mean well over eighty. The dog was no spring puppy either, a grey muzzled retriever who looked as if she'd spent most of her life retrieving cream cakes – and eating them. They sat down, he on a bollard, she on the concrete, and we had a smoke and a yarn. At least, two of us did.

He was John and he'd started life as a tin miner. When that industry died he'd been a trawlerman. Then, he had a little boat of his own he said, trolling bass, potting, whiffing mackerel and squid. 'The wife always told our boys to ask Dad when they were thinking of a career. Then whatever Dad said, do the opposite.' He paused for a puff. 'There's a bass there, my flower.' 'Where?' 'See that raft of weed? She's two feet down tide from it. Give her a go.' I slung my jig to his spot, as it sank a two pounder grabbed it. 'You'll often find them loafing around behind a mat like that,' said John, 'the whitebait and prawns shelter there. Easy pickings. I reckon there's another one there, where the two currents meet.' There was, but only a tiddler. For fifteen minutes John pointed to likely spots, always with a well thought out reason. They didn't all produce, but I released five fish.

I've no idea how many years John spent with his lines and pots, studying the sea. Quite a few, maybe twenty years of mucking about in a boat. But I'm not seventy yet, there's time for me to learn a whole lot more.

A Suitable Case for Treatment

'All he gives is a humbug pill, a dose of dope and a great big bill'
Blind Alfred Reed, *How Can a Poor Man Stand Such Times and Live?*

There's a modern tendency to medicalise more and more conditions. In some cases this is down to better science, deeper understanding, and that's great. When I was little nobody was diagnosed with dyslexia. Children who read poorly were called lazy and their teachers hit them with canes. Or they were written off as thick and sent to colour in pictures while the rest of the class studied *Paradise Lost*. People with autism were tagged as weirdos, those who suffered from depression were softies who needed to get a bloody grip. I'm glad those days are gone. But read the health pages in the tabloids or watch American television advertisements and you realise there are treatments for things our parents never would have recognised as issues. 'Does your bottom itch? You might have IRS, Irritable Rectum Syndrome. And there's help around the corner. Ask your doctor about Magic-Arse and feel better in minutes.' Alternatively stop eating vindaloo three times a day and using cheap lavatory paper made from recycled thistles.

A good deal of this bullshit is driven by money. Once the pharmaceutical companies come up with a name for a problem they can sell a therapy to address it. That works even if the science is iffy. If it's non-existent, that's when the alternative medicine industry jumps in – and it's worth remembering that 'alternative medicine' means shite that never has been proven to do anything at all. Once a formulation produces results in a replicable trial it loses the 'alternative' tag, it's just medicine.

But for all their greed there's one cluster of symptoms the pill peddlers haven't addressed. Those symptoms include mild irritability, dry waterproof clothing, new lures still in their packaging, full bait freezers, obsessive attention to local catch reports, and a recurrent tic in the reel cranking hand. It's a cyclical problem, exacerbated by big tides and onshore breezes: DAWN, Desperate Angling Withdrawal Neurosis. Mild onsets can be relieved by sharpening hooks, making rigs, tying flies, or buying unnecessary items of tackle. Moderate cases call for a brief trip to the water. Severe attacks are remedied only by staying out in vile weather until there's at least one good fish on the shore.

All anglers are a few bricks short of a load, the only reason drug companies ignore us is that we already know how to treat ourselves, we don't need their potions. But even within our nutty ranks there are people who stand out. Never mind a few bricks, how about a few dumpy bags full. And these crackpots are a delight. Take the woman I met on a rocky shore in early summer. She'd a rod but it was lying at her feet as she dipped a small net through the shallows. As I approached she emptied the net into a glass beaker of water. 'What's up?' I asked. 'You're going to find this is odd,' she began. Great build up. When one bass fisher reckons another bass fisher's going to find something odd, it's going to make Lady Gaga look like a conservative dresser. 'It's just that I want a really good look at one of these baby fry.' 'For sure,' I said, 'I call them jelly-fry. The bass go really well to them. I use a size six fly on a dropper in front of my lure. Would you like to try one?' 'Thank you, that's very kind. But it's a bit odder than that. You see I only ever fish soft plastics. And I don't buy them, I make my own. So this is a sculptor's model, if you will. Then when I'm back home I'll start tinkering.' She dug out a mobile telephone, took a few snaps of her tiddler, then released it into a pool. 'It's going to be fun. There's a whole new problem to solve: how do I make something so small and still have enough weight to cast it. Maybe a cavity with a steel rod. And the way they swim, that's interesting as well. Usually I experiment with the thickness of the plastic until the action looks right. Then I test them in the bath. My neighbour has a swimming pool, I'd love to use that. But I'm a GP, my neighbour's parents are my patients, my husband said they'd lose confidence in me if they saw me pulling toy fish around on strings and making videos of the way they move. And I suppose he's right.'

She showed me her lure box: sandeels, mackerel, pollack, worms, squid, whitebait. 'Most of them are hollow. That means I can add weight, or inject oil to make them more attractive.' 'And do they all catch fish?' She smiled blissfully. 'Everything you see has been responsible for at least one bass. And I can't wait to get to work on my fry pattern.'

Now those are proper symptoms, but no need for medication, just a good supply of plastic, silicone, glitter, and dye. And fishing water.

Will You Be Quiet?

'I'd ask him what the matter was but I know that he don't talk'
Bob Dylan, *Stuck Inside of Mobile with The Memphis Blues Again*

One of the many happy memories of my teaching years was when I was giving the class a bollocking. I don't know what the children had been up to, but I thought I was in full disciplinarian mode, finger wagging for emphasis and an extra threatening manner. There was a buzz in the room, then a crystal clear voice cut through the hubbub: 'Will you lot be quiet, I can't hear him properly and I love it when he shouts.'

Some people I meet on the beach bring out the same sentiment in me: 'Will you stop telling me about the bollix you saw on the television last night, I'm in the middle of an important conversation about where the bass might be lurking. The only reason you can't hear anything is that I'm talking to myself.' But once in a long while I run into an angler who's even less chatty than I am.

One August night – I was fishing the morning shift but jet-lag had me up at two thirty – was great fun. The wave was modest, I used joey mackerel with a three ounce bomb weight rolling along in the tide. By four o'clock I was on my last bait, four school bass released. But that last bait must have had a personal hygiene problem, not a nibble, everything seemed to be giving it a wide berth. Then a slim fellow strode along the sand, a fat four pounder swinging from his bag. An eager smile so I braced myself for a five minute blether-fest about Olympic water polo, some television show where hapless amateur entertainers undergo ritual humiliation at the hands of judges so smug you'd like to smack them, or sharp practice in the leek growing division at the flower show. But no, he stopped, uttered one word, and scuttled away along the shore. And that one word was 'Crab'. Unless it was a comment on the weather – which was markedly drab. But he was an angler, lures and baits are our top priorities, so I had a ponder.

A lot of people swear by peelers. I don't. They're a pain to collect, expensive to buy, and most wind up being munched by tiny schoolies. Hard crabs are more to my taste, especially if I can find big fellows, four or five inch shells. I looked up and down the strand for a rock to flip over, a raft of weed to lift. And what I spotted was three pallets, the kind they load onto coasters. They weren't connected, they must just have come in on the same bit of current. They were coated in weed, crusty with mussels and limpets. I flipped one over to see the crustacean version of a mosh pit at a sell-out gig. I stuck a few crabs in my bag, then nipped off the mackerel. On with a 6/0 hook and a big fellow, the hook going in one leg socket and out of another. Almost as the weight settled there was a solid thump on the line, a fat four pounder. Before the light came up I had three more, the best seventy-five centimetres, between ten and eleven pounds. A guess, but I'd say there was a lot of jetsam washing around in the Gulf Stream, collecting marine life along the way. Then it drifted into the choppier shallows and the hitchhikers began to fall off, providing the bass with a swim-through crab shack.

So if the lean and laconic gent should read this I have a message for you, and sorry if by your standards it seems longwinded: 'Yes, and thank you for the advice.'

Production Line Fishing

'I guess you're just what I needed'
The Cars, *Just What I Needed*

Easterly breezes are a pain. In winter they bring chilly days and chillier nights. In summer they're dry. That means watering the garden, either by humping buckets from the butts or using the hosepipe. And the sea flattens out as well. 'When the wind is in the east, that is when the fish bite least.' That could be just a Cornish rhyme, our coast faces south, west, and north. Maybe anglers in Kent and Essex say, 'That's when big bass have a feast' or 'Cast her out and catch a beast'. But certainly not in these parts.

I know one beach that can produce a bit of a wave when the weather's blowing the wrong way. It's not a great spot, too steeply shelving for my taste. It's also a half hour's drive away, so narrow that more than two anglers mean you can't move, and framed by rocky points that make it a natural target for inshore netters. Also you have to pay for parking even in the small hours, the bloke who hands out tickets seems to be an insomniac with a bad attitude. But one summer morning I gave it a shot anyway. It's a sandeel area as a rule, so a packet of big fat launce. As my reserve supply I had a bag of odd and ends. Had there been a label it would have said 'Tiddlers, probably useless'. Most families have a mythical forebear who kept a box of 'bits of string too small to be worth saving'. This was the bait equivalent: a couple of small scad, a whiting, a few other nippers. All had been too far gone to return, too small to eat, and surplus to the cat's requirements because a couple of fish are plenty for her breakfast.

In the cove there was one other angler. As I arrived he lobbed his gear twenty yards into the wave, which showed he was a proper bass fisher. Then he shoved his rod on a rest and picked up another. 'Any good?' I asked. 'Nothing on the bait, I'm on sandeel, quiet as a Methodist supper. I'm just keeping myself busy with the spinning gear, lots of little pollack.' OK, I thought, but you probably have regular eels. Mine are a secret weapon, eleven-inchers built like Fatty Arbuckle. I opened the bag, grabbed a beauty, and its head came away in my hand as a waft of rancid oil hit my nostrils. Rotten, beyond rotten, they must have been thawed out and frozen again. Now I like my bait fresh, I think it leaks more juice into the water. But even had I fancied something smelly, these chaps were so soft they were useless, it would have been like trying to secure chocolate mousse onto the hook.

So Plan B, and the first thing to emerge from the other bag was a nine inch pollack. Tie it on, buzz it out, hope for the best. And ten minutes later my line was slack. I backed up the sand to tighten, a cheery drumbeat on the line, and a four pound bass was zipping about in the wave. 'Beauty,' said the other chap. 'What did she take?' 'A small pollack.' 'Total beauty,' he chuckled, 'I've been putting them back. They'll be even better if we fish them live. Let's have a production line.' We took it in turns with the spinning outfit, bouncing a shad until it delivered a pollack. Meantime the other one fished the previous livebait on his proper rod. Six bass between us, all between three and five pounds. But I still like westerlies best.

The Pied Piper of Bass

'Teach your children well'
Crosby, Stills, Nash & Young, *Teach Your Children*

There are mornings when I wonder why I bothered to go fishing. The feeling never lasts long, it's obvious why I headed out, the alternatives were to sit at home reading grim news on the internet or drink too much coffee until the newspapers arrive at the petrol station, then do the crossword puzzle with fingers that shake from a caffeine overload. Anyway I'm an angler, I live in hope. It may look like a rubbish morning, but it's not over till the fat lady sings, the scrawny gent winds in his gear, and they have a bacon sandwich. And my crazed optimism's justified often enough to make sure the next rotten omen doesn't put me off either.

Early September, light winds, and a small set of tides. There were little bass on the rocks sucking down whitebait, but it felt like time for a change. I love my lure fishing. I also love kippers, just not every day, too much salt and the smell makes the cat go wild. The surf was bound to be tiny so I picked up a few ragworms in the evening. They're not a favourite bait, often a way of feeding schoolies, but at least they produce bites. I followed the advice of Lord Baden Powell as well, being prepared with a couple of frozen joey mackerel. The moon was half, the tide half and ebbing when I arrived, but from afar I could see the wave was indeed tiny. The surfers' website had said two to three feet, maybe those feet belonged to an infant. Or a kitten, the sea was like polished glass. So far so shite.

Worse was to come, there were four headlamps dotted along the shoreline. As I neared the water the lights clumped together and my heart sank to belly button level. Two boys and two girls, fifteen or sixteen years old, all wearing torn jeans and hoodies. If you believe the conservative-leaning tabloids this was likely to be feral pack of delinquents washing down ecstasy tablets with cheap cider before setting fire to a retired vicar. Nonsense, but youngsters tend to be noisy, shattering the peace that's such a vital ingredient of fishing. So by this point I was almost ready to head back to the car, grab the lure rod, and go somewhere else, anywhere else. The only thing holding me back was the ragworms: the tackle shop bloke had given me a generous dollop because they were past their sell by date, ready for the defibrillator. By next day they'd be fit for the compost heap. And I'm too frugal to waste bait for no good reason.

One of the teenagers came up to me. He told me his name but I've forgotten it. I wouldn't be confident spelling it anyway, he was Polish, I struggle with words that seem to have too many consonants and not enough vowels. They were on holiday, himself, his sister, and their cousins. 'Any fish?' I asked. 'Just very little flounders,' he said. 'We've got wonderful worms but the bass aren't interested. Anyway good luck, I'm going to take a break, see what's left in the ice box.'

Again this is where the everything-phobic leader writers in the low rent media would have him smoke some crack, neck down a bottle of vodka, and come up with a cunning plan to claim job-seeker's allowance while selling fake passports to illegal migrants. Bollix again, if I were to find fault with these kids' lifestyles it's that they ate more processed meat in a night than the NHS would recommend for a month or two. And I sympathise, they gave me some of their sandwiches later, kielbasa, wiejska, and several kinds of ham. Delicious.

But back to fishing. Rag wasn't doing the trick for the juniors so I tied on a nine inch mackerel, no weight, and tossed it thirty yards. And that's where it sat, not enough tide to move it along the bottom. So a lift of the rod every couple of minutes, haul it six feet closer to the water's edge. After half an hour I twitched at my bait to feel a solid tug in the opposite direction. A three pound bass. Like a shot the lad who'd been grazing the picnic was at my side, questions flying like raindrops on a Cornish bank holiday. What size, who was I, what bait? Then he said, 'Mackerel? We found a lot when we arrived, before it got dark. Not fresh enough to take them home, we just left them on the sand.' He scurried up and down the beach, coming back with a bucket of joeys and his three companions in tow. 'This gentleman caught a beauty,' he announced. 'What's more he's an angling writer, like a professor of bass. We should hold a seminar, give him our questions, then maybe we'll have a fish to take home for once.'

Some of the things they asked were Zen riddles. Where had all the tiddlers come from? OK, the bridge flows and the water's motionless, why? Obviously they hadn't been pushed ashore by the surf, there wasn't any. Maybe dumped from a boat, maybe a trick of the tide, anybody's guess. Some were easier. Why would bass ignore worms and eat fish? Probably more calories per metre swum to find them. Why no lead weight, why keep reeling in? A moving bait covers more ground. Would I like another sandwich? Stop being silly, of course I would.

By first light we had four decent fish in our bags. Just one of the youngsters was still blanking, Eva. Nothing wrong with her technique, she might have wasted a bit of time scoffing plum tarts and chocolate biscuits. The rest of us stood behind her, polishing off the last few sandwiches and willing something to pick up her bait. I don't believe in ESP, the power of positive thinking's a skip-load of drivel designed to sell awfully written self-help books to people in airports so bored they'll read anything. But just as I was reckoning it was too bright, time to wrap up and go home, her rod tip dived in the direction of the Americas. A four pounder, the best of the session. I grilled our fish on a bed of tomatoes and garlic. It was excellent, almost as tasty as the kielbasa.

In Search of Lost Time

'All I want is a photo in my wallet'
Blondie, *Picture This*

Some people take a picture of every fish they catch. I've very few snapshots, I've only owned a camera for six or seven years. My pals in Botswana were avid photographers, setting up their lenses and waiting days for an elephant to strike the right pose. I thought they missed a lot of what I saw and enjoyed because they were too busy peering at the light meter or adjusting the F-stop to look out of the truck window. The other trouble with pictures is that when you have them you feel the need to show them to people. That can be exquisitely cruel, testing whether 'bored to death' is a figure of speech or a clinical diagnosis.

Some anglers keep a log where they write the details of every outing. They can tell you that on the nineteenth of April 1989 the water was at eleven degrees, the wind was a southerly twenty knots, it rained, and no bass were caught. I've never kept a journal either. Memory's selective, it has an edit function, and that's served me well. In Tanzania we did a lot of boat fishing, trolling for tuna, king mackerel, trevally, and so on. I remember almost nothing about those trips because they bored me stiff. I've fished for flounders when it was so cold I hoped I wouldn't have a bite, putting on a new bait would involve taking my gloves off and watching my fingers turn crispy. Those days are gone too, my brain's deleted them.

I'm lucky. Some people dwell on the mistakes and miseries of the past. My cock-ups disappear, all that lingers is the stuff I enjoyed and learned from. The first time I caught a double figure bass in the 1970s it didn't occur to me to record the date or ask a friend to dig out a camera. But I recall it vividly. One of the old boys on the beach said, 'Proper job, my beauty' and I emptied the water from my wellies. Then I walked home, set up a table in the garden, and cut my fish into portions by the light of a pocket torch. It made eight fish pies. Nobody thought of bass as gourmet food back then, chefs hadn't come up with its posh double-barrelled name, Sea-Bass. The only thing I'd like to reconstruct from my angling past is a simple tally, trout versus bass, how many of each. I became a dedicated bass hunter when we moved permanently to the UK in 1999. For the previous forty-odd years I'd gone for trout as often as I had the chance. Over my life

I'd guess I've caught about the same number of both species, and it's my good fortune that things came in the order they did. Because trout fishing was a terrific way to learn how to chase bass.

Most importantly because one of the first things trout fishers learn is to match the hatch. There's no single fly, lure, or bait you can rely on, you need to work out what's on the water. Trout fans whose last science class was in primary school – before the nature study teacher chucked them out for making stink bombs from the poo in the guinea pig cage – give each other lectures on the life-cycle of the caddis fly. People who haven't read a book since the one where Janet and John took the dog to granny's for a cup of tea argue about the whether *Emphemeroptera* is singular or plural. So when someone on a beach told me lugworms weren't leading to any bites my first thought wasn't 'Dear me, a slow morning'; it was 'Then I wonder what the bass are eating today'. When a sandeel shad didn't do the trick my reflexes told me to peer into my lure box for something to suggest a whitebait or a mackerel. In fresh water I never assumed a slow day meant the trout had mucked off on their holidays, I blamed my ineptitude: I was the idiot punter who hadn't worked out what to tie onto the leader. The same thing's true in the sea.

Another feature both species share is regional variation. Plan a trouting holiday and the first step – after finding a waterside pub – is to read up on local patterns. I've seen flies on Irish loughs that you'd never run into on a Cornish reservoir. And bass behave differently as you move around the country. I stay in my west Cornish bolthole. Down here I expect weed maggots in late spring and early summer. Anglers in Dorset, just two counties over for heaven's sake, find them all through the year. I met a chap from the east who uses small scad as a favourite bait. On my patch, even if the sea's thick with scad, the bass turn up their gills in disgust. So tips you pick up from visiting anglers, though they're sure to be interesting, may or may not butter any bass fillets in home waters. Use an upcountry dodge in the west and people may dub you a creative catching machine; or they may say, 'What's that eejit from Sussex playing at, the daft one that's on a blank?'

Small feeding spots, that's another overlap. Especially in rivers trout have lies where they hold station and conserve energy, waiting for the current to deposit treats in front of their noses. No signs of life, OK, go into pantomime mode, maybe 'It's behind you.' So I wasn't surprised to find bass would hang out by a single rocky structure, that my plug needed to pass through the right square yard of swirly water to do any good. It struck me as obvious that a bait would work best if it trundled along the bottom, pausing in the dips and depressions where dead fish and crabs pile up.

Lastly I knew about stealth. Most bass hunters wade as a matter of course. I wasn't tempted to join them because I'd watched so many fly fishers charging through the shallows in their chesties. It's human nature: once you've spent a packet on high end waders you feel the need to wade up to or just over the maximum possible depth. And yes, often I saw these bold amphibians pouring cold water from their boots. I also saw big trout making eddies, scooting out of the shallows two steps ahead of what must have struck them as a six foot mutant heron waving a big shiny stick. I remember spotting a fellow waist deep in a reservoir. I waited until the silt settled and caught a two pound brownie behind his back. He had a WTF moment, then came ashore and started fishing the margins where the trout were waiting for hawthorn flies on the breeze. Bass are no different, they'll feed close to the shore as long as you don't try to kick them to death or squish them under your titanium studded soles.

So on the whole I don't wish I'd spent more time trying to be an angling Annie Leibovitz or a Samuel Pepys of the shore. I don't need a photo album or a journal to remember thousands of fishing experiences that make me smile, a fair few that help me land more bass. Mustn't grumble.

A Hypothesis Worth Testing

'I'll never understand why or how'
Emmylou Harris, *Boy From Tupelo*

I'm no scientist. My bachelor's degree was in economics, some people call it a social science. Rubbish, that's like describing someone with a lottery ticket as a social mathematician. Real science produces ideas that can be tested in replicable trials, economists peddle guesswork, they're astrologers with boring jargon. Mystic Meg goes on about lunation and the first house cusp, bankers do the same with yield curve inversions and purchasing power parity. But I admire scientific thinking, where you come up with a hypothesis, then devise an experiment to see if it's valid. As I'm retired I don't apply it in business or academia, I use it on bass.

First the hypothesis, part one of two. My surf beaches tend to look flat, which gives plenty of the shallow, stirred up water I like to fish. Walk these spots at low tide and you realise they're not flat at all. Some are scarred with channels that dip into the sand, others have potholes, and these are where bits and pieces come to rest. The space around them's clear, the lower areas are full of scraps of weed, crabs, and dead fish. Given that bass are inefficient at converting protein it makes sense that when the tide's in they'd look for their nourishment in the depressions. Searching a spot where the bottom's smooth is a waste of energy, moving from hole to hole delivers more food for less exercise.

Now for part two of two. There's no reliable way to put a bait into a small pothole thirty-odd yards away in the dark. One day some twisted bass genius might come up with something, maybe a combination of laser guidance to find the hole and a robotic rod to cast to it. But even that wouldn't be much good because beach sand moves with every tide and so do the dimples. The only way forward's to use a weight that doesn't quite hold the bottom, one that bounces about in the wave and the tide, but catches in places where the sea floor drops away a few inches.

There's the hypothesis in all its glory. The experiment was flawed from the start. A rigorous design might have been to fish two rods side by side on a tripod, same bait, same distance, different leads – a bomb that shifts and an anchor that stays put. But science has to comply with ethical standards and societal norms, and I'm a bass fisher. We can't be asked to rest a rod, it's an unnatural act, like skipping breakfast or marrying a laboratory rat. A further snag, I'm not just a bass fisher, I'm a keen bass fisher, I'm mucked if I'm going to use a wired lead any time I think I'd do better with a bomb. Scientific rigour's all well and good, but not if there's a chance I might miss out on a whopper.

So I was stuck with a second rate experimental design, but better than a poke in the eye with a frozen lugworm. There are two local fellows I run into on my marks. I respect them both as thoughtful and experienced anglers. They cast short, hold their rods, vary their bait with the season, and stay back from the water when it's calm. In other words they fish the same way I do, we're comparable; except that they both use wired leads regardless of the size of the wave. So over eleven sessions I kept track of our catches. That's a small data set, any conclusions are tentative at best, but it's a start.

And now for the findings. When the report on a commercially funded trial says, 'The results were not statistically significant' often that means 'We didn't see what we were hoping for'. The superfood supplement designed to improve cognitive function and memory was less effective than a placebo made from ginger nuts and custard. In a five hundred person preference test the new double caramel skinny latté scored lower than instant coffee mixed with dishwater. But my experiment, at first reading, showed nothing at all. I had twenty-six fish, my companions had twenty-four. It seemed neither the wired lead nor the bomb weight was better, it was a short head on the line. But here's the interesting bit: exclude schoolies under two pounds and the bomb scooted clear to win by a distance, twenty-two against nine.

OK, so back to the start and now we have a new hypothesis. It isn't bass in general that hunt their food by moving from depression to depression, it's bigger bass. Tiddlers swim around at random, their small mass means they don't need to conserve energy. Big ones sit tighter. Propelling five or ten pounds of bodyweight through the water burns off more calories, whoppers can't afford those wasteful journeys hither and yon. And this ties in with what I see when I watch fish from the cliffs on calm days: babies are in groups and they're never still, fat girls are solitary, washing around in the wave and moving only when they have to.

Of course a brand new hypothesis means I need a brand new experiment, more data, more comparative catch reports. I'm thinking of a rigorous long term study, extending over at least a couple of hundred sessions. Nobody said the scientific life was easy, I'll have to carry on fishing for quite a while.

Pass it On

'If there's one thing I can't stand'
Jason Isbell & The 400 Unit, *Codeine*

The other day I had a message on a fishing forum site, someone looking for advice, he was blanking on one of my local beaches. I did the best I could, and back came a reply: 'Thank you, you're amazingly kind.' Not really. I almost never tell people where I fish. I'd be as narky as a cat in a bubble bath if the word got around and one of my beaches were rammed with pup tents belonging to the some upcountry angling club, if a favourite cove were taken over by hooligans who leave tangled line and beer tins on the rocks. But when people are fishing on one of my marks that stable door's open already, the horse is down the pub and on its second pint. If I'm catching bass and they're not I feel like a man tucking into a monster pasty while some scrawny wretch gives me the Oliver Twist look. 'Not even more, sir, I just want something.' Of course there are a very few gits who enjoy flaunting their success and rubbing other people's noses in failure. Psychologists might diagnose them as sociopaths or narcissists, the rest of us think just they're arseholes. And there's no excuse for joining their number.

One late July morning I was on a long Mount's Bay beach in a light surf. The tide was big enough to create a cross-flow, a three ounce bomb weight was bouncing merrily, half a mackerel trailing behind. I was whacking a three and a half pounder on the head when a small figure approached. 'Excuse me sir,' a youngster, maybe fourteen, 'but would you mind telling me what bait you're on.' 'No worries, mackerel. And why would I mind?' 'Well,' he said, 'the man over that way just caught two small ones and I've had nothing, so I asked him. I think he's using rag, I saw him dipping his rig in the water, maybe toughening them up before casting. But he told me to mind my own bloody business and work it out for myself.' 'Oh well, it takes all sorts, I suppose. Worm's OK, lots of bites as a rule, but mostly tiddlers. Have you got any mackerel?' He hadn't, just lugworm. No bombs either, six ounce breakaway sinkers. So I sorted him out and away he went.

An hour later he was back. 'Thank you. I just had my personal best, three pounds twelve ounces. Another question. My mate just showed up, is it OK if I tell him about the mackerel?' 'No,' I said, 'tell him you're using a microwave curry and attaching the cooking instructions to your swivel. Of course you should tell him. And grab a few more baits while you're here, there are plenty in the bag.'

By first light the lads had kept a four pounder apiece and were heading to their caravan site. They stopped for a yarn and I gave them one last bit of advice. 'Hang your fish from your bags so they're on show. And when you pass the bloke who told you to mind your own business, stop and take a few pictures.' So am I amazingly kind? Not a chance. Show me an ill-mannered petty minded creep and I'll show him petty mindedness in a top hat and Cornish tartan underpants. But with a polite angler who's happy to help his friend, that's another story.

Bass in Cyberspace

'What a long strange trip it's been'
The Grateful Dead, *Truckin'*

When I started fishing in the 1950s advice was thin on the ground, maybe thin on the water. There were books, magazines, and local experts. A lot's changed in sixty years. Farmers used to take their carts to the beach after storms and load up with seaweed to use as fertiliser. Nowadays the council sends a JCB and shovels the offending flotsam into a pile before burying it. Children messed about on bomb sites instead of skateboard parks. Olive oil was something you bought from the chemist' shop and dripped into your ears to soften the wax. Cars and refrigerators were for toffs, working class Cornish people relied on bicycles and meat safes. And we still had polio. Happy days.

But the great revolution's been around information, its volume and ease of access. No need to leave a request at the public library – *Salt Water Fishing in Ireland*, Clive Gammon – and wait for an amnesiac hoarder to return it to the shelf. Just type 'bass' into Google, ignore references to Fender, Charlie Mingus, Jaco Pistorius, and Bill Wyman, and you'll have enough reading matter to last a lifetime. It comes at a price, some damned fool algorithm's going to bombard you with supposedly targeted advertising, but so what? Google seems to think I'm looking to meet a young bride from eastern Europe; also to join an American political movement led by a right wing religious fundamentalist bent on deporting gays and Mexicans and providing his followers with discounted Californian Shiraz. And I don't even like wine.

But there's no shortage of information and advice about bass fishing. The challenge is sorting the wheat from the chaff-like bollix, and posts about tackle call for scepticism that would make Pyrrho look like a sucker for a good yarn. I've always suspected some writers are nobbled by manufacturers and when my first articles were published I found I was right. Five hundred quids' worth of kit was mine as long as I promised to say it was better than a full English with extra bacon. I was polite, just that I didn't need new gear right now, and anything they sent would be evaluated on its merits. That shut them up in two shakes of a whiting's tail. Even honest comments on equipment need a pinch of salt and a sliver of garlic. I've used my beach rod for six or seven years, I'm used to it, it's my baby. And although all infants look like a late period Winston Churchill superimposed on an overweight Sharpei, I know my daughter was the prettiest child ever to pee in a nappy. So an eager beaver blogger may say, 'This spinning reel's the best I ever hope to own, deffo you should get one'. What it means is, 'It's part of my family, one of my children. It suits me and the way I fish, you might like it too. Or not.'

Some advice doesn't add up at all, it contradicts itself. I saw a discussion about braid, swear words at dawn, this brand casts further than your old shite, yes but this one lets you put your plug into orbit you ignorant tosser. Woven through the thread was another thing to look for, shock absorption. Everyone agreed that most of their big fish had taken close to the angler's feet. So why do we need line that lets us chuck a lure to the Azores? And it's nothing new, I remember reading Des Brennan in the 1970s. He said you must stand thigh deep in the surf and cast to the third breaker. Then he warned you not to be alarmed if you saw lots of big bass swirling between you and the beach. Again this goes on bended wader to beg a question: does it make sense to fill my boots with water when I could stand on the shore and cast to whoppers in the first wave?

Another thing to look out for: regional bias, and I don't just mean Cornish people slagging off Bedfordshire clangers and Forfar bridies. Bass behave differently as you move around, a dodge that's idiot-proof in Sussex might guarantee you a blank in Devon. And by the way, the Definitive Pie Map of Britain from Buzzfeed shows Devonians live in a pastry-free desert, any claim they invented the pasty should be treated with outrage and contempt. That said they have some good bass, but crossing the Tamar can mean changing your style. I met a top lure fan from Seaton. He was startled to see me fishing from the rocks, all his marks called for deep wading so you could put your plug close to the reefs. A chap from Norfolk had taken casting lessons, his home beach is sheltered by a ridge of sand a hundred yards out, the bass feed on top of the bar. So tips from distant parts always are interesting and worth looking into, but you can't just cut and paste them from Dumfriesshire to Dorset. Anyone who says 'This technique works' is a few words short: 'This technique works on my favourite mark', that's more like it.

Which brings us back to local knowledge, where the internet often yields slim to skinny pickings. Most bass nuts keep favourite marks under their spiffy baseball caps or tatty woolly hats. We'll say we were on a south coast beach or a headland near Land's End, the rest's up to you. And even the best and most specific guidance isn't always up to date. Take the May morning when I went up to the north side of the peninsula. It was my first trip of the year to this particular beach, but it's a mark I know well. As I parked a holidaymaker introduced himself, he'd read my reports on a website, where should he start? 'Come with me,' I said, 'at half tide there's an area that's all scoured out, lots of ups and downs on the bottom. The local boats are on the early mackerel, their discards seem to wind up in the low lying bits.' An hour later we were fishless. My man decided to move a hundred yards east, then I leapfrogged further along the shoreline. Still not a chuffing wibble, he shifted again. And first cast he hooked a two pounder. I joined him and the bites were steady until dawn, seven fish to four and a half pounds. By now the water had dropped so I took a look at my normal spot. It was as smooth as a rattlesnake's bottom. All the depressions and potholes had wandered quarter of a mile across the strand.

So yes, these days you can find any amount of information about bass, but there's no substitute for clambering into your waders and going for a hike. And I wouldn't have it any other way.

Chaos Theory

'Hand me down my walkin' shoes'
Guy Clark, *Walking Man*

About half my double figure bass have come from one small area. Eleven and counting, the best a twelve pounder. To avoid needless suspense and cruelty I'll be clear, I'm not going to say where it is. In Cornwall. Where land meets water. And that's your lot. But one thing I'm prepared to let out of the bait bag, how I came across my whopper-land. Maybe then you'll find one of your own.

It was October, when our beaches stop smelling of sunscreen, in comes the autumn aroma of squid and rotting seaweed. A big improvement, some cosmetics must be made from the nastier by-products of the chemical weapons industry. And this October the iodine tang was strong, the shore was knee deep in wrack. After a calm summer we'd had a three day gale, the first big blow rips up all the loose fronds and flings them into the shallows. But the surf was roaring, the tide was big, and I went in search of fishable water. I knew it was going to be a slog so I emptied as much as I could from my bag and pockets. Bomb weights, for instance, they'd be as much use as waders in a discotheque, two pounds of lead I could leave in the car. I dumped the sand-spike too, I only use it when I'm baiting up. The spare spool and the filleting knife as well. Then off I went.

I started on a small beach near our house. The wind was out of the west, the headland gives a bit of protection, maybe all the mess would pass us by. It didn't. In fact the shelter seemed to make things worse, there was a whirlpool effect with all sorts of junk piling up. I'm not sure anyone knows how currents work, the whole business is very complicated, like chaos theory where the butterfly flaps its wings and a few months later a tornado picks up a shopping centre and drops a frozen food shop onto an iceberg. Or something like that.

Long strands can be good. Even if the bit you're fishing has hideous amounts of flotsam, you can keep moving until you find a clear patch. I spent two and a half hours walking five or six miles along a couple of them. There was variation, in some places the weed was thick, in other places it was solid. But my line stayed dry. By now it was an hour before first light, plans A, B, and C had come up maggots, and I couldn't manage much of a plan D. In the end I thought of a really unlikely spot. I was driven by desperation, but I'm going to dignify my choice by saying it was perverse logic: if beaches that tend to be clear are full of shite, a beach that's shite central might be clear. Not much of a rationale, but who knows, it's all chaos anyway. You wouldn't expect a cabbage white to bombard the polar ice cap with frozen peas and raspberry ripple, my idea was just as daft. Because the last throw of the squid was at a spot where often you can't find the sand, it's buried under a couple of feet of seaweed, lost commercial fishing gear, plastic bags, and empty water bottles. And sure enough I had to scramble over a slippery barrier of assorted crap to get to the water's edge.

But even though I was standing knee deep in the sort of stuff that snaps off terminal tackle like a malignant brush cutter, the surf was fishable. It was almost dawn, I had time for just two casts, a six pounder then a seven. And lots more to come. Perverse logic, what a brainless idea, I feel a self-help book in the offing.

Not Quite Molly Malone

'They got some hungry women there'
Bob Dylan, *Just Like Tom Thumb's Blues*

Fishing tips can come from strange places and people. In Cornwall we describe some of our local folk as pixielated. Not pixelated, that's derived from pixel and it's something to do with the blobby look of a photograph from a cheap digital camera. Pixielated comes from pixie and it refers to a person who spends too much time chatting with small, imaginary creatures that dance around on west country moors and give misleading directions to holidaymakers; a role that's diminished in importance lately, the satnav sends drivers all around the houses anyway. If you're eccentric you march to the beat of a different drummer. If you're pixielated you can't hear the drums at all.

I met one of these odd ducks on a surf beach at dawn. I was packing up after a decent morning, a couple of three pounders, but nothing like as good as I'd hoped in such an appetising wave. Across the sand came a tiny elderly lady with two hessian sacks. And when I call someone 'elderly' I'm not talking about pensionable age, I'd say close to ninety. She was barefoot, wearing a studded leather waistcoat over a pink cashmere jersey and a pair of men's rugby shorts, size extra large at a guess, held up with twine. She was singing as she strode along, *Jumping Jack Flash* at full volume. We introduced ourselves, she was Morwenna, and she was foraging. One bag was almost full of dried wrack from the high tide line. The other held a few leaves of sea spinach. She admired the bass in my bag, I asked her about the weed. She was going to wash it, then put it in a pot of water in the bottom oven of her range for eight hours. 'Then you get something that's just like nettle soup.' I wondered why, if you wanted nettle soup, you wouldn't just pick some nettles and save eight hours, but I'm a novice when it comes to wild food, she was the real thing. To keep my end up I pointed to her spinach and told her there were some good clumps at the edge of the carpark. 'Thank you, my lover,' she said, 'that's good to know. Only I haven't been down here since the equinox.' OK, I thought, the equinox, maybe for some Cornish pagan ceremony, sacrificing wild garlic to the gods of Mount's Bay. 'The big spring tides, I always come here for them.' So not a druid, could she be an angler? Of course she could, a perfect match with the profile: out at odd times of day, a bizarre outfit, clearly obsessive, belting out a Rolling Stones tune to the seagulls, classic fishing behaviour. Then she went on. 'See on a really big tide there's a huge mussel bed straight out from where we're standing. Even at slack low water they're a couple of feet deep. But I bring my friend Annie, she's got long arms.' Then Morwenna dropped her voice to a whisper. 'I like it to be low tide very early or very late, not when there are too many people around.' An even more secretive tone. 'Annie's strange. Not crazy, but she wears the funniest outfits.' Says her pal who's sporting a leather jacket, a shocking pink jumper, and shorts borrowed from a second row forward. Since that day I've had my eyes peeled for Annie. She'll be a long-limbed lady dressed as a Womble, a member of the Swiss Guard, or a lobster.

As to the fishing tip, it was obvious. As long as it's rough enough to wash a few into the wave, that spot's great with mussel baits, bass with a few gilthead bream as a bonus.

A Two Pipe Problem

'Rain is falling just like tears, running down my face'
Tom Petty & The Heartbreakers, *Louisiana Rain*

I like rain. If you've ever had a Cornish seaside holiday you may be thinking, 'Then you live in the right place, you soggy Celtic prat. Two weeks of expensive indoor theme parks and wondering when the bloody caravan's going to float away to somewhere with sunshine.' If so I'm sorry, but I like rain anyway. It waters the garden and fills up the butts against an unlikely drought. It makes the hedgerows blossom. It turns the pastures lush and the cows moo merrily. And most important, it tends to come in on westerly winds, the ones that put a wave into the rocky coves and a surf onto the beaches. And I don't need dry weather, I dress sensibly for the shore, no skimpy bathing costumes, waders and a rain jacket. But there's one fly in the ointment when it's wet – runoff.

In cold conditions it can be a monster, not so much a fly as an overweight albatross. The Atlantic almost never drops below eight or nine degrees, rain can be as low as two or three Celsius, and a gully-washer produces a stripe of chilly water along the shore. Bass behave like our summer tourists, they hate the cold. They don't search for heated cafés or amusement arcades, they just move out into the milder depths. Summer precipitation's warm but it can play hell with the fishing too. Most of my marks are overlooked by dirt cliffs or dotted with pipes that drain roads and carparks. A soggy spell puts tons of gunge into the wave, the blue that drew artists to Newlyn and St Ives is replaced by something that looks like weak cocoa in a filthy mug. Bass tolerate muddy water, they run up turbid estuaries, but they don't seem to care for it. Like me I suppose, I don't spend my weekends firebombing shops that peddle alternative therapies to vulnerable people who should be seeing a GP, someone to provide real medical treatment without picking their pockets; but I'd never choose to set foot in one.

So coming back from a July work trip I faced a challenge. From the train window you can see stretches of Mount's Bay. Four foot breakers, but the board jockeys could have been riding in a gravy boat, light brown with darker streaks. Never mind that, I'd been away two weeks, I needed a fishing trip if only to blow the air-conditioned junk out of my lungs. But where? There's a north facing beach with no cliffs, just white sand dunes, that might be OK. Then I wondered about bait. It was too late to pop into the tackle shop for a face-to-face report so I looked at a few posts online. I'm sceptical about tackle recommendations from websites, but when people say they're doing well with mackerel or ragworm I take them at their word. And the consensus was sandeel, the rock hoppers were catching pollack and garfish, the beach brigade small turbot and bass. Good news, I had a few bags of whopping eels, by-catch from mackerel-fishing. Just a hunch, but I reckon a bait that's the same species as what the bass are feeding on, almost identical but just a tiny bit larger, can be irresistible. I know they don't think, but it's the psychology of the serving platter. When four slices of steak pie come to the table you'd take the one closest to you – if someone was watching. If you were on your own you'd spin the plate around and grab the biggest piece. And my launce were chubby beauties, tempting belly-buster portions fit for the most gannet-like appetites.

Early next morning I was on the sand, a three or four foot surf, no mud. Encouraging, but it was odd nobody else was fishing. The middle of tourist season, I'd expect a few all-nighters. Maybe the weather was putting them off, a light drizzle with the odd five minute downpour. Not everyone, I reminded myself, is daft enough to enjoy a soaking just because the rain's coming in from the Atlantic. But an hour later I began to wonder, maybe those catch reports should have been in the creative writing forum – not a nibble. And maybe the people who'd stayed at home had a point, the rain was lashing down, better pressure than we have from our terminally

Weever fish

inept water company. I moved along the shore, cast short and long, tried a squid from the reserve bait supply, and beached one small weever. Then as the surfers started arriving – they don't care about the weather, they're dripping all the time – I had a pull from a three pound bass which took as I was reeling in. There were peas in the garden along with the last of the broad beans and early potatoes, the fish came home to join them.

I cleaned her on the lawn, a practice I recommend. Scales on the counter can lead to harsh words, scales on the floor and ceiling to a full-scale domestic dispute, and it's hard to blame them on the cat. Once the fillets were ready I ran my normal autopsy. The bass had a stomach like a cushion stuffed with black puddings, but the lumps were mackerel heads, not a sandeel in sight. The day-boats land a lot of mackies, in high summer they sometimes fillet a bunch at sea and sell them pan-ready to holiday visitors on the quays. Then the frames go over the side. Maybe that was the story. Anyway I could see why my eels had been ignored. They were like slices of that pie, even a giant wodge wouldn't tickle my fancy if I could see another plate piled high with whole steak and kidney puddings.

Next morning I was back with a bag of mackerel. I had five bass to five pounds. And the day after that mackies were useless, not so much as a wibble, it was back to launce. Why? Who knows? There's nothing to beat a good mystery.

Intelligence Gathering

'Well the first days are the hardest days'
The Grateful Dead, *Uncle John's Band*

When I was working, bass fishing was a way of having some balance in my life, it kept me sane. More accurately it kept me nutty, but in a socially acceptable way. If a client drove me round the bend I didn't look for a drug dealer or run naked into the boardroom with a samurai sword, I just planned my next trip to the shore. When I retired I was a bit nervous. Some people are concerned they won't have enough to keep them busy. My fear was that I'd want to do too much, that bass would take over my life. A local newspaper runs stories about elderly people and their odd achievements. A woman's made a cake from every recipe ever presented at her Women's Institute meetings. There was a photo, she's looks as if she's eaten most of them too. A man's had a pint in every pub west of Barnstaple. That story carried a picture as well, I'd guess it was a pint, two pies, and a pudding. With no job to keep me out of mischief I wondered if I'd fish compulsively every day, pausing only to stuff my face with bass, chips, and more chips. Then one day I'd be on page five, a twenty-two stone oldie with a rod and a satisfied smile. I needn't have worried. Right after I stopped travelling Shelley and I set up our little charity to help Yezidis after the genocide of 2014 and if I'm obsessive about anything these days it's raising enough money to keep it running.

But I still manage to go fishing a lot. And if I don't have a rod in my hand, bass are never far from my thoughts. Some mornings I go for a walk. My route doesn't vary, down to the beach and back. The excuse for being such a dull dog: it's a stiff climb on the way home, that's a good workout. The real reason: I can look at the surf and decide where my next fishing trip's going to take me. I always pick up my newspaper from the filling station, not because it's convenient, it means driving past a different stretch of the coastline.

Even food shopping can be a chance to do some research. I don't buy fish – that would be an admission of failure – but sometimes I pick up mussels, crab, or prawns. You can buy them from the supermarket, that's no fun. Ask the so-called fishmonger where the bass are from and you'll be directed to the little label, 'Sustainably caught, produce of the UK' or 'Cyprus, imported'. Fishmonger my arse, the blue and white stripy apron comes from the wardrobe department, tomorrow it'll be red and white, move over to the meat counter and read a script about beef sourced from British farms, your rump steak came from a Hereford bullock called Bertie who lived an idyllic life on a Cotswold farm run by Bartholomew and Belinda. But we have a couple of small shops in Newlyn where the people who fillet the haddock have brothers, sisters, husbands, and wives on the trawlers. They know what's going on. 'Matthew brought the bass in, seven boxes he had, fishing over the stones. He stood two rounds in the pub. Paid cash too.' That's a fishmonger. One April I popped in for some mussels and the ice counter was a foot deep in little mackerel, eleven or twelve-inchers.

In the spring most of the mackerel seem to come from the Scots vessels, I think they fish deep for them. But no, these were local, one of the day-boats in Mount's Bay, Trevor. He'd been out pulling his pots when they showed up on the fish finder, he landed twelve stone. That was interesting. No, it must have been exciting, I was half way to the car before I remembered why I'd come to Newlyn in the first place, I had to hoof it all the way back for my mussels. And they're not the sort of thing I forget as a rule. Milk, teabags, soap, possibly; but mussels with shallot, garlic, cider, cream, and parsley, they stick in my imagination.

I was excited because the bass had been sparse of late, and finnicky, like people who take their dietary advice from unqualified prats in halfwit newspapers – by the time they've decided to give up lactose, gluten, spices, spuds, brassicas, onions, mushrooms, and meat, every trip to Tesco turns into a two hour scavenger hunt with slim pickings. One day I'd have a few fish on ragworm, another day it was squid, then hard crab. And whenever I took one home to eat, its stomach was almost empty. But if the bay was filling up with mackerel, that could be the start of something. Lots of grub means lots of bass – they can follow the shoals. And they find tiddlers hard to resist, maybe the fussy eating would be a thing of the past. I looked at three beaches on the way home, and took a bag of joeys out of the deep-freeze to thaw overnight. Next morning I went through the whole lot, five baits, five bass, the best a six pounder.

And maybe that's the best thing about fishing in retirement: more time for reconnaissance.

Of Course it isn't Fair

'None is crying out for justice'
Peter Tosh, *Equal Rights*

We like to believe people get what they deserve. A clumsy child who spends thousands of hours catching balls in the park winds up captaining the national team. A veteran hospital cleaner wins a massive lottery prize, buys her mum and dad a house, and gives millions of pounds to charity. But things don't work like that. A lot of sports stars were identified as talented toddlers, then coached and hot-housed at public expense while their less coordinated pals cleaned kit and mowed the pitch. The lucky ticket holder turns out to be a skeevy stockbroker who pisses away the prize money on cocaine, sports cars, and settling sexual harassment cases. The reward of industry and virtue is the knowledge that you did your best and tried not to be a dick, that's all you get. No surprise if you're an angler, we know life isn't fair. Fish like champion all night for a few schoolies, some total incompetent's going to pitch up as you're heading home, make one cast, unpick the resulting tangle, and beach a ten pounder. Spend two hours digging lugworms so big and juicy you're tempted to add them to your sandwich, you'll arrive on the mark to find the fish are on squid and your lumbago means you can't concentrate because the paracetamol's making you groggy. Our patron saint's Peter, he must have a twisted sense of humour.

One example was in May. The weather was sunny so it must have been the middle of the month, between the imaginatively named Early May Bank Holiday and the equally evocative Late May Bank Holiday. Long range weather forecasting's easy in summer, just look at the calendar. If it's a day off, a pop festival, Wimbledon, or a test cricket match you can be sure of high winds and heavy rain. But it was calm and dry, one of my local tackle dealers had taken his boat out, shot a little net, and come back with the year's first good haul of sandeels. So I arrived on my rock mark brimming with optimism. Make that drowning in it, anglers always brim with the stuff even if conditions are rotten, I was in up to my woolly hat. Often that's a recipe for a long blank, when everything seems spot-on, that's when the bass decide to take a break and visit their cousins in Dorset or Dingle. But there were quite a few about, I had four on a skinny shad before the light began to change.

All small though, the best was two pounds, and I wanted something a smidge bigger for supper. I keep bass. Not a lot, I'm never close to butting up against the official limits, I'm what they call 'a sustainable harvester'. A bit of a mouthful until you look at the alternative: 'a chap who eats fish and gives a few to his friends but doesn't fill bin bags or otherwise behave like a selfish git'. And what I wanted was a three pounder, ideal for fillets chunky enough to stay moist in the pan.

Now one of my unproven theories is that larger fish feed closer in than littler ones. Another is that the changing of the light can bring bass into very thin water: in full sun they avoid it, but dawn gives them one last chance to scoop up a few treats from the shallows. So I clipped on a weightless silvery soft plastic and started chucking it at forty-five degrees to the shoreline. Three or four casts and I saw a healthy swirl. I reeled in, aimed my softie at the vortex, and gave myself a pat on the back: good thinking Bassman, you know how to find them. Another sucking slurp and my rod keeled over. Then the lure flew from the water. If I wanted to feel good I'd say the fish took short. If I'm honest I tightened too soon and too vigorously. When bass take a plug, a shad, or a spoon they hit it hard. Strike or don't strike, generally they hook themselves anyway. But with a squishy bit of latex they seem to suck gently, take it into their jaws, then turn. Once they've done that raising the rod sets the hook neatly in the scissor. But too much adrenaline, I'd yanked the softie out of her mouth. And now it was fully light, almost time to up sticks. Maybe I could pick a bag of sea spinach on the way to the car, arrive home with something to eat at least.

Then I saw a seatrout. And it was a fashion model or an influencer on social media, it wanted to be seen, it splashed into the drink and leaped again, all the way clear of the water. A cracker no less, I'm sure it was four pounds. It was sixty yards out, there's a lump of rock that creates a funny-shaped wave. I'd always reckoned there must be bass around it, but there's a kayak fishing couple I run into, they've hammered it time and again: mackerel, pollack, garfish, wrasse, never a bass. But a four pound seatrout, that would be fun. I rummaged in the lure box, the only thing hefty enough to cast that far was a two inch wedge. It didn't look much like a sandeel, maybe a baby sandeel that swallowed a new potato. What the hell, I slung it at the horizon anyway and started cranking like a pastry chef whisking egg whites. But no meringue, no seatrout, a three and a half pound bass. There's no justice either.

Two Chances, Slim and None

'You ain't going nowhere'
The Byrds, *You Ain't Going Nowhere*

There's something magic about reverse psychology. Tell a toddler, 'Eat your vegetables or there won't be any pudding' and you might as well have the mop ready to wipe them off the kitchen floor. But 'There's no way you're going to manage all those peas, impossible' and you're looking at a clean plate. Maybe we should try it with politicians: 'Ladbrokes have you at four to eleven to tell more than ten lies in the next five minutes, nine to four between one and ten, thirty-three to one against you telling the truth. Your time starts now.' We all like to pull off a longshot.

So when a fellow in the carpark told me I was wasting my time I took the bait. Common sense said he was right. The tide was small, the wave was puny, it was the middle of summer, and he'd been on the beach six hours for a weever fish and a pocket-sized schoolie. Not a pocket on a pair of those weird cargo trousers, a waistcoat pocket. 'I tried the lot,' he told me. 'Peeler, lugworm, squid. Useless. I'm going to have a kip in the caravan, maybe when the sun comes up there'll be some mackerel from the point. But right now you've got no chance.' There must be some etiquette around accepting a challenge, perhaps I should have slapped Mister No Chance in the face with a bit of seaweed and said, 'Honour will be satisfied, ragworms at dawn'. I didn't, I just wandered onto the sand. My tackle bag stayed in the boot. It turns into a stool, my arthritic knees appreciate that, but I didn't expect to be sitting down for a sea like this.

As I see it, the problem with static water is that there's nothing to concentrate the things bass like to eat. In a decent surf, worms, crabs, tiddlers and squid are pushed into the shallows. When it's flat they're scattered all over the sea bottom. If there's a current running that can do duty for a missing wave. It sweeps the flotsam along the shore, often piling it up in just a few spots. Not this morning, a big tide in my parish runs six metres above datum, today's was a three point eight. So the Atlantic ocean was like a giant pond, the fish could be anywhere. The mountain wasn't coming to me, I didn't mind coming to the mountain, but I'd have to find the blasted thing first. And maybe it was a molehill anyway. I put on a two ounce bomb weight and a sandeel. A thirty yard cast, a very slow walk along the shore, and when I'd dragged the bait around and almost onto dry land, repeat the dose. As often as necessary. Maybe there should have been another instruction, 'Do not use more times than recommended', it was painfully boring, between drying paint and growing grass.

Then I saw a pair of seals. Most anglers don't like seals, they're accused at best of scaring off the fish, at worst of eating everything in sight. I love them, especially those faces, like retriever puppies that found the Sunday roast and had a picnic on the lawn. And I've never seen a seal scoff a bass – mostly rays, scraps washed from the decks of trawlers, and flatties. As if on cue I felt a tug on the line, a mini-flounder. At least that meant my one person-power trolling operation wasn't a total loss. Maybe a bigger bait would do the trick. I took off the weight, tied on a pair of 4/0s, and mounted a whole mackerel. And in a stroke of tactical brilliance I decided to turn around and wander in the opposite direction. Actually the about -face was to help my legs: I'd walked a mile on a right to left slope, time to reverse the camber. I was almost back to the end of the beach and the sky had a purple glow when the gear suddenly felt light. The line was close to parallel with the water's edge but there was no drag. The bait's fallen off, I thought, better reel in and have a look.

And that's when the rod almost jumped out of my hand and the drag started buzzing. I could see my fish, she was in such shallow water that her tail beats were sending up spray as she ran. By the time she was on the sand the prophet of doom from the carpark was at my side, a spinning outfit in his hand. 'Jeepers, that's something I never expected to see. She must be four pounds at least, more like five. That's a whopper for a flat calm in July. Good fishing, my man, good fishing.' I did my best to be nonchalant, the old 'I knew I'd sort one out' look, but I've never had a good poker face. 'I didn't expect it either. The only reason I kept grinding away was that you'd said I had no chance. So half the credit's yours. D'you want half the fish?' He did indeed, and I think he deserved it.

A Crime Scene Investigation

'We never loved a shovel'
The Clash, *Bankrobber*

One September evening I pulled into a Mount's Bay carpark. I hadn't had time to read the paper and for my first look I like the sea in the background. When I see a repulsive comment from a politician I don't bang my head on the wall, I just watch the waves until the red mist clears. Beside me were two minibuses. About twenty-five people emerged with forks, bait diggers. I had a chat with one, they were a club from Lancashire, next day they were going to fish a competition. If you've seen films of the wheat harvest on the prairies, this was the worm equivalent, an army crossing the beach in line abreast formation, loads of churned up mud. That, I thought, is groundbait on steroids. Once the tide covers the trenches the bass are going to feast in the spoil. I chatted with one of the Lancastrians, she gave me a couple of dozen rag. In return I told her to try close in for their match. I hope she won, they were cracking worms.

Soon after midnight I was back. The surf was small, but no need for a wave, I knew where to find the buffet table. Sure enough the lead was settling when I felt a sharp tug. And that, I thought, is why you so rarely use worm, too many babies. A new bait, another stripped hook. But they didn't feel like schoolies. Even small bass thump. I'm not sure what they do to a regular bait, on a lure or a livebait they often introduce themselves with a head butt to knock their victim for six. These bites were like something grabbing hold, swimming a foot, then dropping the hook – a fishy shoplifter overcome by sudden remorse. It was too early in the year for whiting, what could they be? I switched to a 2/0 and finally landed one: a little mackerel. At which point I turned into whirlwind of busyness, a cooking show contestant when the judge says, 'The judges are starving and seriously pissed off.' A puddle to keep the mackie frisky, on with a 6/0, nip it behind the aft dorsal, and lob into the darkness. I kept the bailer open, the braid between thumb and forefinger. After ten minutes line started melting from the spool and I tightened into a seven pound beauty.

I sat on my backpack and wondered: what would Sherlock Holmes say? The dug-up area must have brought in the mackerel, the bass in their fin-steps. But hard to be sure. The livebait was an ex-livebait so I gutted it, Doctor Watson hoping for traces of worm. No luck, an empty stomach. And mackerel eat anything and swim anywhere. OK, they go well on spoons, jigs, feathers, sandeels, strips of fish, and prawns. But I've seen them take bread, one bloke had a dozen using the filling from a sandwich – cheese was too soft, ham was a winner. For all I know the Lancashire Anglers may have had nothing to do with anything. But I had fun, I'll always think of them kindly. And on reflection I don't think you'd catch mackerel on tofu. That's a challenge. Someone's going to prove me wrong.

The First Rule of Bass Club

'Your useless and pointless knowledge'
Bob Dylan, *Tombstone Blues*

When experience and logic send the same message you'd be crazy to ignore it, so I fish close in. Thousands of hours with a rod in my hand tell me that's where bass browse, especially bigger bass. I don't know how many people I've met who were blanking until I persuaded them to stop trying to fling their gear to the Scillies and focus on the water twenty or thirty yards from the shore. And it's obvious why the fish feed where they do, their treats are easier to find in the shallows. Tiddlers have fewer escape routes in thin water, they're cornered. Edible debris washes right up to beaches, lots winds up on dry land, most's not far from it. If Isaac Newton had been a bass hunter he'd have added a fourth law of motion: 'The angler who casts too far may be in motion, but the rod will remain at rest because the dafthead won't have any bites'. But bass don't obey laws.

I was on a storm beach one October morning, a five foot wave and colour in the water. Ideal conditions for a squid at close range, and sure enough I had a four pounder within twenty minutes. Then a surfer came up to me. 'Wow,' he said, 'your lead's only going thirty metres. Does that work? Some people send theirs way out into the ocean.' So I told him more than he wanted to know about bass behaviour and my well-tested theories. 'Interesting. It's not just that you can't send it further then?' 'Not at all,' I told him. 'It's like Roger Federer,' there'd been something about him on the *BBC World Service* as I drove to the beach. 'He doesn't hit the ball as far as he can. If he did that, it would be, well, silly.' I should have learned my lesson when I worked in America, everyone used sports analogies, the full court press, a *Hail Mary* pass, a triple play, I never had any idea what they meant. And now I couldn't remember what it's called if you whack a tennis ball into the next county. It's 'out', but that came to me later. To cover my confusion I said, 'Here, I'll give it some welly this time' and chucked seventy yards into the gloom. The chap wandered off and I started to reel in, put my bait back where it belonged. But my gear was snagged. I tightened harder and the snag thumped twice before taking off for the depths. I'd never caught a decent bass on such a long line, it took ten minutes to bring her in. A seven pounder. I had two squid left, two good fish, both at range.

I scratched my head. Most likely there was a channel out there or a deep scour. I took bearings so I could plop myself back in the same spot the next morning. Which is what I did. Nothing on my first couple of casts, seventy yards again, so I flung out even further. Still not a chuffing wibble, try winding in a bit at a time. And when my squid was in the first breaker,

Bass

thirty yards from my boots, a six pound bass grabbed it, a five pounder to follow. So were my faraway fish the exception that prove the rule? A freakish stroke of luck? A hallucination? I taught introductory statistics for a couple of years, not long enough to be an expert, but I learned how to sound like a pedantic prat. And I reckon – in pedantic prat-speak – that the way big bass feed is defined by a probability distribution, something like the famous bell curve. Most of the time they're in the middle of the curve. In my area of the country that's thirty-odd yards from dry land. Sometimes they're twenty or forty yards away. And once in a very long while you'll find them kissing the shore or lurking far beyond the waves. That's a mathematical explanation. An angler's take's more useful: bass don't follow laws, they do what they do.

Professional Advice

'Maybe just a hand, stranger'
Richard Thompson, *Hand of Kindness*

Anglers wind themselves up about commercial fishers. Lots of ranting about how we take care of bass stocks while they're guilty of wholesale destruction. I've no time for the criminal scum who set illegal nets or sell off-the-books catches to dodgy restaurants, but we should expect skippers with a lawful quotas to use them. Anything else would be like asking employees if they'd mind donating a chunk of their pay packets to help the underprivileged fishies. And good luck with that. I'm more inclined to moan about the bloody fools who set policy in the first place, but even there I'm more understanding than some. The fishing and fish processing industries account for about one eighth of one percent of national income, much the same as *Harrods*, less than some football clubs. So little wonder the minister in charge usually seems barely qualified to manage the cabinet's tea and digestive biscuits, certainly not to be trusted with anything as tricky as cappuccino or custard creams.

What's more I live near Newlyn, I run into men and women daily who work in and around the commercial boats. It's hard to demonise people you see in the pub and the post office, they don't have horns and tails, and they aren't buying flash motors or designer togs with the proceeds of slaughter.

One autumn morning I was after mackerel on the pier when a huge pleasure yacht set sail. As she slipped from her mooring some wanker picked up a coil of grubby nylon rope and a bucket of rubbish from the foredeck and chucked them into the water. I picked the slimy sandwich wrappers and soggy paper hankies from my line and made a rude gesture as the floating gin palace cleared the jetty. About fifty yards away a day-boat was coming into port. I pointed at the rope, which was unwrapping itself across the harbour mouth, I jumped up and down and yelled, and in the nick of time the chap at the tiller slowed his engine and gaffed the tangle of shite aboard. Ten minutes later he was beside me. 'Thank you, my pet.' That's normal usage down here, on a par with 'mate'. 'If you hadn't let me know I could have had all that crap round the propeller.'

We sat on a stone wall and had a smoke. He was Dennis, mostly he went after mackerel and squid. Of course I asked him about bass. 'Too much like hard work,' he said. 'And no matter how many I caught, Father would laugh at me. Back in the eighties, when they were decommissioning trawlers right and left, he couldn't find a berth. He was a qualified engineer, had his mate's ticket, but there were three or four people chasing every job. So he fished bass from an old Morris Minor. Did all right as well. He took me along now and again, and I tell you my lover,' (that's normal too, 'mate' again) 'we went to places you wouldn't believe.'

Then Dennis told me about a rock mark on the north coast. There are sandy gullies between the boulders, some of them reached by the sea only on high spring tides. 'The water was a foot deep at the most, but those channels were heaving with bass. Big ones too. Father reckoned all sorts of stuff built up there in the brackish water when the tides were smaller, dead fish, what have you. They were like a great big larder. Then a few days a year, the old bass could get in there and eat till they were fit to burst. He liked it best on a black dark night, creeping around on his hands and knees. No tackle either, just a hook on the end of his line, a sandeel or a crab. Drop it in, pull out a bass, on to the next mark.' I've tried Dennis' dad's spot four times. My best fish was seven pounds. Twice I blanked, I think the moon was too bright.

As we walked off the pier we met the harbour master. Dennis told him about the rope and the garbage. 'Did you notice who dropped it?' asked the harbour master. Yes, I told him, the posh ocean racing yacht from Portsmouth. 'Right, she's going over to Scilly. We can't penalise the skipper, he'll just say it was an accident, slipped off the deck. But someone's going to have a quiet word, tell him not to be such a prat in future.' Dennis grinned. 'My brother-in-law runs a crab boat on Scilly. I reckon Mister Portsmouth may find his posh boat doesn't smell too good in a day or two. She's at least fifty foot, lots of places to tuck away a mackerel or two.'

I'll Keep my Amateur Standing

'Using vulgar words of language'
Woody Guthrie, Pretty Boy Floyd

People ask why I don't set myself up as a bass guide. My first answer: 'How much time do we have?' Because there are more reasons than you can shake a squid at. I tried guiding in the Gambia. Lots of my clients were lovely, some drove me round the bend. And I reckon I'm less tolerant now than back then, less confident in my patience. What's more I spent twenty-odd years as a management consultant selling advice to companies and their managers. That's made me even warier of eejits.

A lot of the executives who hired me wouldn't tell the truth about what was going on in their organisations. 'We're doing fine, we just want to move things to the next level.' A few days later you realise this abject shower's last sale was in pounds, shillings, and pence, and you hope they'll pay your fee before they go bankrupt. With anglers I always asked how much experience they had. Some had never been fishing in their lives. Easy, spend ten minutes chucking lures along the beach until they could handle the tackle, stand close and hold their hands once you were on the mark. Some were very competent, they just needed a few tips about local conditions. These people tended to be modest. 'I've done a bit', then it would come out as we chatted that they'd spent twenty years after salmon or cod. The horrors were the ones who wanted to sound impressive. One fifty-ish Swedish fellow said, 'I started when I was ten.' As soon as the rod was in his hand I thought, 'Right, and you gave up when you were ten and a quarter', he was clueless. Another claimed he'd had whoppers from every one of the world's oceans. That meant he'd sat in lots of charter boats where the skipper finds the fish, the mate hooks them, and the geezer with the credit card sits in a fighting chair and does what he's told. He couldn't even cast.

Cash can be a snag too. Corporate types seemed to think giving me a cheque guaranteed results. Not if you pay stuff-all attention to the advice you bought; it would be like hiring a personal trainer to sort you out with a programme and leaving it at that. You don't lose your spare tyre by sticking a list of exercises to the refrigerator door. Even buying an ugly lycra outfit won't improve your muscle tone, you have to do the damned sit-ups. And stop scoffing an ice cream every time you go into the kitchen to look at your fitness plan. I had angling clients convinced the fee meant they were sure to land whoppers. A couple from Denmark wanted to catch trevally. I said I'd pick them up at five. 'But we have cocktails at five, can't we go on the rocks at three so we'll be back for our gin and tonic?' No, I told them, the fish came on around sunset. 'But we're going to give you all this money, you must be able to find something earlier in the day.' Maybe they thought I split my earnings with the trevally, give them a few extra quid and they'd change their feeding habits.

Another pain in the neck's the person who uses 'I know' or 'That's obvious' like a call and response gospel choir. In business it's a passive-aggressive way of whining about costs. 'Nothing you're telling me's new, how come it's so expensive?' I never rose to that fly, I'd just smile. I knew if we got into it I'd wind up saying something rude: 'If it's so fecking obvious, how come you've done stuff-all about it for ten years? Drink? Drugs? Or just bloody bone idle?' One of my Danish fishing clients wanted a barracuda. They can take off like a Jack Russell after a flying sausage, so twice I told her to make sure the drag was loose enough. 'Yes, of course it is, stop saying that.' Then a fish hit and the rod was yanked from her hand into the drink. My rod too, it took half an hour to find it. And Britta added to her English vocabulary: prat, cretin, and eejit...

But the clients I struggled with most were the ones who were delightful, such fun that I felt guilty asking them to pay. It was liking having a pal over for a barbeque, then saying, 'That's ten quid for chicken, twelve for booze, fifteen percent for service.' And most of the anglers I meet these days would plop neatly into that bait bucket, people I enjoy being around. If they need a tip they're welcome. In return I'll take a smile when they land their bass. Maybe a bacon sandwich if they have one to spare.

Like a young chap who came into the carpark near one of my rock marks. He opened the driver's door, introduced himself as Kirk, and offered me a coffee. A kind thought, I must look dozy at four o'clock on a May morning. He'd driven twenty miles to have a go in this cove, he'd looked at the Ordnance Survey map, it ticked the right boxes. 'But I'm new at this game, I'm chuffed to see a veteran like you thinks it's a good spot too.' By 'veteran' I hope he meant a bloke whose waders and tackle showed plenty of wear – not 'geriatric old fart'. We walked down to the shore together,

Kirk quizzing me all the while. How deep was the water, was there much current, what were they feeding on? Not the questions of a novice, it turned out he was a keen bass fisher. 'But I'm from Kent, I'm sure it's different here.' I told him I'd been doing best with flies to suggest jelly-fry. 'Right,' he said, 'I thought I saw a dropper in your line. Can I have a closer look?' I offered him a leader, a muddler minnow in front of a soft plastic. 'Very kind, thank you. But you might need it in a hurry if you snag bottom. If you've got a spare fly, that would be great. I can tie a dropper.'

I'd love to say we had a red letter session but we didn't. No trophies, a fair amount of weed, and not that many fish, three apiece, the best a two and a half pounder. We took a break to look in each other's lure boxes. Not the shopaholic chat, this is ten percent off this month. We had a proper job bass conversation, here's a good one when the mackerel are in, I lost a six pounder on this little shad. And then it started lashing rain so we scuttled back to our cars. 'Thanks for your help,' said Kirk, 'that was brilliant. D'you want some porridge? I just bought a little cooker thing that plugs in the cigarette lighter.' Again I wish I could tell you it was delicious. Not really, it was warm and filling, like eating wallpaper paste straight from the oven. But I enjoyed it a lot more than saying, 'You owe me fifty quid, plus two for the muddlers.'

Suspend that Disbelief

'Would I say something that wasn't true?'
Eurythmics, *Would I Lie To You?*

I must look approachable. When I'm on the shore people come over and have a yarn. I think it's the white beard, a skinny Santa Claus in waders. Or maybe it's just that there's nobody else to talk to, and as scruffy as I may be I don't match the stereotype for a mass murderer or a professional bore. And anglers almost always say hello to one another anyway. People with dogs greet strangers with strange dogs, people with rods are the same. An introduction I remember was from Bill, a visitor from Manchester. 'I,' he announced, 'am Cornwall's most sustainable bass fisherman.' I said I thought hook and line was a very sustainable method, so yes indeed. 'Oh no, that's not what I mean at all. I'm a real conservationist. I've been fishing for Cornish bass for seven years, an average of two weeks each year, and I've never caught a single one. Not even an undersized one to put back.' As we were chatting my line went slack. I backed up the sand and in came a three pounder. Bill stared at it. 'D'you want one to take home?' 'Yes, but not that one. I want one I catch myself. And one day that's going to happen.' I asked him what bait he was on. Ragworm, not a bad choice in summer when there are lots of small fish. And how far was he casting? He grinned. 'Promise you won't laugh, because it's improving. I measured my distance in a field. Pretty crap, eighty yards. But a year ago it was more like sixty-five. I'll get there.'

The beach we were on has channels running parallel with the tide line. As a rule the better bass are in the closest channel, the babies in the second. It's a place where I'd as soon fish an omelette on a kedge anchor as cast more than thirty yards. But Bill was a tough sell, a Mancunian cynic. 'Are you sure that isn't just something you tell the emmets, pull their legs and steal their trousers?' So I put on a new bait and made a twenty yard lob. 'That's what you do when I'm watching. Then as soon as my back's turned, you'll belt it out miles.'

He lit a ciggie. I had one in the turned up bit of my woolly hat so I dug it out. And before I could find a lighter the rod tip dived again, another three pounder. 'Holy shit,' said Bill. 'So you weren't having me on. Here I've been trying to cast further and further, making a bit of progress along the way, and I've been going in the wrong direction.' I reassured him, over-casting's the commonest mistake on our local beaches, nobody can imagine decent fish feeding where they do. Everyone thinks I'm taking the mick when I tell them where my bait is.

Twenty minutes later Bill beached his first bass. He took it home for lunch, which means he's not Cornwall's most sustainable bass fisher any more. Because I'm sure there are anglers out there right now who keep chucking their baits fifty yards outside the feeding area and blanking. I'll never meet them all, I hope a few might read this and break their ducks.

Strange Ambitions

'My analyst told me that I was right out of my head'
Joni Mitchell, *Twisted*

I remember a stand-up talking about psychoanalysis. His best line was that he needed to manage his neuroses but he didn't want them to go away, they were what defined him as a person. Quite right, without our odd traits we're dull dogs indeed. Businesspeople often work hard to hide their quirks. I worked with shirts so stuffed you could have put them in the oven and served them with apple sauce. No hint of personality as they chuntered on about maximising shareholder value and embracing the corporate vision. But after a few drinks their real interests came out: writing haiku in Latin, collecting Appalachian dulcimers, using beer mats to build scale models of Bob Dylan, a do-it-yourself tofu operation. Sober and in the boardroom they made ditch water seem thrilling. In their cups in an airport bar the mask slipped, they were weird, fun, and delightful.

The great thing about anglers – especially when we meet fellow anglers – is that we don't try to hide our nuttiness. Pointless, I'm holding a rod, so are you, game over. We both know we're talking to a person who's a few bananas short of a bunch.

One February I was spinning from a pier. I think it was 2014, the year the railway at Dawlish fell into the sea – we had the wrong kind of waves. But the herrings and pilchards enjoyed the storms, they stuck around all winter. Along the breakwater came a chap in a suit. No fishing gear, but his cap had logos. 'Penn' and 'Shimano', they might as well have said 'Loopy' and 'Obsessive'.

He greeted me, then asked if he could look in my fish bag. Another eccentricity, you wouldn't buttonhole strangers in the Tesco carpark to admire their parsnips and loo rolls. 'Ever see any bass?' he asked. The odd schoolie at this time of year, I told him, but I tried to avoid them in the close season. 'How? D'you know where they live?' he asked. 'Sort of. When the tide's ebbing they often hold in one spot. There's shelter from the current, but all the junk flows right past it. Scraps from the boat decks, prawns, tiddlers. It's ideal for an ambush. Right there.' I chucked my rig to the edge of the drift. On my third or fourth cast, as the jig sank, I felt the thump of a small bass. 'Wow, amazing. How much longer's it going to be ebbing? Have I got time to run to my car? I've got a pack rod in the boot. I'm from Southampton, I'm only here for a board meeting, but the rod lives in the car just in case.' I assured him he had a couple of hours of good tide. 'Great. You see we've got a challenge, me and three mates. We're each trying to catch a bass on a lure in every calendar month. I managed one at the end of last March, hard work but I made it. April to December, no problem. Early January there were winter fish still about. But February's been useless. Until now.' So off he sprinted in his shiny shoes and pinstripe bags. And fifteen minutes later his travel rod was bouncing. I unhooked his bass, I didn't want him to show up for his meeting smelling fishy.

As he snapped a photo of an undersized out-of-season schoolie he grinned like a Cheshire cat in a comedy club full of nitrous oxide. Then he darted off to have breakfast with his company's finance director. And none of it struck me as even remotely strange. An angler who's a total fruitcake, whose three fishing chums are covered in marzipan and royal icing, business as usual. Thank goodness for that.

Healthy Exercise

'I'm gonna leave here running'
Big Bill Broonzy, *Key To The Highway*

I bash on and on about the need to be flexible when you're fishing. You might say I'm like a broken record, except that broken records won't play at all, and the scratched LPs I remember didn't say a whole lot. Astral Weeks produced two or three notes from the bass, then a long hiss. Blonde On Blonde sounded as if Bob Dylan was singing in Gaelic with asthma and a sack over his head. Maybe I'm more like a defective MP3 file, but I stand my ground. You can't predict what bass are going to do, you need to find out and respond to what's happening in the water. Sometimes the plans you start out with are wrong. And sometimes you spend a whole session switching from one rubbish idea to another, the angling equivalent of a speaker whose mouth opens only to allow for a change of foot.

This outing was in May three or four years ago. I know that because my car still had doors you could lock, that let me keep my rods in the back. More recently the central security system died and a new one would cost a lot more than the whole banger's worth, so I leave it open. Nobody's likely to nick the vehicle itself, but spare tackle lives in the garage these days. Anyway it was calm and windless with high water due at dawn. There's a long shingly beach not far from our house, it's steep at the top of the tide, and bass sometimes push fry up against the shoreline. Ideal for the fly, at least for a poorly coordinated fluff chucker whose efforts at long casts usually end in tears, not to mention tangled leaders and a line that touches down as gently as a cow belly-flopping into a hot tub. It was warm and dry as well, ideal for a gentle stroll with a few schoolies.

After a mile I realised two things. First there weren't any schoolies, the water's edge was deserted, not so much as a baby mullet disturbing the surface. And second it's hard work slogging along through gritty pebbles, your boots sinking to ankle depth with every step. But peering out into the bay I could see a patch of dimpled water. Too still for it to be a wind lane, it had to be a shoal of something, mullet or mackerel most likely.

Grey mullet

Mullet often show up in late spring, they feed on tiddly shrimps and they go well to the fly. Mackerel come and go at random, you'd think they'd booked one of those mystery bus tours where you hope you might wind up in the Trossachs or Shakespeare country, then find yourself spending a week in a series of service stations on the M5. But either way the shoals were well out of my range, eighty-odd yards away, so I pludged back to the carpark for my spinning rod, a pair of baby feathers and a hefty metal jig. Forty minutes scuttling along scanning the horizon and I realised all the shoals had moved further offshore, close to two hundred yards.

Then at last something took, a nine inch mackerel, and as I swung it to my feet I saw a whole lot more wobbling around in the oily calm. Some were dead, some needed CPR, a few were swimming normally. I reckon a boat must have shot a net, these were escapees. I rummaged through my pockets for a big hook. Some weights, my tobacco and lighter, two torches, a receipt from the filling station, half a pasty of doubtful vintage, and two plastic bottles I'd picked up on the high tide line. No hooks. That meant another trip back to the car, and by now the light was starting to change, no time to waste. If walking on shingle's hard work then running's the sort of thing you'd expect as a judicial sentence just before they give you forty lashes and a one way trip to Botany Bay. There was a 4/0 on the dashboard so I tied it on, baited up with my joey, then dumped my sweat-sodden jacket on the passenger seat.

Back to the water's edge and I jogged along until I could see my crippled mackerel again. A gentle lob before I collapsed onto the beach to get my breath back. The eastern sky was pale when line began to vanish from the spool. Five yards, ten, and then I tightened into a four pound bass. In the still water she ran three times before I could slip her onto the shingle. A well-earned fish, I told myself, the mark of a chap who has some clue what he's doing. And that was when Murphy's Law received the royal assent: I heard a rumble of thunder, there was a flash of sheet lightning, a few seconds later the heavens opened.

When I arrived home there was a puddle in the driver's-side foot well, I emptied rainwater from my waders, and I stripped off my dripping togs in the porch. And yes, you still need to be flexible to catch bass. Sometimes it helps to have a few fitness sessions with an Olympic sand running squad. And the well prepared angler carries a waterproof top even if the weather seems settled.

The Angler on the Clapham Omnibus

'A kind of welfare state of the soul'
Lambchop, *Up With People*

It's hard to explain a lasting affection. Shelley says she married me for my spaghetti sauce, I say I fell for her cat and she was part of the deal, but we're kidding. At least I am, maybe it's time I made another batch of Bolognese just in case. But one thing I love about fishing's the way anglers help each other. Sure, now and again you run into a prat who refuses to let on what bait's doing the trick, a snotty eejit who sneers at cheap tackle, an oaf who says, 'Mine's bigger than that'. But you meet creeps in everyday life as well. And the angling equivalent of the person on the Clapham omnibus tends to be a bloody decent stick, even if the other Clapham-bound passengers need to make room for all those rods and to put up with the smell of old bait.

I think it's because the most valuable asset when we fish can be shared without being exhausted. Stuff like money and status is limited, the more you get the less is left for the rest of us. What turns people into dicks is a zero-sum game where you succeed only by shafting the other bod. Stock market trading for instance, or politics: 'I win' means 'You lose'. Anglers have different goals, we're not all trying to catch the same fish, so we're inclined to cooperate. One of us wants a tasty supper, another's after a double figure trophy, a third cares only about bass on poppers, so winners don't need to create losers. And more important, the currency of our sport's knowledge, you can dish that out all over the place without making yourself ignorant. Tell a blanker the bass are on sandeel and you don't immediately forget what they're eating today, your skinny shad keeps its magic. You're still having takes, now someone else is as well. And that's something real anglers enjoy.

Twenty-odd years ago I was starting to take lures seriously. I was pottering through a series of little coves when I spotted a tall gentleman of sixty or so with a rod in his hand. I sat on a rock, lit a ciggie while I watched him fish. Except he didn't fish, he just stood and stared at the water. Then he walked ten yards and stared at a different bit of water. I was down to my last puff when at last he cast his lure. Right away his rod started bouncing. He released a two pounder, checked his hook point, and set off for yet another little hike along the shore.

When the sun was fully up we headed back to the carpark together and I interrogated the poor man, a thorough grilling. Was he sight fishing? Could he see his bass before aiming a lure in their direction? No, not at all, he might notice the odd sandeel flipping on the top, but mostly he was looking for good spots. 'It's the shape of the water,' he told me. 'When there's a bigger wave it's easy – as the swell sucks out, you see eddies and foam. That means it's washing over a rock or a lump of weed, and that's where the baitfish are pushed around, easy for a bass to catch them. On a day like today, flat calm, you really have to focus. When the tide's running you can see where the current's disturbed by an obstruction. Sometimes it looks oily, even flatter than the rest of the bay. Sometimes there's a little whirlpool effect. Sometimes there's an extra ripple, like a cat's paw in the breeze. And when I see any of those things, usually that means a lump on the bottom, a feature that's going to bring in the fish. Let's sit down for a while, I'll show you.' For quarter of an hour he pointed out irregularities on the surface. And for another fifteen minutes he gave me an exam, I'd notice what I thought was a bassy spot, he'd tell me if I was right. That half hour turned me from an optimistic punter who chucked it out and hoped for the best into someone who really fishes his lures.

Another morning I was on a storm beach bouncing half a mackerel along in the cross-flow. Modestly chuffed, I'd been at it an hour, two schoolies. Then an older couple came across the sand. They walked a few hundred yards and stopped. Ten minutes later they were heading back to their car. 'No good? Too much weed?' I asked. Then I looked closer, they each had a four pounder. 'So is there a really good spot down the way there?' No, they told me, the shoreline was unstable, the current was different from week to week, even day to day. The best bass areas moved as well. 'So we look for a place where the weed's getting dumped on the shore or building up in the shallows. Where's there's weed, that's where the bass are going to find dead worms and fish.'

Once they told me, it was obvious, as obvious as the fact that bigots are self-loathing failures, that people who drive too fast through built up areas are narcissistic cretins. So obvious that I'd have worked it out for myself, given a few years and a few hundred fishing trips. But I didn't need to work it out for myself because a couple of seventy-year-olds from Land's End gave me a great tip.

And maybe that's what I really love about our sport. When the newspapers are full of stories about malignant sociopaths, slimy fraudsters, self-obsessed prats, racists, homophobes, sexists, and common or garden scumbags, anglers remind me daily of an important truth: most people are good.

Review highlights for James Batty's

The Song of the Solitary Bass Fisher

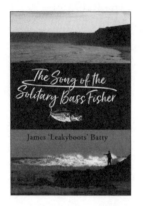

'The 192 pages are not only the how and why of bass fishing, but also contain hilarious accounts of his fishing and notable catches.' – *Sea Angler magazine*

'He loves to fish in those pre-dawn hours beloved of insomniacs, when the tide brings the big feeding bass close in to the shore. And so the book's real focus is on understanding bass behaviour, then using that understanding to work out the place, time and method. James Batty offers ideas as to how to catch bass in any weather or sea-state. But his book isn't just about the hows-and-whys of bass fishing, it is a wry look at life and it will make the reader laugh.' – *Western Morning News*

'This book is bursting with observations, ideas and advice which can't fail to educate and inspire the budding bass-fisher. The insights and tactics described in these pages will be valuable to beach bass-fishers anywhere – and James's approach to locating fish and understanding their feeding habits can be applied right across the angling spectrum.' – *Angling Trust*

'Batty's writing is funny and to the point, and he doesn't mince his words. What I most enjoyed about the book is how accessible it made bass fishing seem, finally. By encouraging me to look closer to the shore, Batty has somehow hauled bass fishing within reach. When I finally finished this book, I realised it wasn't going to be long before I picked it up again in the seasons to come, where I'll be putting my mind to work with my old rod and, thanks to Batty, some new ideas. Merlin Unwin should be applauded for publishing this refreshing book.' – *Fallon's Angler*

'I found the book hard to put down.'
                    – *BASS* (Bass Anglers' Sportfishing Society)

£14.99

Further reading from Merlin Unwin Books
full details: www.merlinunwin.co.uk

The Secret Carp Chris Yates £20 hardback

Falling in Again Chris Yates £20 hardback

Fishing with Harry Tony Baws £15.99 hardback

Flyfishing for Coarse Fish Dominic Garnett £20

Hooked on Lure Fishing Dominic Garnett & Andy Mytton £25 hbk

Canal Fishing Dominic Garnett £20 hardback

Confessions of a Carp Fisher BB £20 hardback

Fishing with Emma David Overland £9.99 strip cartoon paperback

Get Fishing Allan Sefton £9.99 hardback

Flytying for Beginners Barry Ord Clarke £14.99 hardback

Pocket Guide to Matching the Hatch Peter Lapsley & Cyril Bennett £7.99

Pocket Guide to Fishing Knots *Step-by-Step Coarse, Sea and Game Knots*
Peter Owen £5.99 paperback

GT – *a Flyfisher's Guide to Giant Trevally* Peter McLeod £30 hardback

How to Flyfish – *from newcomer to improver* John Symonds £9.99 hbk

Fishing Forever David Churchill   ebook £3.99

Once a Flyfisher Laurence Catlow £17.99 hardback

The Healing Stream Laurence Catlow £20 hardback

Tying Flies with CDC Leon Links £14.99 paperback

The Fisherman's Bedside Book BB £20 hardback

Flycasting Skills
John Symonds £9.99 hardback

Trout from a Boat
Dennis Moss £16 paperback

Fishing on the Front Line
Nick Sawyer   ebook £6.75

The One That Got Away
Multi-contributor   £20 hardback

The Countryman's Bedside Book BB £20 hardback

The Naturalist's Bedside Book BB £20 hardback

The Best of BB £20 hardback

The Shootingman's Bedside Book BB £20 hardback

The Way of a Countryman Ian Niall £16.99 hardback

The Sporting Gun's Bedside Companion
Douglas Butler £15.99 hardback

The Complete Illustrated Directory of Salmon Flies
Chris Mann £20 Paperback

The Poacher's Handbook Ian Niall £14.95 hardback

That Strange Alchemy – *Pheasants, trout and a middle-aged man*
Laurence Catlow £17.99 hardback

The Yellow Earl – *Almost an Emperor, not quite a Gentleman*
        Douglas Sutherland £20 hardback

James Batty writes about the charity he runs with friends:

One And All Aid is a registered charity that funds two school projects around Sinjar in northern Iraq. Sinjar was the centre of the ISIS-led genocide of 2014, and many Yezidi families are still living in tented camps as their homes and livelihoods were destroyed.
One And All Aid's main fundraising effort is running a charity shop in Penzance. This earns enough to provide an education to about 300 Yezidi children. A wonderful tribute to the generosity of our donors, shoppers, and volunteers. But we are only scratching the surface, and we would love to help more youngsters.
If you would like to support our work, please visit our website:

sites.google.com/site/oneandallaid